SO YOU WANT TO BE A WRITER

SO YOU WANT
TO BE A WRITER

Robert E. Moore
Grossmont College

Boyd & Fraser Publishing Company
3627 Sacramento Street, San Francisco 94118

Robert E. Moore: SO YOU WANT TO BE A WRITER

Composition by Dharma Press, Emeryville, California.

Library of Congress Catalog Card Number: 73-90424

ISBN: 0-87835-046-2

2 3 · 6 5 4

Contents

Part I

GENERAL INFORMATION

Chapter 1
Introduction

There are many possible reasons for taking a creative writing course, joining a writing workshop, or reading a book about writing. Maybe you were just looking for a few easy units. If so, you will probably drop the course as soon as you get the facts. Perhaps you were advised by your marriage counselor or psychiatrist to write as a means of outlet or catharsis. In that case, you may or may not get what you need out of this book, and you may even find out that you enjoy writing. Or are you studying writing because your beloved is mad for it and you hope to achieve togetherness? A situation like this has lots of possibilities. For instance, you might find out that you are better at it than he/she is just about the time he/she decides to give it up.

The chances are, however, that most students of writing fall into one or another of the following four categories:

1. *People who want to be writers.* These are starry-eyed individuals who have sidestepped the normal ambitions to be nurses, airplane pilots, firemen, or short-order cooks and decided that they wanted to become writers, preferably rich

and famous ones whose pictures appear in the news magazines surrounded by admiring members of the opposite sex. Or perhaps their fantasies are not so glamorous and they just want a job where there is nothing to do but a little writing instead of hunching over a hot stove or desk forty hours a week.

2. *People who want to write.*   This group may include graduates of Group 1 who have faced the unpalatable fact that to become a writer one must write, and are now eager to get on with it. It also includes all the people who have said, "*I* could write a better book than that," as well as those who have had so many interesting experiences that it is a shame more people haven't heard about them, and the ones who have a wonderful story, if only they could find time to sit down and write it. There have been many successful writers who have started out in each of these ways.

3. *People who do write.*   This select group contains everyone who writes poems for his friends' birthdays (even for just one friend), the shy individuals with a trunkful of writings at home that they can't bear to let anyone see, and the people who have papered a bedroom wall with rejection slips. They are already over the biggest hurdle; now they only need to improve on what they can already do.

4. *People who write and have published.*   This, of course, is the smallest group of all, and the reasonable question might be asked, "Why should they take a course or read a book? Haven't they already arrived where the rest of us want to go?" The answer is different for each one, naturally. Some have placed one poem in a local newspaper and would like to get a bigger audience. Others may be having great success, but in the wrong field. I once had a student who had already published more than a hundred novels, but none that she cared to put out on the coffee table and show members of her church society. What she wanted were techniques for writing something besides pornography. Published authors are always welcome additions to a workshop or a class, because their experience has made them able to give sound advice and encouragement to the less-advanced.

The general purpose of creative writing instruction should be to take each student at whichever level he is now on and bring him up to at least the next step. Success will depend on many factors: The capabilities of the instructor; his relationship with the student; the interaction of the class or workshop as a whole; and, most important of all, the potentials of the student himself and his determination to succeed.

LIMITATIONS

There are quite a lot of things no creative writing workshop, course, or book can be expected to do, no matter how brilliant the instructor, how supportive the rest of the class, or how incisive the text. None can give you a vivid and original imagination or an unfailing insight into the motivations and actions of human beings, although they may give you suggestions as to how best to sharpen and control however much of the above attributes you already have. None can teach you spelling, punctuation, and sentence structure.

Nor will this book or any workshop or course make you able to save the world tomorrow by the brilliance and compelling logic of your presentation of the solution you have worked out for all the problems of mankind. Poets, novelists, and playwrights, not to mention religious prophets and philosophers, have been going after these problems for millenia, and the world still seems in no danger of being saved. You may be the person who will do it, but not because you have read this book or taken a creative writing course.

And there is very little likelihood of either your instructor or this text providing you with the perfect formula for writing The Great American Novel (or Poem or Play). If he and I knew this secret, we wouldn't be about to impart it to you, at least not until we had published the G. A. N. ourselves. Of course the truth is that there is no such formula. Great works are usually the result of great and original genius. Critics and researchers may be able later to reduce them to formulas so that lesser writers can imitate them mechanically—to produce mechanical imitations.

BENEFITS

Now that we have covered some of the limitations of creative writing books, workshops, and courses, let us consider what they *are good* for, before you decide to give up and see if the book store will give you your money back for this text. There are a number of specific benefits, and probably the first and most important is to give you an incentive to write more than you have been writing. It is not always true that practice makes perfect, but there are very few competent writers who got that way without having done a substantial amount of writing.

Not only will a course or a workshop "inspire" (euphemism for "force") you to write, but it should also encourage you to rewrite what you have written, improving your craftsmanship as you do so. Good writing is almost always a result of rewriting—frequently many weary times.

Next, for students enrolled in creative writing classes or workshops, there is the important experience of reading or hearing (both, if possible) the works of your fellow students and discussing and criticizing them in class. There are a lot of things to learn from criticizing the writing of your peers. One is that they have problems too (already you can feel less lonesome), some of them the same ones you have. Better still, they may have solved some of the problems you have, and you can learn how they did it. They may have fallen into traps that you can learn to avoid. But best of all, criticizing their work may develop your ability to criticize your own before you do the last final rewrite and hand it in.

Last, and certainly not the least important, a course should give you the opportunity to hear your own writing being criticized. This is probably the most painful ordeal you will have to suffer during the course—much more painful than the writing or even rewriting—and some students find themselves unable to endure it at all. It's no fun to sit and listen to a bunch of insensitive clods who obviously don't know the first thing about writing themselves profaning the limpid outpourings of your innermost soul and, worse still, showing that in their boorish way they have completely missed the point of what you are saying. And furthermore, they can't even agree among themselves as to what are the faults, and virtues if any, of your work. Let me give you a little well-meant advice on how to handle the situation, both during and after the carnage.

1. *Keep cool.*   Listen in silence, masking as well as possible your true feelings, whether murderous or suicidal. You have heard what piranha fish do when they smell blood; don't let it happen to you. If you allow yourself to reply, you will only find yourself getting defensive and the attackers more truculent. Set your jaw and take notes or doodle.

2. *Absorb.*   Don't dwell on what was said, but don't forget it either. Try to tuck it into a closet in the rear corner of your mind and keep the door closed for at least 24 hours. Then open it a crack and examine the criticisms again. Most of them will still seem vicious and witless, but you may find that some of the ones that hurt you most have, alas, possibly the least bit of validity. Not much, mind you, but . . . . Reclose the door.

3. *Evaluate.*   After another 24 hours, take another look. By this time the criticisms may be beginning to sort themselves out into two stacks: Those that are applicable enough to justify having action taken on them and those that are clearly off the point and should be forgotten.

4. *Utilize.*   By the end of the third day, you should be in the right frame of mind to rewrite, carefully considering the comments worth considering. And while you are at it, even take another look at those which indicated that the critic didn't understand the piece. Why didn't he? Is it because he is stupid or he failed to read it carefully (both possible), or is it that you didn't make it clear enough? If it was even a little bit your fault, try to clarify it. Not all your readers will be careful scholars, and very few will be clairvoyant.

When you get to the point, perhaps before the end of the term, where you can accept unfavorable criticism without losing confidence in either yourself or the basic worth of your writing; when you are able to distinguish valid criticism from that which is inapplicable (even though it came from the instructor himself); and when you can rewrite, using the good advice and ignoring the bad, congratulate yourself. There is hope that you will become a writer.

CHAPTER 2
I DON'T LIKE YOUR PLATITUDE

Style is the characteristic your writing has that sets it apart from the writing of anyone else. You will probably notice as the term progresses that you can recognize the writing of one of your fellow-students, just as you are able to recognize the voice of an old friend on the telephone, even when he is trying to disguise it. A certain amount of the style is a part of your own personality, but it can also be cultivated, just as prospective actors and disc jockeys cultivate their voices by exercises and imitation of other effective speakers. Robert Louis Stevenson claimed to have developed his by imitating those of already-established writers. In his own words, he "played the sedulous ape" to a dozen or more in turn before they all merged into his own clean, apparently effortless style. Imitation, even to the point of parody, is one way to develop style; another is to build up the strong points in your own natural style systematically, at the same time trying to eliminate the weak ones. This chapter will make a few suggestions that seem applicable to style in general.

MAKING THINGS PERFECTLY CLEAR

Probably the most essential single characteristic to develop in your style is clarity. It is hard for many beginning writers to make their meaning absolutely clear, for several possible reasons. The commonest is that in order to write about a character at all, the author must be pretty well acquainted with him, to the point of identifying with him and thinking the same thoughts. When you are that intimate with a character, it is hard to remember that he is a stranger to the reader. What the character is thinking is obvious to you, because you are really doing the thinking for him. However, the reader has to be told, sometimes in such disgusting detail that you are afraid of insulting his intelligence. Don't worry. "No one ever went broke underestimating the intelligence of the American public," as one cynic has said. And if it should be brought out in criticism that you have erred in hitting your reader over the head too hard, it is always easy to delete a line or two. And at the very least, you will have made sure that everything is clear in *your own* mind.

Another important reason for obscure writing is the trend in Twentieth-Century literature toward subtlety. Readers no longer expect to be told in so many words what conclusion to draw from a story (like the "MORAL" in Aesop's Fables). It is easy to confuse subtlety with obscurity. Such thinking results in an inexperienced writer leaving out necessary facts in order to avoid being "too obvious." But leaving out necessary facts is not playing fair with the reader, and he will be quicker to resent that unfairness than he will any implied insult to his intelligence. To see genuine subtlety in action, examine any well-done detective or mystery story. You may have missed some of the clues as you read, or misinterpreted their significance, but they were all there, and when the solution comes, you are able to look back and see every wisp of evidence that was available to the Master Mind. Your reaction as reader, then, should be, "Of course," not "How the healthy heartburn could I have been expected to get that?" If you don't like books about dicks or private eyes, take a look at Faulkner's classic short story "A Rose for Emily." The story goes through more convolutions than a five-deck freeway interchange to keep the vital clues from appearing in logical order, but when the hair-raising denouement is reached, every element of Miss Emily's eccentric behavior has been clearly set out well in advance. Just be sure that you try to do as well.

Most examples of really great literature, particularly poetry, contain layers of meaning and suggested significance which underlie the surface story or picture that the reader sees at once from a casual perusal. This "layer" characteristic is what makes a piece worth rereading, because often new interpretations come bubbling to the surface on the third or even the twelfth time through. In your eagerness to make sure your own works have such depths to plumb, however, do not be betrayed into neglecting the "on top" story that even the lazy reader can see. Unless a reader finds that story worth his time, he won't even bother to finish the first reading, let alone pause to reread and find all the extra goodies you have built in for him. Remember the old advertising slogan: "Save the surface and you save all."

PREPACKAGING

Artists are at the mercy of their media. Portrait painters are expected to make human likenesses with nothing but canvas and paint. We have to do the same thing with only paper and words. The English language contains many thousands of words, but some are so technical and esoteric as to be unsuitable for creative literature (galactagogue or thiosinamin, for example). So we find ourselves using and reusing the same words and combinations over and over again. Is that bad? Not necessarily. Prepackaged phrases are often the quickest way to express a meaning so common that there is no point in wasting space on elaboration. "Just in time to ...," "in the wind," "broke the law," "barely enough," or "under duress" write themselves out on the page as if each were all one word, like damyankee. They are handy timesavers, although like most words, they get monotonous if overused.

Where one may get into trouble, however, is in the use of clichés. These are prepackaged expressions, frequently similes or metaphors, which are not yet common enough to have the status of the standard timesavers mentioned before, but have been used often enough to remove all suspicion of originality or freshness. They are often used to describe a situation or feeling that is sufficiently individualized or complex really to deserve fuller or at least more original treatment. The trouble with these little nifties is that they come so close to fitting and that they often come to mind disguised as your own ideas, so beautiful that you can hardly believe your own cleverness. When you get that feeling, Beware! You are probably getting it from your memory banks rather than your imagination. Here are a few examples:

calm before the storm	by the skin of his teeth
eye of the storm	butter wouldn't melt in her mouth
an eye for an eye	which side his bread is buttered on
tooth and toenail	bred in the bone

OVER-OBVIOUS EXPRESSIONS

Perhaps even more insidious than the cliché is the platitude, a trite repetition of some generally-accepted truth (or untruth) made as if it were something new and exciting. "There is sanctity in motherhood," "The race is not always to the swift," "Freedom is worth fighting for," and "We must make the world safe for democracy" are a few obvious examples. Now it is understandable that young students who have just begun to explore the mass of different philosophical concepts available suddenly discover for themselves principles that many educated people have been embracing ever since they began to learn. Naturally, the young student wants to share his exciting discoveries with his readers. However, it would be unfair to say that only the young writers deliver platitudes. Many people with gray hair are still using excerpts from Fourth of July oratory that they heard in childhood and have kept stored away as dim memories.

DEFENSE AGAINST THE TRITE

How does a writer learn to avoid clichés and platitudes? The same way he learns any kind of self-criticism. Classmates are usually quick to note them in each other's work, and to comment. There is a Dictionary of Clichés usable as a helpful reference after you have learned when to be suspicious. But there is no substitute for eternal vigilance, which we all know is also the price of peace (see how easy it is to notice clichés in other people's work?).

Don't think, however, that clichés and even platitudes have no place whatsoever in creative writing. Some writing is intended for unsophisticated audiences who tend to think in clichés and platitudes, and who would be confused by any more complex and individualistic an approach. If you want to write children's stories, confessions, or men's magazine stories of the Blood, Bosoms & Biceps variety, you will be catering to readers who can often accept triteness with more comfort than genuine originality.

Again, even in sophisticated writing, clichés, platitudes, or mixed metaphors (Birds of a feather gather no moss) are often used in dialogue to help characterize the person speaking. Does he think in platitudes? There is no better way to show that than to have him say a couple every time he opens his mouth. My late father, who spent most of his life in the men's clothing business, continually betrayed his farm origins in picturesque cliches like "That coat was cut out with an axe," or "It fits like a saddle on a sow."* He had some that showed approval, too: "That's as pretty as a speckled pup under a brand new red

---

* One of my colleagues from Oklahoma tells me that she learned "It fits like stockings on a rooster" for the same situation.

wagon," or "it fits like a sock in the mud." For further examples, see e. e. cummings' poem "next to of course god."

KEYS TO DESCRIPTION

Watch for the use of modifiers: adjectives, adverbs, and the phrases and clauses that do the same job. They are useful. Without them, your style would look pretty meager, and you could not make your meaning very clear. But they can certainly be overdone, particularly if allowed to fall into a regular pattern. Take this sentence (if you can): The beautiful blond girl came down the winding walnut staircase into the gracious grand ballroom. Note that there are only three nouns in the sentence, and that each is embellished with two alliterative adjectives. The sentence is so symmetrical that it looks absurd. Play with it awhile. Try putting three adjectives, or, better, one, with a couple of the nouns. Does it help? Why?

In some cases you can avoid using modifiers by simply using more specific nouns or verbs that contain implied modifiers themselves. Thus:

Staggering, the drunken man came down the walk.
could be compressed into
The drunk staggered down the walk.
The picture is just as complete, and probably a little stronger.

For some reason or other, adverbs ending in *ly* are more obtrusive than others. This is unfortunate, because so many of them do end that way, but it is wonderful practice to check over your work and see how many you have used. If there is one or more per sentence, check each and see if you could (1) do without it, (2) eliminate it by merging it into a verb, or (3) substitute another adverb without the *ly*.

Another thing about modifiers, and other words too: Try to make them specific rather than Size Fits 'em. "It was a beautiful scene" doesn't really tell us much except that we are supposed to be looking at an area, probably outdoors, that conforms to the author's standard of aesthetics. But what does the author like? Huge flat desert covered by a vast arching blue sky? Bright green rolling hills with stone farmhouses in the foreground? A restless gray-green ocean pounding the granite cliffs? None of the above?

Beautiful is a fine adjective to avoid, especially in describing a person. I can think of no greater disservice that you can do your heroine than to describe her as beautiful, unless it would be to describe her as divinely beautiful. All your female readers will immediately hate her. Who can possibly identify with someone perfect? If she has a wart on her right kneecap, a twitch under her left cheekbone, or one leg slightly shorter than the other, then she is forever set apart from all other women, yet somehow likeable, because we all have warts or twitches or worse, and we can sympathize.

KNOW THE STOPS

Choice of punctuation is a stylistic problem too. I assume that you know pretty much when commas should be used and what to do about punctuation that goes with quotation marks. If I'm wrong, you should find out, preferably before your instructor has a heart attack. There are a few perfectly legitimate punctuation marks that should be used sparingly. Nobody can object to an occasional exclamation point, but if as many as fifteen percent of your sentences end with them, your reader will become bored with exclamation points or develop sufficient immunity to them as to make them ineffective. When you find yourself tempted to put in two or three of them together to show that something is *really* exciting (!!!), it is time to review all the single ones to see if any of them are really necessary.

Another bit of punctuation that should be kept in its palace is the quotation mark when used to set off a word or phrase used out of its normal context. There is nothing like an "overdose" of such "elevated commas" to make your "opus" look "silly," as this sentence should demonstrate.

Dashes, too, have their purposes. One of them is *not* to evade the responsibility of deciding whether to use a comma or a semicolon. A dash is a dramatic sort of mark; don't use it where a more pedestrian mark, such as a comma or parenthesis, would be just as effective.

VARIETY

Another stylistic problem is the use of sentences. Sentences may be categorized as to length (long—more than two lines or 20 words; short—fewer than 10 words; and medium). Or they may be classified as simple, complex, and compound. If you are not quite sure what these mean, you had better look them up. The smoothest, most readable styles are usually the ones that mix up both sentence length and structure. Of course this does not mean that every sequence of three sentences must include one short simple sentence, one long compound one, and a medium-length complex one. It does mean that if you look over your work and find that most of your sentences are about four lines long and consist of several main clauses bound together by commas, semicolons, or *and's*, you should consider replacing some of the commas with periods and subordinating several of the main clauses. Or maybe they are all short. If so, nail several together so they will provide variety.

If you plan on choosing a great author to imitate in developing your style, I would highly recommend that you cross the following really first-string writers off your list: Ernest Hemingway, William Faulkner, and Henry James. Hemingway is noted for his terse, punchy sentences, which work well—for him. But I am afraid he has preempted the market. Faulkner's sentences are often more like long obstacle courses than attempts to communicate. (When asked about this, he is said to have replied that he feared he would not live long enough to write the next sentence, so that he had to put everything he knew into the first one.) Henry James' sentences are frequently tests of the reader's memory.

The fact that each of these gentlemen had a flawed style in no way indicates that he was not a great artist. On the contrary, it proves it. No reader could possibly put up with such style if there were not other compensations. So if you feel that you are in a position to compete with the trio mentioned, go ahead and write that way. If you still have a way to go, it's better to make your style a pleasure to read.

There are times when a mixture of sentence lengths and structures is not what is needed. Special requirements sometimes dictate the use of a series of short, choppy sentences, perhaps to show a brisk interchange of conversation:

"You mean," she bit her lip, "you don't care what I need?"
"If that's how you want to put it."
"But George—"
"But George," he falsettoed. "Forget it, you slut. I'm splitting. Now."
"But—but what shall I do?"
"I could care less. Drop dead if you want to."

A series of short quick sentences may give an impression of breathlessness or excitement:

She turned, tears blinding her burning eyes. Head down, step off the curb. Horns blaring, suddenly right in her ear. Brakes screeching into a whine. The pavement slamming up to meet her. Then, through the haze of pain, a sound. A police whistle skewered her eardrums.

You have already noticed that several of the sentences in the examples above aren't really sentences at all, but fragments, the bane of composition teachers everywhere. In creative writing, fortunately, the fragment has its uses. One is to get the confused effect shown above. Another is to make natural-sounding dialogue. Few of us consistently talk in complete sentences. Still another is the technique of unhooking what would normally be an adverbial word, phrase, or clause from the end of a sentence and making it a separate sentence instead to give a startling, usually comic, effect. Probably the most famous is the quotation attributed to the late W. C. Fields: "It's not true that I hate children; I'm very fond of the little monsters. Fried."

CAN THEY BELIEVE YOU?

Verisimilitude is a big word meaning realistic—like the real thing. No story, poem, or play is actually exactly like real life. For one thing, there just isn't room to put everything in. For another, most writers impose a certain amount of order or logic into the sequence of events depicted, and such logic is not often readily discernible in reality. As a matter of fact, all writers require their readers at least occasionally to make a "voluntary suspension of disbelief" in order to follow the story. However, readers are more likely to accept an occasional improbability if most of the work has verisimilitude. This is true of even the wildest fantasies, which tend to show you life as it really would be if you are only willing to accept a few minor variations from normality, such as that horses are vocal and intelligent whereas human beings aren't, so that horses maintain stables of people who can be harnessed to pull wagons.

Verisimilitude is gained by the judicious use of little details that everyone can identify: tipping over a chicken croquette before attacking it with a fork, or heading for the bathroom right after getting up in the morning. It is much easier to put in such details if you are thoroughly familiar with the situation described. Rarely can a person whose only contact with journalism is scanning the sports page do a really convincing job of a story set in the city room, particularly if some of his readers are reporters. So if you were planning a story about life in a pewter mine, I suggest that you forget it. It is likely to fall into the hands of some metallurgist who knows that pewter as such cannot be mined because it is an alloy of tin with lead, brass, or copper. The same for watermelon orchards.

Chapter 3
Writing Habits

Unless you are a pretty remarkable person, you sometimes have trouble getting started on your writing. And once you get started, if you are interrupted by something like having to eat or go to work, you may have trouble getting back with it. This problem, gaining momentum and keeping it, has bothered even some of the greatest writers. Samuel Clemens (Mark Twain) was once congratulated on being paid the fantastic sum of a dollar a word for his output, but had to admit glumly that there were some days when he couldn't even produce a dollar's worth. It is true that the American writer Mary Roberts Rinehart produced a considerable volume of fiction writing with a fountain pen during the occasional odd moments she could squeeze in between keeping house, raising two children, and acting as substitute office nurse for her M.D. husband. And almost everyone has heard the inspiring story of British novelist Anthony Trollope, who got up at an outrageous hour every morning so he could write for three hours before going to work, and who always wrote the same amount each morning.

It is immediately evident that Mrs. Rinehart and Mr. Trollope had several things in common: (1) They had enormous drive, discipline, and stamina. (2) They must have had clearly in mind what they intended to write when they picked up their pens. (3) They didn't expend much time "getting in the mood" to write. Also, though it isn't evident, note that (4) Each was a capable craftsman, but not a genius.

If you are a Mrs. Rinehart or a Mr. Trollope, don't bother to read this chapter. For the rest of you, here are a few suggestions on what to do when you find yourself staring at a blank virginal sheet of paper that seems to be staring back at you, daring you to start something. No one of the hints will work for everybody, but one or more should be of help to you.

DON'T JUST SIT THERE

Probably the first rule is one that applies also to housecleaning. When faced with a problem so vast and mind-boggling that it is patently impossible, like cleaning up a room where several unsupervised children have been fingerpainting for two hours, *start in a corner.* Put on blinders, if necessary, to keep the entire scene from frightening you out of your last meal, and do a small, manageable section of the job to build up confidence before proceeding. When the four corners meet in the middle, the task will be over. Similarly, if you are at a loss as to how to start a book, don't start the whole thing. Start one part of it that you *do* know how to start. Write one stanza, one chapter, one episode, one page, possibly from somewhere in the middle. Even if you throw it away later, you will have started, and proved to *that* smug piece of paper who is boss.

Note that the suggestion is to write something that you *know* how to start. But what if there isn't any such thing, so that your mind is idling and your emotions are in neutral? How can you be sure of not getting caught with nothing to write? Well, there are some ways. Many writers find it easier to write from an outline which shows what is to be covered, and more or less in what sequence. Of course this brings up the problem of how to start writing an outline, but since outlines are shorter and need never be seen by anyone but the writer himself, it is a less terrifying project—a sort of corner itself.

And some writers spend a substantial amount of time between writing stints in mentally going over parts that are coming up—what she is going to say to him and he to her—or repeating endlessly a line of poetry which has to be made to scan. These people are inclined to go around mumbling to themselves and tripping over small objects, so that they are unsatisfactory as brain surgeons or school-bus drivers, but they generally know what to write when they sit down to it.

If these systems do not work for you, you might try writing or typing nonsense syllables or finger exercises (if you are tired of quick brown foxes, try "Pack my box with five dozen liquor jugs" or "A quick move by the enemy will jeopardize six fine gunboats") until the paper starts looking messy and you are less loath to use it for your own messy ideas. Some people even find that using the backs of discarded computer print-outs for the first draft is less intimidating.

If you are a naturally greedy person, it may be well to take advantage of your own weak character by promising yourself a treat after you have completed a given section of your task. The nature of the treat will, of course, be up to you, since you know your own appetites. Some writers will settle for a cup of coffee, while others will hold out for a chocolate fudge nut sundae, a pitcher of martinis, or a sexual indiscretion. I recommend against alcohol or hallucinogenic drugs as a bribe. You are going to have to get back to writing later, you know.

MOMENTUM

And that brings us to the second, and scarcely less serious, problem—how to keep going on something you started yesterday or last week. This area is further complicated by the fact that there appear to be at least two different kinds of dynamics from which writers operate: intellectual and emotional. I expect that both driving factors operate to some extent in every individual, but there are some who lean more heavily on their minds (call them "head" writers), and others whose main thrust comes from the emotions ("gut" writers, or in the romantic idiom of an earlier generation, "heart" writers).*

I know a husband and wife team who collaborate. I do not believe that there is enough evidence to indicate that these are sex-linked characteristics, but it happens that the man is a head writer; the woman, a gut writer. The husband complains that when it is his turn, he sits down behind the typewriter and, after a few minutes of fumbling, starts to write where he had left off before. His wife, on the other hand, composes with a pencil and often spends most of her writing time chewing the pencil and trying to regain the emotional mood she had been in when she wrote before, so that she can continue on the same note. Husband admits, grudgingly, that Wife, once she does get started, can produce at a much higher rate of speed than he, and that her work is of at least as high a quality.

This example indicates that gut writers have, if not more problems in maintaining momentum, at least different ones. That may account in part for the fact that each of the suggestions given here will work for some people but not for others.

One way to get yourself ready to move is to reread, correct, and revise what you have already written on the piece. Hemingway claimed to have carried this to its ultimate by starting in each morning and rewriting everything he had ever done before on his story. By the time he reached the point where he had left off before, he would be ready to keep going (I trust this applied only to short stories; I cannot imagine his starting at the beginning of *For Whom the Bells Toll* every time he sat down to write). This system certainly has merit, especially for the gut writer, and it has the additional values of forcing self-criticism and making sure you start off at the right point in the manuscript.

---

* If you believe that all poets are necessarily gut writers, I recommend that you read Edgar Allen Poe's essay "How I Wrote 'The Raven.'"

Another method might be called the Cliff-hanger technique. "Cliff-hanger" is a term for a low trick used, particularly in drama and fiction, to keep the audience from departing during an intermission or forgetting to pick a novel back up again after finishing Chapter 7. The most famous and dramatic use of the cliff-hanger was made by Queen Scheherazade, reputed author of *The Arabian Nights.* Her husband had the regrettable habit of garrotting each of his wives at dawn after the wedding night. Scheherazade started telling him stories every night, and managed to time each so that at daybreak she had just arrived at a climax so suspenseful that he would grant her a twenty-four hour reprieve to find out what happened next. After 1001 nights of this, he issued her a full pardon—so he could get some sleep, one presumes.

The same method, somewhat refined, accounts for the fact that it doesn't work to say, "I'll just finish reading this one chapter and then go to bed," and is the reason that your parents or grandparents were unable to miss a single Saturday matinee featuring the serial *The Perils of Pauline.*

Another, and less well-known, use for the cliff-hanger is as a device for the writer to use on himself. The job is not as hard as Scheherazade's. You don't have to end a day's work at a suspenseful point; perhaps it's better that you don't, lest you find the next day that you don't know yourself how to get Pauline off the cliff before her fingernails give out. The main goal is to avoid stopping at a logical place. Do *not* quit at the end of a chapter. Stop in the middle of a paragraph. Stop, if possible, in the middle of a sentence. If you have enough will-power, stop in the middle of a word. This is a way to avoid the sickening sight of a mocking blank sheet of paper when the time comes to start again. Suppose, for instance, you finished yesterday's stint like this:

> She gazed into his eyes, her breath coming in little gasps between parted lips. His arms were tight around her—painfully tight, but with such a delicious pain. "Darling," he whispered, "darling Pe

At this point it is conceivable that you are not quite certain what her answer is going to be, or even whether his question will be a proposal or a proposition, but at least you should know that the girl's name is Penelope, and by the time you have that written or typed, you will have had some time to think up the rest of the sentence, and you are off. Now isn't that simpler than sitting down and looking at a page that says

CHAPTER 12?

If you make a habit of leaving yourself a cliff-hanger, you may eventually get to the point where you can end a year's work on your candidate for the Great American Novel by writing

> "I didn't expect you," she said.
> "I just couldn't do it," he admitted. "After I split, I just kept thinking about the commune, and you, and the baby, and I had to come back. I guess it's my bag."
> Her fingers were making marks on his bare shoulders. "I've always wanted to be your bag," she whispered.
>
> The End

then immediately whip the page out of the typewriter and, inserting another sheet, write thereon

> STAR-CROSSED HEARTS
>
> by
>
> Perspicacity Smucker
>
> Chapter 1
>
> The warm June breeze caressed the swaying tendrils of the pepper tree. The moon made a patt

Another trick that many good writers use is to have some little procedure to go through regularly each day before start-ing. It doesn't have to be an elaborate ceremony—just enough to remind you that when this is over you always start writing. Some may say a brief prayer, others sharpen seven pencils or clean the type on the typewriter. Almost anything that works for you is all right.*

Perhaps I should add a word of warning. There are certain activities that are not usually effective. Don't try reading a chapter of the current best seller for inspiration, or looking up three words in the unabridged dictionary. Almost any activity that involves reading is a disastrous prelude to writing. Reading is so much easier. More fun, too.

WHERE?

I must include one more point that is equally applicable to getting started and to keeping going. That is the surroundings in which you work. It is a good idea to find a place with as few distractions as possible. If you share a studio apartment with three other people, a television, and a stereo, you clearly have a problem (there are writers with such powers of concentration that they could write in a boiler factory which has caught on fire, but you probably aren't one of them). It may be possible to find a time when everything is serene in your home, and it may not. If not, it may be advisable to go somewhere else. Your college library or a public library is a good possibility, particularly if you don't compose on a typewriter. Libraries are traditionally kept as quiet as the traffic will permit, and rarely do we find a traveling salesman singing "Marian the Librarian" in one of them. Of course there is the counter-balancing problem of having all those books around and available.

Ernest Hemingway and William Saroyan did much of their earlier writing in restaurants, in Paris and San Francisco respectively. It might be worthwhile to find out if there is a convenient restaurant with a manager who doesn't mind vagrants occupying tables for long periods of time while buying only an occasional cup of coffee or glass of sauerkraut juice. It

---

*. . . as long as it doesn't take up your entire work day.—Ed.

would help if your available writing time coincides with the restaurant's slack period.

If home turns out to be the best place available, it would be desirable for you to find a corner somewhere that could be kept sacred to your use as a place to write. A whole room would be ideal, of course, and an old-fashioned roll-top desk would be nice, but anything down to a space on a table about two feet square could be used. It should be a place where your manuscript would be safe from compulsive housekeepers and nosy snoops, and where a dictionary and your writing materials would be always available. Mary Roberts Rinehart, mentioned earlier, partially attributed her ability to pick up her writing at any time to the fact that she had a corner where her writing was the only thing that ever got done.

Even if you cannot find a suitable spot, so long as you feel you must write, it still can be done. But developing a routine set of working habits that fit you will be even more important.

JOIN THE TWENTIETH CENTURY

One last thing should be mentioned while we are discussing work habits. Can you operate a typewriter? If you can't, at least to the extent of using three or four fingers, you should take whatever action is necessary to learn. Some writers do even their first drafts on the typewriter, but whether you do them in pencil, with a ball-point pen, or in charcoal on the back of a shovel, sooner or later they are going to have to be re-done in as smooth a draft as possible on a typewriter. It is not fair to a creative writing instructor to expect him to decipher every student's scrawl (some of your classmates have terrible handwriting, quite unlike yours), but even if he will pamper you to that extent, I can assure you that no editor, nor even a publisher's first reader, will bother to look at a manuscript that is not typed, and typed rather neatly and free from careless error as well.

Maybe you know someone who will type your manuscript for money or love, but even that is only a stop-gap solution to the problem. If you are going to continue to write, sooner or later the price (whichever) will grow onerous, and you will wish you could do it for yourself. Besides, almost every writer who types his own final draft finds that he is still modifying and improving as he does so.

Chapter 4
Once More, With Feeling

I was recently asked to address a meeting of a writers' club. During the meeting, one of the members leaned forward earnestly, cleared her throat, and asked, "Mr. Moore, don't you think that some writing is done in such a heat of inspiration that it is not only unnecessary to revise it, but that it would actually ruin it to try?"

There was no hesitation in my answer: "No."

That reply may have been too brusque, but with a very few exceptions, most of which have become famous only because they were unusual, it was correct. Good literature is not written; it is rewritten, perhaps dozens of times. Most of the work that is done in a "heat of inspiration" comes quickly because it is largely composed of cliches which the heat has made to look like inspiration, just as heat waves make desert sand look like cool water. Face it. Practically all of your work will have to be rewritten or thrown away. The question is not whether to rewrite, but how to go about it.

Perhaps it sounds a little arbitrary to say flatly that your work will have to be done over again. Let us examine some of the reasons that may require it, so you will know what to look for.

CONSISTENCY

One of the most obvious reasons is that in early drafts of a piece more than a page or two in length, there are likely to be discrepancies between the beginning and the end. Some of these may be caused by carelessness, and some because you, as writer, have changed your mind. Perhaps you start out with a heroine who has a head of raven-black hair, and somewhere in the middle it becomes convenient, for purposes of the plot, for her to have flaming red hair. If the story has a contemporary setting, there will be no problem except to decide whether to send her to the beauty parlor or let her do the job at home with the help of her sister. But if it happened in Victorian England, you had better go back and rewrite the opening (if you change the time to present, that will require even more rewriting). Or maybe you want to change her name from Elsa (which sounds too much like Elissa, the downstairs maid) to Betsy. (Incidentally this would be one of the most difficult revision jobs you could set for yourself. Four drafts later, overlooked "Elsa's" might still be floating to the surface.) Besides, the very act of revising one part may throw another so out of kilter that it needs changing too.

Unfortunately, I cannot assure you that the need to repair discrepancies is going to go away even after you become experienced and professional. In the classic *Vanity Fair,* Thackeray portrayed a vulgar housemaid wearing dress-up clothes so flamboyant that he referred to her forever after as "Ribbons." However, at some time or other he decided to cut out the original description in which the nickname was earned, and the reader today is confronted with a "Ribbons" but no hint as to who she is. And in *Madame Bovary,* a most carefully written novel, the heroine's eyes are brown, but so dark as to appear black, in one place; blue, but so dark as to appear black, in another. There were no contact lenses in those days, either.

BE CRAFTY

Even more important than taking care of the inconsistencies is the matter of craftsmanship: of putting the story together so that it is told in the most effective way possible. Craftsmanship includes many problems. Is it told in the best possible sequence? (Some stories are done best in strictly chronological order. Some are better when told in a series of flashbacks, so that they begin just before the actual ending. Others need to be done by telling, one at a time, several story elements which happened simultaneously.) Is the climax strong enough? Is there enough suspense? Are unimportant matters dwelt upon at too great length? Are the characters believable? Can we love, hate, or feel compassion for them? What about the motivation? Is the story told from the most effective point of view?

All these questions, and a thousand others like them, can be answered only after the original writing has been criticized. The criticism may come from your instructor, your classmates, or almost anyone who can read. Ideally, a lot of it should be self-criticism, and one of the purposes of this book or any class or workshop should be to make you more capable of doing more and more effective criticism of your own work.

In Chapter 1 a number of points were made about how to develop a healthy attitude toward criticism, so it will help you rather than destroy you. In summary, they were to listen with an open mind and closed mouth (even if you have to clench your teeth around a pencil), and to give the criticism a chance to settle before evaluating it. Criticism definitely must be evaluated, and the writer himself is the only person who can make the final decision.

Decisions as to the validity of comments must be made on an individual basis, of course, but here are a few test questions that may be used to help you decide:

(1) Is the critic really talking about *your* poem, story, or play, or or is he talking about a different one that he

would have written instead? The temptation to rewrite someone else's work is often overpowering, and in all fairness, sometimes the suggested piece would be better than the actual one. But it would be different, and probably therefore irrelevant to the work at hand.

(2) What kind of criticism does the person who made the suggestion generally give? If his comments on other students' work tends to be shrewd, you should probably give his opinion more consideration than if he never utters anything but drivel (although he possibly might not be acting true to form).

(3) Does the consensus of other critics' comments agree with his? This would certainly improve its credibility, although in writing it is unsafe to take a vote, for you must make the decision; you will be stuck with it.

(4) Is the critic a spouse, lover, relative, or close friend of yours? If so, beware. He is probably too emotionally involved to be objective. His percentage may improve if he happens to be an expert on writing, but not necessarily, if I am to believe some of my students who are married to editors. (The publisher-husband of Anita Loos enthusiastically declined to publish her novel *Gentlemen Prefer Blondes,* an all-time best seller.)

(5) Is the criticism *right?* This of course is the ultimate and only important question. If you can look at the comment and decide out-of-hand, all the other questions are unnecessary.

FACING REWRITES

Now that we know why re-writing is necessary and some of the things to consider in doing it, the next question is when to do it. Of course if someone in authority, like an instructor or editor, tells you, "I want that rewrite on my desk by three this afternoon," you have no big decisions to make. But usually this is a doubly important question, since you probably have less time than you need for writing anyhow, and certainly none to waste.

Unfortunately, there is no nice clear-cut answer. I cannot say, "Always start rewriting exactly eighty-two hours and seventeen minutes after receiving the last criticism," or even, "Start revising as soon as the black-and-blue spots have all turned yellow." Each case has a different answer. But here are a few rough guidelines:

Wait a little. Rewrite only after any pain and bitterness from hearing adverse comments has abated enough for you to make some sort of fair evaluation of it and decide which suggested changes are feasible. Feasible changes are those which can be carried out without altering the complete course and intent of the piece. They also must improve the writing without requiring so many compensating changes that the whole thing will be ruined.

That sounds pretty abstract and complicated, so let's look at an example. Some years ago, an acquaintance of mine wrote a novel based on combat experiences during World War II, of which he is a certified graduate. It went on the market in 1965. He got a number of nice letters from publishing companies, but no contract. The general tenor of comment from those who liked it otherwise was that World War II had been over for twenty years, and who would want to read about it when a nice fresh conflict was going on in Viet Nam? Some well-meaning friends suggested that he change the time to the early '60s and the place to Viet Nam. *This was a non-feasible criticism.* Virtually none of the events of the story could or would have happened in Viet Nam. The same soldiers that graced his pages might be visualized in Nam, but none of the incidental characters playing darts in English pubs, standing by their ruined homes in Germany, or cheering the advancing troops in central France would have worked in a rewritten story. The very fighting tactics were different. And he could never hope to reproduce the authentic local color by writing about a place he had never visited.

Wait for a constructive mood. Besides your attitude toward the criticism, the other factor is your feeling about the writing itself. Somewhere in the process of producing a poem, a piece of fiction, or a play there comes a point at which the author gets sick of it, so that he is sorry that he ever began it and hopes never to see it again. This is obviously no time to be working on revisions; even if you could drive yourself to do it, you would be unable to distinguish between what is truly loathsome and what only looks loathsome to you. You will easily recognize this phase when it hits you. It is a good time to be working on something else, something that you can feel enthusiasm about. Probably the best time to revise would be before this awful feeling gets to you, but if you miscalculate, about all you can do is wait until the sick feeling goes away, or at least abates. How long that will take depends on your mental and physical health and the length and quality of the work itself. I still have the manuscript of a novel on which I worked off and on for about seven years. It has been lying fallow for almost twelve, and I doubt if it is ever going to be resuscitated. It has been too long. Shorter works generally have briefer recover periods, measured in weeks or even days instead of years.

Avoid piecemeal rewriting. If you are doing a long writing—a novel, three-act play, or epic poem—you may choose to turn it in and receive criticism a section at a time. If so, it is usually best to wait until the first draft is completed in its entirety rather than rewrite the first couple of sections right away. This is because what you decide to put into later parts may require changes or foreshadowing in the earlier portions, and you might as well take care of everything at once. Novice writers sometimes even find that the best thing to do with a first scene or chapter is to throw it away and pound the few essential bits of information it contains into cracks in later scenes. Making such a devastating decision is much easier if you haven't already revised that part twice before.

GETTING THE JOB DONE

Now is the time for a few helpful hints on the mechanics of rewriting. Even if you have the ideal motivation and working conditions; even if you have selected a time when the piece doesn't look completely hopeless, rewriting is an upleasant task like cleaning up after a party, and the easier you make it for yourself, the better for us all—provided, of course, that the job is thorough.

In the first place, do not start rewriting or retyping the whole thing from the beginning. No matter how much of a disaster it may have been, there are plenty of parts good enough to save, and there is no use doing an elaborate copying job. Yet.

Go through the piece to be revised with a pencil or pen in your hand. Make the needed changes in pencil or ink if you can, crossing out and writing between the lines (I *hope* you double-spaced it) or in the margins (that's the reason for wide margins). If there are long portions that you have to eliminate, cross them out with big X's, but not so thoroughly that they can't still be read. There might be a phrase or sentence worth salvaging. Should you need to add a portion that is too long to write on the existing paper, write or type it out on another sheet and carefully mark the place it is to be inserted. If you find a paragraph or stanza in the original that is well enough written but really should have come somewhere else in the text, cut it out with a pair of scissors and mark the place where it belongs.

After you have done all this, take scissors, cut out all the deleted parts, cut the pages in two at the places marked for inserts, and reassemble the whole thing in the correct order. Paste is the traditional means of sticking the scraps together, although I prefer staples myself and editors swear by rubber cement. Attach the cut sections in proper sequence to backing sheets of plain paper.

Now you have a ragged, sloppy-looking mess of paper, but at least one that is technically better written and can, we hope, be read. If it can, read it again, picking up and changing any little rough spots you may have missed before and any inconsistencies that may have cropped up as a result of the changes themselves.

There are people, gut writers mostly, who find this piecemeal method of revision impossible because they lose the emotional effect they can only recover by rewriting the whole thing in sequence. If you are one of these, let me give you a couple of precautions. (1) Write notes to yourself in the margins of the draft you are copying, so you won't sail on by the part that needs changing. (2) Do not try to write a final smooth draft while you are making the changes. Make it a rough so that you can x out words and write them right instead.

Now, regardless of which system you used, you are ready to start typing a clean fair copy of the very best writing you can do—at least until the next time you have to revise it. And there is no reason why the new version can't give you just as much thrill as the first time through. Revision is practically as creative as original composition, even more professional, and absolutely essential to anyone who hopes to lose his amateur standing as a writer.

Part II

POETRY

Chapter 5
A Matter of Form

Poetry is the most controversial of the types of creative writing. Perhaps the commonest reaction among students when the subject is brought up is a kind of fascinated revulsion, like the immediate recoil on seeing a snake. On the other hand, no form of literary expression has so many loyally enthusiastic supporters—poets, students, and readers who feel that poetry is the only means for communicating anything more delicate or less mundane than directions on how to assemble a child's Irish Mail. If we examine the subject closely, we may be able to see the reasons for the polarization of opinion, and to find a position for ourselves a little less extreme than either of those mentioned.

WHAT IS THIS STUFF?

First, a definition. There really isn't room here for all the definitions that have been attempted, nor is there much real need for it, since all of them fall short of being complete. Let us just say, then, for the purposes of this textbook, *poetry is writing wherein the length of the line never depends upon the location of the right margin.* Perhaps this is too mechanical a definition; certainly there are many other important characteristics that poetry has, and which will be discussed in this chapter and the next, but this is a good working definition that enables you to tell at least the *intent* of the author at first glance. If the lines are different lengths (other than the ends of paragraphs), it is poetry.*

Poetry is our oldest form of literature. All the most ancient surviving examples of creative literature, from whatever culture, are in poetic form, many of these old poems predating the development of writing. I would guess, in the total absence of evidence, that there were prose fiction compositions just as old, but that they all got lost before writing was developed. In the days when literature had to be remembered in order to survive, poetry had the inside track, because poetry, at least all old poetry, contains built-in memory devices which make it easy to pass on from mouth to mouth (although different versions frequently develop).

Some of the memory devices, such as rhyming the last words or sounds in lines according to a certain pattern, and the use of rhythm, or meter, with a given number of beats in each line, are connected with the definition, for they are a reason for the irregular lengths of lines. Other devices include the repetition of key phrases or lines at fixed points in the poem (a refrain, or chorus), and the use of repetitive sounds in other ways than by rhyming. Examples are *alliteration* (repeating the beginning sounds of words—"a bouncing baby boy" or "Peter Piper picked a peck of pickled peppers"), *assonance,* a sort of half-rhyme in which the main vowel sounds are alike but not the consonants ("Leave them *alone,* and they'll come *home*"), and its companion, *consonance*, in which the consonant sounds agree, but not the vowels (*think-tank*).

---

* Here's Bob Dylan's definition of poetry (at least according to the graffitti on the wall of the john in the Berkeley Barb office):

"A poem is anything that walks by itself."

This note was contributed by our typesetter.

Because of these memory devices, particularly the meter and rhyme, poetry has always been popular with children, who like to repeat simple rhymes from writers as diverse as Mother Goose and Dr. Seuss. And of course we hear a variety of play poems and songs that go with children's games:

> Here comes the doctor, here comes the nurse
> Here comes the lady with the alligator purse.

> Red Rover, Red Rover
> Let Susie come over.

In the little farm town of Laurel, Nebraska, where I learned the one above, we said Red Clover instead of Red Rover. That is how variations in folk poetry occur. If Shakespeare's father had been a farmer rather than a glover, the expression might have been "Hay nonny" instead of "Hey nonny."

Considering this youthful appeal, we can understand why so many great poets were fully developed by the time they had reached voting age, certainly younger than the age at which novelists or playwrights reach their peak. John Keats, for example, died at age twenty-six, his friend Percy Bysshe Shelley at thirty, and Lord Byron at thirty-six, each having already produced some of the English language's greatest poems.

Closely akin to play songs are work songs, like the sea chanteys, which have been used for centuries to keep workers moving in rhythm. I don't know, but I suspect that in addition to the whip-wielding overseers shown in pictures of the construction of the Egyptian pyramids, there were also song leaders to give the laborers the beat. Military recruits learn to march better singing the responses to the "Jody Cadence":

> Ain't no use to go áwol
> Four more weeks and that is all
> Sound off!
>   ONE, TWO

Sound off!
THREE, FOUR
ONE, TWO, THREE, FOUR
ONE, TWO; THREE-FOUR!

Naturally, work songs give rise to protest songs, folk songs, and all the other poetry-to-music that students with guitars like to sing. All these are cornerstones of poetry. If you keep this in mind, the subject seems less awesome (or awful).

BECOMING AN INSTANT POET

There are a few kinds of poetry that anyone, even you in the back there, can write with very little practice. Try the *diamante*, for example.

The diamante is a new poetic form designed by Professor Iris M. Tiedt, University of Santa Clara. It is named after its diamond shape. It does not require rhyme or rhythm—only knowing a little about the parts of speech. The first line consists of one word, a noun. The second line is two words, both adjectives related to the first line. The third line consists of three participles (verbal forms ending in -ing or in -ed, -en, etc.). The fourth line is made up of four nouns designed to start swinging your thoughts from the subject on line one to that on line seven. The fifth line is three more participles which go with the seventh line. The sixth is two adjectives. The seventh is one noun, generally one which *contrasts* with the first. The following examples were written by students after about the same amount of instruction as you have had:

1 noun	life
2 adjectives	free, mysterious
3 participles	awakening, moving, delighting
4 nouns	rules, regulations, order, entrapment
3 participles	bleeding, stumbling, falling
2 adjectives	dark, gloomy
1 noun	death

death
silent, lonely
depressing, frightening, alarming
friends, sympathy, tribute, memory
satisfying, believing, loving
beautiful, glorious
resurrection

birth
new, unwilling
shocking, dangling, squalling
cradles, cribs, beds, coffins
failing, dangling, sighing
unwilling, old
death

Try writing a couple of diamantes yourself. Please ignore the fact that all the examples shown mention death. That is a coincidence, not a requirement, although death is one of the primary subjects of all creative literature.

HAIKU

If you made your way through the diamante without serious trauma, take a look at a traditional Japanese form of poem, the *haiku*. Haiku (the word is either singular or plural) are poems made up of seventeen *syllables*, written in three lines, usually of five, seven, and five syllables respectively. They do not need to rhyme or have any particular meter. Now and then one will even depart from the seventeen-syllable rule, but not by more than one or two.

They usually give two distinct pictures which have some symbolic or sensory connection (not usually an obvious one, like a trailer to a car or a chair to a table, but something that can be noticed if pointed out, like a vapor trail to a chalk mark or a sunflower to a spectator at a tennis match). Many modern haiku, however, give only one word picture, as do most of the examples given here. Although there may be action in haiku, they are intended to give static pictures, like camera slides rather than movies. Japanese haiku are usually associated with one or another of the four seasons of the year; most of their images come either from nature or from the interaction of people with nature.

Haiku are written in such condensed form that non-essential words are frequently omitted: articles, or even parts of verbs. This feature makes it easier to fit the poem into the syllable count.

Here are some examples of contemporary American haiku written by creative writing students like you:

Cars in the sunlight
Crowded in concrete deserts
Lakes of bright metal

Shrouds of wind spirits
Blow off the mountain's shoulder
Rising of the fog

Fold across her breasts
Staples transfix her thighs
Playmate for April

Light, through stained glass window,
Filtering through April rain.
An opening umbrella.

Sallie Ruthven Whitney

Miracle — it grows
Sticking its long head out
Pick it for a weed

Harry J. Keehan

New flowers of Spring
covered by expended brass.
Beauty gone so long.

Polka-dotted hills
Blue sky seen through green lace trees
Windmusic whispers

Dorothy Burger

Now go outdoors. Look, listen, smell, feel, and if it's sanitarily possible, taste. If you have a beautiful green vista, great! If all you can see is smog, with your view of it obstructed by electric wires or TV antennas, that's good subject matter too. Fill yourself up on sensory impressions for about five minutes, then come back and see how many haiku you can create from the experience. Two would be good, three or more excellent. And if even one of them is *good* haiku, you have real promise as a poet.

TRIOLET

Another poetic form you might try is a *triolet*. A triolet is an eight-line poem in which the first line is repeated as the fourth and seventh lines, and the second line is repeated as the eighth. Lines three and five also rhyme with line one; line six with line two. Since you must be confused by now, let's look at an example written by the English novelist-poet Thomas Hardy. The letters in the column to the left are a guide as to what to look for: the capital **A** indicates the first line or a repetition of it; the small **a** indicates that the line rhymes with the first line. Capital **B** is for the second line or its repetition; small **b** for a line that rhymes with it.

How Great My Grief*

A   How great my grief, my joys how few,
B   Since first it was my fate to know thee!

---

* From *Collected Poems of Thomas Hardy.* Copyright 1925 by Macmillan Publishing Co., Inc. Reprinted by permission of the Trustees of the Hardy Estate, Macmillan London & Basingstoke; and the Macmillan Company of Canada Limited.

a   —Have the slow years not brought to view
A   How great my grief, my joys how few,
a   Nor memory shaped old times anew,
b   Nor loving-kindness helped to show thee
A   How great my grief, my joys how few
B   Since first it was my fate to know thee?

Write a triolet, using the following first two lines. As you can see, that doesn't leave much for you to write!

A   My car broke down the other day
B   So now I thumb my way to school
a
A   My car broke down the other day
a
b
A   My car broke down the other day
B   So now I thumb my way to school

If that went well, make up your own first two lines and try again. That should be easier, because if it doesn't work out, you can alter one or both of them.

LIMERICK

Another form that you might like to try for fun is the *limerick*. Limericks are short, usually funny, poems five lines long. The first, second, and last lines rhyme with each other, and the third and fourth, which are shorter, also rhyme with each other. Limericks are not always dirty.

Examples:

There was a young lady from Kent
Who said that she knew what men meant
When they asked her to dine,
Gave her cocktails and wine,
She knew—oh she knew—but she went!

A tutor who tutored the flute
Once tutored two tooters to toot.
   Said the two to the tutor,
   "Is it harder to toot, or
To tutor two tooters to toot?"

All set? If you want to make it a game, choose two fairly common rhymes (words that rhyme with "game" and "try" would do) and let everyone in the room see how good a limerick he can write using one rhyme for lines 1-2-3 and the other for 3 and 4.

You probably noticed that the second limerick example uses another device common in limericks—the pun, based on the similarity in sound of words with little connection in meaning. A similar limerick trick is to use a word with a ridiculous spelling (like "enough" or "victuals") in the first line and to spell all the rhyming words in the same way. Probably the most outrageous of these is one made up by someone who knew that English place names frequently have weird pronunciations. *Warwickshire* is pronounced *Warem* and *Hampshire, Hants.** Hence

There was a young curate from Warwickshire
Whose manners were quite harwickshire-scarwickshire
   He wandered 'round Hampshire
   Without any pampshire
Till the vicar compelled him to warwickshire.

By now you are probably noticing that a poem has a lot to do with *form*. In most pre-Twentieth Century poetry, the form is clear and obvious, but even the apparently "free" verse written nowadays follows its own patterns for its own reasons.

There are many other standard poetic forms: the ballad stanza, the couplet, and the sonnet, to name a few of the

---

* *Hants* is now an approved spelling.

commonest. If you are interested in knowing more about forms and in doing more of the mind-stretching exercises of putting a poetic idea into a set form, you should look into a book that goes into the matter more thoroughly than this. One such is Babette Deutsch's *Poetry Handbook*.

CHAPTER 6
THE PROOF OF THE POEM

In the last chapter poetry was defined as "writing wherein the length of the line never depends upon the location of the right margin." Then it was brought out that a poem also has a form or structure of some kind, so that, although no two poems are identical and interchangeable like two three-sixteenth inch stove bolts three inches long, they have patterns like fingerprints: not an exact match, but recognizable as fingerprints. But this doesn't quite solve the problem of whether to saw up your writing into poetry-length lines or to call it prose and let it run clear across the page. Let's take a look at some of the characteristics that we find commonly in most poems.

This is neither a simple nor a secure operation, because many of the elements to be mentioned exist also in good prose writing, and probably a poem which contains *all* of them is extremely rare. However, I think it can be said that all good poems have some of these characteristics to a sufficient extent that we could recognize them as such even if they were written clear across the page.

IMAGERY

Imagery is the use of one object or concept in such a way as to make the reader think of some totally different concept or object. For example, when Robert Burns tells us,

"My luve is like a red, red rose,"

we can be pretty sure that his "luve" is not really like a red, red rose in very many respects. For one thing, except when in a state of extreme embarrassment or sunburn, her complexion must be far different. For another, her temperature, presumably near 98.6° F, would not be a viable one for a rose. Besides, a rose would be much less fun to nuzzle, unless you happen to be a bee. Then is Mr. Burns lying? Of course not. He is telling a poetic truth, and the reader can quickly draw his own conclusions about how Burns' "luve" is like a rose. Maybe she is a delight to watch; perhaps she emits a seductive fragrance. Or she might be temperamentally thorny, so that one has to be careful in handling her. Or maybe she is fragile—let us hope that she is more durable than a rose, though, at least—or inclined to lose her petals (gloves, handkerchiefs, keys) wherever she goes. The ideas that imagery of this kind bring up will be different for each reader, yet probably any and all may be valid in appreciating the poem.

Does this mean that a poem can mean different things to different readers? Definitely, yes. Once a poet has published a poem, he has lost control of it. Readers can and will interpret it differently, no matter whay you say or want. It also means, however, that the use of imagery gives extra depth and meaning to the poem: there can be a surface story or picture of something quite simple and ordinary, like a fork in a little-used path through the woods, pretty and nostalgic, that suddenly through the magic of poetic imagery becomes a symbol of decision-making. Before we realize it, we are thinking of the big decisions in our lives—whether or whom to marry, whether to go into the family business or a commune—and how we have to live with the results.

DEVICES OF IMAGERY

There are several ways to create an image. The first and probably simplest is the *simile*. In it, we merely say that this thing resembles that one. The word "like" or "as" is generally used. "My luve is like a red, red rose" is a typical simile. Similes are common in all forms of imaginative literature and even in ordinary speech: "My car goes like a bat out of hell," "That soldier marches as if he was looking down a microscope," and "She spends her money like a drunken sailor."

A *metaphor* is a simile with the "like" crossed out. If Burns had said "My luve *is* a red, red rose," it would have been a metaphor. Metaphors can be more subtle than similes. Here, for instance, from a sonnet by the Elizabethan poet Sir Philip Sidney, are a whole galaxy of metaphors crowded in so closely that one hardly notices:

> Come Sleep, O Sleep, the certain knot of peace,
> The baiting-place of wit, the balm of woe,
> The poor man's wealth, the prisoner's release,
> Th' indifferent judge between the high and low. . . .

In the first place, it is suggested that sleep is a person, who can be talked to. (This is also another literary device called the *apostrophe*: the addressing of a remark or a question, often rhetorical, directly to someone or something. Apostrophes vary from the one shown above and Byron's "Roll on, thou deep and dark blue ocean, roll" to the term "gentle reader" used by many early novelists to turn temporarily from the story and speak directly to you, the reader.) In addition, sleep is compared directly to a "knot of peace," whatever that means, "the baiting[feeding]-place of wit [intelligence, as in 'keep your wits about you']" and a number of other things, all in four lines. The metaphors, in fact, come so fast here that unless the reader plows laboriously through them, no single metaphor has time to make a full mind-blowing impression, and the total effect is simply to make one realize what a blessing it is to be able to sleep, which is probably what the poet intended.

SYMBOLIC IMAGERY

Next on the list of kinds of imagery is *symbolism,* made famous by Dr. Freud, who maintained that the things we dream about represent (are symbols for) what we are really interested in. Without debating Freud's psychological theories, it is clear that whether dreamers use one thing to represent another or not, poets do. For example, let's look at another of Burns' poems, "John Anderson My Jo," surely one of the loveliest of all British love poems. In the first stanza, the speaker addresses John Anderson, her husband and "jo" (joy, or darling), reminding him that she knew him when he was young and handsome, but that now he is old and frosty-headed. Here is the second stanza, which I have taken the liberty of translating, possibly to the horror of Burns-lovers, from its broad Scots dialect into contemporary English. Aside from spoiling one good rhyme, I don't think I have damaged the poem.

> John Anderson my jo, John
>   We climbed the hill together
> And many a happy day, John
>   We've had with one another
> Now we must totter down, John
>   And hand in hand we'll go
> And sleep together at the foot
>   John Anderson my jo!

Few people will have any trouble recognizing that climbing a hill and tottering down have a double meaning, since they symbolize the living of a life. And if anyone missed the beautiful triple meaning of "sleep together" in the next-to-last line, he should read the stanza again.

ALLEGORICAL IMAGERY

Closely related to symbolism is *allegory,* used in fiction and drama as well as poetry. In allegory a story is told, usually one with a strong moral lesson, in which each character represents something else—a group of people, a philosophical point of view, or a famous personality. A classic example is John Bunyan's *Pilgrim's Progress,* in which characters with names like Christian, Mr. Worldly Wiseman, Law, Religion, and others equally subtle, portray the search of an individual for religious truth. Several contemporary newspaper columnists use allegory extensively to lampoon points of view or well-known figures in public life. Perhaps the most notable is the San Francisco columnist Art Hoppe, who records the exploits of Captain Buck Ace, Private Oliver Drab, Sir Ronald of Holyrood, and Nick Dixon, among others.

PUNS

Puns, which were mentioned in connection with limericks, are another means for creating an image of one thing while talking about another. While in limericks puns are used to make us laugh, they may be used in serious poems to make us think. Take Emily Dickinson's poem:

THE BUSTLE IN A HOUSE *

The bustle in a house
The morning after death
Is solemnest of industries
Enacted upon earth,—

The sweeping up the *heart*
And putting love away
We shall not want to use again
Until eternity.

---

* "The Bustle in a House" by Emily Dickinson. Reprinted from *The Complete Poems of Emily Dickinson,* edited by Thomas H. Johnson, by permission of Little, Brown and Company.

I (not Miss Dickinson) put the word *heart* in italics. Generally we don't sweep up hearts, but one of the symbolic acts of domesticity has long been to sweep up the *hearth* of the fireplace. The pun, then, draws special attention to the comparison that exists throughout the poem between the re-arrangements that have to be made in a household (first stanza) and those made in the mind or heart (second stanza) after the loss of a member of the family.

ALLUSION

Another species of imagery is *reference to common experience,* a device often used in other forms of literature also. It is one of the simplest ways to create an emotion that will be similar, if not identical, for all readers. Most of us have, or had, mothers we can remember, and mere use of the word creates some sort of response in each of us. Since mothers are human, many have been drunks, child-beaters, or purse-snatchers, but for most of us the concept of "Mother" is a pleasant one surrounded by a halo of nostalgia.

Similarly, most adults have experienced the death of a friend or relative, and so bring quite a bit of their own impressions along when reading the Dickinson poem we just looked at. And all of us know about sleep and insomnia, so we can understand what Sidney was talking about in the opening lines of his sonnet.

One common experience that all readers of poetry will have had is that of reading itself. Not everyone will have read the same things, of course, but there are certain parts of literature so widely read that the poet can assume that everyone has either read it or heard something about it. Reference to this particular kind of common experience is called *literary allusion.* A poet who mentions Little Lord Fauntleroy or Pollyanna, for instance, can be pretty sure of getting an image. (Practically no one born in the past thirty years or so has read the books, but everyone has heard of them.) When Rudyard Kipling entitled one of his poems "Uriah the Hittite" he felt he could count on most of his readers being familiar enough with the Old Testament to remember an unsavory episode in King David's life very similar to the events in the poem. Shakespeare was an inveterate user of allusion, particularly allusions to Greek and Roman mythology, which were popular in his day. Now the works of Shakespeare himself (particularly *Julius Caesar, Hamlet, Macbeth,* and other plays commonly taught in American high schools) are mined for allusions. Aesop's Fables, Homer, and the parables of the New Testament are only a few of the sources still used. Even dirty jokes ("who is doing what, and to whom") have been used when there are enough people who are familiar with them.

Of course, literary allusion, like any other poetic device, can be overdone. Many of T. S. Eliot's poems, some of Ezra Pound's, and a great deal of James Joyce's prose seem to assume a breadth and depth of literary background that most of us simply don't have. Some readers accept the challenge and feel that understanding the poem is worthwhile enough to do the requisite research; others turn off (and away). Perhaps how esoteric your allusions should be allowed to get depends upon the audience you want to appeal to. In general, if I had a choice between an allusion to Jack Horner and one to Orestes, I'd opt for Jack Horner. The mythology buff who knows about Orestes has probably heard of Jack, too.

TYPOGRAPHICAL TRICKS

Besides imagery, the next most common characteristic of poetry is use of typographical tricks (arrangement of the words on a page) to add to the effect of the words themselves. We have already mentioned one of them, length of line. In most traditional poetry, line length is dependent on the meter (so many down beats to a line) and the rhyme (rhyming words usually come at the end, or occasionally in the center, of a line). Innovations during the past century have changed and loosened the custom, so that the end of a line has become almost a kind of punctuation, indicating a pause in reading. In Walt Whitman's poems, most of the lines are long, and they usually end at the completion of some grammatical unit: a clause, sentence, or phrase. Lewis Carroll, in "The Mouse's Tale" from *Alice in Wonderland,* makes his poem fit the contours of a mouse's tail, so that it draws a picture on the page. e. e. cummings, a painter as well as a poet, sometimes scattered his words all over the page to create a more impressionistic picture. Poems like these are intended to be looked at rather than listened to; indeed, some of cumming's poetry could be nearly impossible to read aloud. But most free verse uses line length as punctuation or to emphasize a particular word or short phrase by giving it a line to itself. See how the line length works in the poem "Vacancy":

> It was odd how she left
> I never realized
>   the size of the room
> empty
>   of her presence.
>
> I sat there quietly
>   thinking,
> trying to separate the events
>   that were history;
> yet they blurred together,
>   Indistinguishable,
> leaving my mind hollow, vacant
>
> The room's too large
>   now, I thought.
> Much too large . . . . . .
>   One can hardly think in
> a room this large . . . . . .
>   one can hardly think.

Harry J. Keehan

Notice that the poet has used other typographical effects: the strings of periods ending the third and fifth lines of the last stanza and the use or non-use of capital letters at the beginnings of lines.

Of course it is easier to make up typographic effects if you are a printer with all different type sizes and styles at your disposal. However, notice what another student poet was able to do with only an ordinary manual typewriter to work with:

I HATE YOU

I hate you.
I wish you pain and sorrow and dread.
I hate you.

You who walk so proud and laugh at the pain of others.
You who talk so loud and listen not to the words you say.
    But only say them for the noise they make.

I HATE YOU!
I wish you anguish and sleepless nights.
I HATE YOU!

You who laugh by yourselves and share not your joy.
You who take love and use it to please your fantasies .
    But don't even know what love is.

I HATE YOU !
I wish you sterile days and ever running tears.
I HATE YOU !

    Do you want to know why I hate you?

Because you made me look inside myself and I didn't
    like what I found.

                                       Karol Jaye

STANZAS

It is customary to write prose in paragraphs, which are groupings of sentences on the same or allied subjects. Poetry is usually divided into groups of lines called stanzas (except for very short poems, which can be thought of as being one stanza in length). Stanzas in much formal poetry are of standard length and standard pattern (rhyme scheme, meter, line length, etc.). But even free verse is usually divided into stanzas of some sort, although they may be of varying lengths and patterns. Stanzas are useful because they make the poem look less formidable to a reader than a solid mass of lines (there are points at which one may stop without losing his place), and because, like paragraphs, they may be used to show a switch in subject matter or approach. Note the use of stanzas in "The Bustle in a House," "Vacancy," and "I Hate You."

ONOMATOPOEIA

Onomatopoeia is a horrendous name for the poetic device of using words whose sound is like that of the thing or action it goes with. Bobolink, katydid, snort, and roar are onomatopoetic words. Aardvark, peanut butter, and walk are not. Poetry often gets extra mileage from a word by reinforcing its meaning by its sound. Edgar Allan Poe was one of the masters of the technique, and his poem "The Bells" is the proof. Here are the first two and the last lines of each long stanza of the poem:

I

Hear the sledges with the bells—

Silver bells!

*   *   *

From the jingling and the tinkling of the bells.

II

Hear the mellow wedding bells—

Golden Bells!

*   *   *

To the rhyming and the chiming of the bells!

III

Hear the loud alarum bells
Brazen bells!

❋   ❋   ❋

In the clamor and the clanging of the bells!

IV

Hear the tolling of the bells—
Iron bells!

❋   ❋   ❋

To the moaning and the groaning of the bells.

Does anyone question that these four kinds of bells all sounded different?

While we are still looking at part of this poem, notice that Poe made full use of line length, making the left margin as well as the right irregular, and that there seems to be a recurring pattern in the stanzas, at least so far as the opening and concluding lines are concerned.

PARALLELISM

In addition to the use of line length, stanza pattern, rhyme scheme, and a repeated refrain, there are other rhetorical devices which tend to give poetry coherence and make it easier to memorize. Chief among these is parallelism, a technique which places several successive and similar ideas into the same grammatical pattern. Line length can be used to reinforce the effect.

Parallelism is also used in good prose; in fact, one of the best-known literary works which makes extensive use of it is usually written in prose—Abraham Lincoln's Gettysburg Address:

Fourscore and seven years ago our fathers brought forth on this continent a new nation, conceived in liberty and dedicated to the proposition that all men are created equal.

Now we are engaged in a great civil war, testing whether that nation or any nation so conceived and so dedicated can long endure. We are met on a great battle field of that war. We have come to dedicate a portion of that field, as a final resting-place for those who here gave their lives that that nation might live. It is altogether fitting and proper that we should do this.

But, in a larger sense, we cannot dedicate—we cannot consecrate—we cannot hallow—this ground. The brave men, living and dead, who struggled here, have consecrated it, far above our poor power to add or detract. The world will little note, nor long remember, what we say here, but it can never forget what they did here. It is for us the living, rather, to be dedicated here to the unfinished work which they who fought here have thus far so nobly advanced. It is rather for us to be here dedicated to the great task remaining before us—that from these honored dead we take increased devotion to that cause for which they gave the last full measure of devotion—that we here highly resolve that these dead shall not have died in vain—that this nation, under God, shall have a new birth of freedom—and that government of the people, by the people, for the people, shall not perish from the earth.

RORSCHACH EFFECT

One well-known psychological personality test is given by letting the subject look at a casually shaped ink-blot and tell what he sees in it. The ink-blot doesn't really look like anything but an ink-blot; however, most people can see something in each one, just as most people can see images in a cumulus cloud. *More is seen in the ink-blot or cloud than was put there on purpose.* Much good poetry affects the reader the same way; he looks at the surface meaning (if any), and then, if he looks longer, new shapes begin to form, either on the page or behind the reader's own eyeballs. An elegant example of how much Rorshach effect a single brief poem can have on the reader is in John Ciardi's essay "Robert Frost: The Way to the Poem," which you will find in Appendix A. It shows what can happen between a great poet and a tremendously sensitive reader. Take a closer look at "The Bustle in a House," "Vacancy," or "I Hate You" and see what you can find in those inkblots.

DEVIATION FROM THE EXPECTED

Because poetry does normally have a pattern of some kind, the reader is brought up short when the pattern is not carried out. Take this limerick, for instance:

> There was an old man from St. Bees
> Who was stung on the arm by a wasp.
> When asked, "Does it hurt?"
> He replied, "No, it doesn't.
> I'm so glad that it wasn't a hornet."

Most people laugh, although there is certainly nothing funny about the events we are told. But limericks are supposed to rhyme, and this one doesn't. Furthermore, limericks are supposed to have a punch-line ending. This one doesn't. So, not quite knowing how to deal with it, we laugh. The bawdy old folk song "Sweet Violets," which I will not quote here, uses the same sort of surprise. Each line seems inevitably headed into a rhyme—one involving a naughty word—and then abruptly veers off at the last moment into a non-rhyme, then swoops back to the brim of another disaster, only to duck again.

These are examples of humorous effects from deviation from an expected pattern, but the method can be used for serious effect too. The last two lines of Robert Frost's poem "Stopping by Woods on a Snowy Evening" (see Appendix A again) constitute a break in the established rhyme scheme of the poem, which is, in each four-line stanza, aaba. The last stanza goes aaaa, and the third and fourth lines are the same:

> The woods are lovely, dark and deep
> But I have promises to keep,
> And miles to go before I sleep.
> And miles to go before I sleep.

The double unexpected change makes us do a double-take at the last line, and before our eyes, the words "miles" and "sleep" take on an unexpected new meaning. And impact.

A note of caution. This device works well if it comes at a point which needs emphasis. But *don't* use it any time you can't think of a good rhyme. All that will call attention to is your awkwardness.

These, then, are some of the characteristics found in poetry. Many of them appear in fiction and drama as well, and most poems haven't room for all of them, but a poem without any would be a weak thing indeed.

Chapter 7
Free—But not Cheap—Verse

Several times in the preceding chapters I have mentioned Twentieth Century free (apparently formless) verse. Since it is in common use today, and because many of you will prefer to write it rather than the conventional rigidly structured poetry, it would be a good idea to examine the reasons for it, its advantages and disadvantages compared with conventional rhymed and metered verse, and some of the responsibilities a free verse poet must face.

WHY FREE VERSE?

Probably the basic reason for writing non-conforming verse is much like a young man's rationale for wearing a beard—because his father didn't. It is a human characteristic, perhaps even a need, to have a change occasionally just for the sake of change itself, as a housewife may have a sudden urge to move the console TV to another corner of the room. Obviously there cannot be progress without change (chalk up another platitude on the record you're keeping), and there isn't likely to be any regression either. Right now, even after all the years since free verse became popular, it is hard to tell whether it is a step forward, backward, or merely sideways. But one thing *is* clear. It's fashionable.

S. I. Hayakawa, the great linguist and general semanticist, suggests that modern advertising has made such heavy use of jingles and rhymed slogans that the reader of a new poem in the old structure immediately looks to see what the poet is trying to sell, instead of reading the poem. This may be true. We are certainly bombarded by singing commercials, slogans that rhyme and are set to dance tunes. "Winston tastes good, like a cigarette should" was an historic example. A number of well-meaning English teachers made it even more famous by objecting to it on grammatical grounds. When the advertisers came back with their taunting riposte "Which do you want, good grammar or good taste?" they may have lost their rhyme, but they gained some Rorschach Effect—with me, at least. I am still considering the improbability of getting either grammar or taste in a cigarette advertisement.

A third important reason for writing free verse is that it is easier, at first glance at least. You don't have to worry about finding a rhyme for "orange," only to give up eventually and change the word to "gold," which isn't quite what you meant. Sometimes in writing metered verse you may find yourself forced by the need for a word with two light beats and one heavy to put in something that you not only did not mean, but that doesn't seem to mean anything at all. Free verse would save such situations.*

ADVANTAGES OF FREE VERSE

The first advantage a free verse poet has is the one just discussed—freedom to say exactly what he means without a lot of artificial form restraints. (Robert Frost, a holdout for rhyme,

---

* John Keats faced this dilemma when writing "On First Looking into Chapman's Homer." He stoutly grasped one horn and changed the name of the explorer from Balboa to Cortez—because *Cortez* has the two syllables he needed to make his line scan.

likened writing free verse to playing tennis without a net.) Logically we might expect that the newer free poetry would be much clearer than formal poetry, but close scrutiny of the works of T. S. Eliot, Ezra Pound, Wallace Stevens, e. e. cummings, William Carlos Williams, Sylvia Plath, and others fails to indicate that it is so. Each of them would make a fair match for Robert Browning, a conventional rhyme-and-meter poet notorious for the obscurity of his poems.

Why should this be? Are they deliberately trying to be hard to read? If so, there might be a couple of reasons. Perhaps they want to make sure of being distinguished from advertising poetry, which in addition to being catchy, must be clear enough for anyone with the price of the product to read and understand while traveling at seventy miles an hour on a freeway. Or they may want to make sure that anyone who reads their poems will have to be a sincere student who will study them so carefully that the Rorschach Effect will take over (maybe this is the reason that there are so many bewildered poetry-phobes around, too).

The obscure phase in the development of poetry may conceivably be on the way out, too. Many of the newer poets, such as Bob Dylan and his contemporaries, seem to be backing away from the fog and toward a clearer exposition, if not lesson. At any rate, clarity is one of the options which free verse gives the poet.

Another advantage is that it lends itself well to experimentation with new and unheard-of patterns and forms of poetry. The diamante, discussed in Chapter 5, is an example of form growing out of freedom. It may sound ridiculous to talk about using formlessness to create new patterns, but in all phases of human life there is a constant tension, struggle, and interplay between the desire for individualism and freedom on one hand, and the need for discipline, formality, and cooperation with others. Literature is one of the battlegrounds, and this struggle has provided a theme for many poems, as well as a personal problem for the poets.

DISADVANTAGES OF FREE VERSE

Free verse has its problems. In the first place, no matter how immortal yours may be, nobody is likely to memorize it in sixth grade and recite it years later for the edification and amusement of other guests at a cocktail party years later. It may be available in every library in the land, but not in people's heads.

Let's see why. Here is the first stanza of Ezra Pound's poem "Commission":

> Go, my songs, to the lonely and the unsatisfied,
> Go also to the nerve-wracked, go to the
>   enslaved-by-convention,
> Bear to them my contempt for their oppressors.
> Go as a great wave of cool water,
> Bear my contempt of oppressors.*

This is Pound at his most lucid. We can tell what he is talking about. But try seeing how long it takes you to memorize these four lines, compared with the four opening lines of Longfellow's "The Day Is Done":

> The day is done, and the darkness
>   Falls from the wings of Night
> As a feather is wafted downward
>   From an eagle in his flight.

Well, you may object, despite the pretty imagery here, Longfellow was writing a Mickey-Mouse poem, while Pound was saying something pretty heavy. Without necessarily agreeing with you, let me submit the first stanza of Robert Browning's deeply philosophical poem "Rabbi Ben Ezra":

---

* Ezra Pound, *Personae*. Copyright 1926 by Ezra Pound. Reprinted by permission of New Directions Publishing Corporation.

> Grow old along with me!
> The best is yet to be,
> The last of life, for which the first was made:
> Our times are in His hand
> Who saith, "A whole I planned,
> Youth shows but half; trust God: see all, nor be afraid!

I learned that stanza in high school, and I have just written it from memory, then checked my memory against the poetry in print. I had omitted two words and made several errors in punctuation (which I don't generally memorize, because it's hard to hear). I doubt if that would be possible with Pound's poem—by me, at least. And incidentally, Pound's poem would be harder to set to music to make into a song, although I will admit that songs nowadays are made more often of free-form lyrics than they used to be.

Another disadvantage of free verse is that, in not confining yourself to a set form or pattern, you miss the chance to find yourself forced into saying something *you had never realized that you had meant.* (For a fuller treatment of the subject, take another look at Ciardi's essay "Robert Frost: The Way to the Poem" in Appendix A.) Unfortunately, you may not be the kind who tends to find pearls when trying to slop the hogs, or when looking for a rhyme for "thanks," discovers that a word meaning a tailless domestic cat is exactly the word you should have wanted had you thought of it in the first place. Take a look at the triolet you wrote (Chapter 5) and compare it with these two:

Liquor's Quicker But Thumbs Are OK

> My car broke down the other day
> So now I thumb my way to school.
> New girls I've met along the way.
> My car broke down the other day
> And older "girls" have bade me stay,

But Jeez—I'm not a fool
My car broke down the other day
So now I thumb my way to school.

L. J. Scott

My Car Broke Down

My car broke down the other day
So now I thumb my way to school,
For I cannot mechanics pay.
My car broke down the other day.
If only I could have my way
I would not ever break a rule
My car broke down the other day
And now I thumb my way to school.

If yours looks more like the second, with lines that rhyme, but don't mean much in conjunction with the poem as a whole, it may be that free verse is a better bet for you, at least for the time being. If yours all mesh in together, like those in "Liquor's Quicker But Thumbs Are OK," if your thoughts seem to reach out for rhymes and meter comes naturally to you, and if your ideas seem to complete themselves just about the time the form runs out, you should try working with various forms and patterns of traditional poetry until you find your natural means of expression.

RESPONSIBILITIES OF A FREE-VERSE WRITER

If you decide that free verse is right for you, there are certain responsibilities you have to a greater extent than has a writer of formal verse. The first is that you have to decide where to end *each* line. In a formal poem, you make that decision when you set up the pattern, and from then on you are stuck with it. In free verse, however, make sure that there is a good reason for ending the line where you do, that it really helps to give the effect you want. Take this one, for example:

Poem for My Son

The baby's fine they
    said you were fine
How was I to know that
they said that to all the women
and so
belly emptied   I slept at last
leaving you breathing in your new
       chrome casket

They let him see you but he didn't
       really look

I would have I
   would have

And when I woke you weren't (I'm
sorry but the baby expired   they
said   as if you were a credit card)

He said you were small and wet
      I tried
to see you through his being

I guess we never had much in common
     I live alone now and
the only thing that
he took with him when he
    left was
what you look like   How I wish
Oh Baby how I wish

           Patricia Traxler—1970.

Notice that there is no punctuation whatsoever in this poem
except for the eccentric use of line length and arrangement and
for the wide gaps within the lines to show the reader when to
pause. Some of the line endings and gaps (those in lines five and
six of the first stanza, for instance) come at points where punc-

tuation would normally be used. In other places, like the third stanza

> I would have I
> would have

the pause signal is at a completely unexpected and abnormal place for punctuation. In normal prose writing, it would go

> I would have; I would have.

which gives an entirely different effect.

When this student poem was being discussed in class, one male class member objected that the pauses were put in capriciously and that they made the poem hard to read. Another student, a woman who had herself lost a baby right after its birth, immediately took issue. "That's just exactly how you feel," she assured us.

Since I have never gone through the ordeal myself, this poem is probably as close as I will ever come to understanding the combination of the aftermath of labor pains plus the sense of loss (nine months of travail and anticipation gone—for nothing) all reinforced by the post-partum blues. And the lurching gasp-and-sob is conveyed almost as much by the length and positioning of the lines as by the words themselves. It is hard to imagine this poem being as effective if written in formal rhymed verse.

The next responsibility a free verse writer has is to use enough of the characteristics of poetry shown in Chapter 6 to make it obvious that a poem is on the right side of that thin boundary line between prose and poetry. Imagery ("new chrome casket," "as if you were a credit card"), typographical tricks, onomatoepia, division into stanzas, parallelism (see "I Hate You" in Chapter 6) or other patterns such as repetition of a refrain ("I Hate You"), and perhaps most important of all, the Rorschach Effect are included in this category, and some of them should be included in each poem if it is really to be a poem.

Lastly, a free verse poem must be effective and memorable in itself because it reveals a truth so important or so originally and brilliantly told that the reader cannot forget it. Limericks are almost impossible to forget, no matter how much one would like to. They keep running over and over in the mind like a sound-track of Ravel's "Bolero," endlessly repetitous, endlessly monotonous. That is because of their built-in tricky form. The free verse poem has no such gimmicks. It must go out and compete on the basis of worth alone.

CHAPTER 8
WHERE DOES IT COME FROM?

The material of poetry, like the material of any other kind of imaginative writing, comes from a variety of places—personal experiences and observation, things read or heard, and the unfettered imagination, which usually synthesizes several of the others. But that is like saying that all living things are made up of carbon, hydrogen, oxygen and a few trace elements. That doesn't tell us how they came to be alive. Where does the spark of life come from? Scientists are still working on it.

Luckily, it is easier to identify some of the internal sources of the spark of poetry, the magic impulse that draws together and shapes the raw materials into a recognizable work of art: a poem. This is a good time to look over the geneses of poetry.

STORYTELLING

The first kick-off for poetry is the same as the impulse that starts out most fiction and much drama: the desire to tell a story. Why the poetic form is used rather than one of the others is largely a matter of personal choice, but it might be based on the fact that the story is a little short or too allegorical to be ideal fiction or drama. Or that the material is poetic rather than prosy. Or just that the writer does better in poetry. Here is a student's poem that tells a story:

LOVE STORY

Henry was a labrador retriever   and
Isabelle   was a cow
Henry   often said that he would leave her 'cause
retrievers hardly ever like cows   anyhow

so she stuck her head in a drinking fountain
but it overflowed before it could extinguish her
"boo   hoo"   she cried out so he'd hear
but since she was a cow the sound did not distinguish her

So Isabelle   started chasing after rabbits   and
rolling over   playing dead   fetching sticks   and
Henry started sitting up to notice   He said
"Wow   how'd a stupid cow learn all those clever tricks"

So he followed her around 'till he learned all that she knew
but she said she had a few she hadn't taught him yet
He's still with her now though he couldn't tell you why
It must be one of those things she taught him to forget

Isabelle is very happy now
and though I think she is a crappy cow
her retriever   didn't leave her

Mark Montijo

This particular poem was intended to be a song, and it goes rather well with a guitar accompaniment. The story is so bizarre that it is funny. But even if it makes us laugh, the poem does more than tell a ridiculous story: it has a strong Rorschach Effect which varies with the individual reader. To me, the absurdity of a cow trying to make a dog of herself to please her boyfriend brings pictures of career women trying to make housewives of themselves to save their marriages, or house-painters trying to make portrait artists of themselves to keep their wives happy. But that's *my* ink-blot. What's yours?

SOUND-DOODLING

Starting at the age of about three months (give or take six), a baby will start taking interest in sounds. Some will lie on their backs for hours, waving all four feet in the air and solemnly repeating "Ga-ga-ga-ga-ga-ga-ga-guy-guy-guy-guy-die-die-die-die-die—" Every now and then he will hit on some sound combination so killingly funny that he cracks up completely and laughs for awhile before he can regain his control and get back to work.

That same fascination with sounds makes older children —and altogether too many adults—into punsters who guffaw and slap their thighs when they get off a good one. It is also a characteristic which makes poets—the fascination with words and the sounds they make. A poet may play with a word for hours, like a basketball player practicing handling the ball, testing rhymes, making alliterations, punning, using it in all its meanings and connotations, fitting it into phrases, perhaps making a poem around it. Here is a student work which sprang from a bout of sound-doodling:

SUNNY DAZES

Birds, bees
Flowers, trees,
Sunny warm,
Life is born
And me—I gaze
On sunny days

Birds alive
Swoop and dive,

Up and down,
Far around,
Surround the breeze
Escaping trees,
Life's simple maze
Is with sunny days.

Blues, yellows, greens,
Breathtaking scenes,
Twos and threes,
Nature's keys,
Show no haze,
For sunny days.

Third phase,
Whether gulls or jays,
Yeahs or nays,
Always pays,
Forget those A's,
On sunny days.

Frank Michael Sgobba

Not a great poem, perhaps, but one with a rich interplay with word sounds plus an ability to create a spring-feverish mood —one that most of us are only too willing to have.

Try an exercise in sound-doodling. Pick a nice common word with plenty of rhymes. "Sound" would be a good one. Scribble down all the rhymes you can think of for it (using a rhyming dictionary should not be necessary). Think of possible alliterative words and write a series of silky, sensuous S-sounds. Consider all the possible meanings for the word and possible rhymes and alliterations that go best with each. Select some of the words out of the mish-mash and try stringing them together into phrases or sentences, adding "and," "is," or some other short connective word as needed to hold it together. Does it start making sense almost in spite of you? If so, maybe you are working your finger exercise into a poem.

PATTERN-DOODLING

Pattern-doodling is like sound-doodling, arranging and rearranging words to make a sort of visual pattern on the page. Crossword puzzles, Scrabble, and acrostics are kinds of pattern-doodling that have been formalized into games. When combined with word-doodling, it makes a sort of dual pattern, one which can be seen and heard (or at least read) at the same time. Then it is poetry, and poetry with an extra dimension. Here is a student's work which demonstrates the point:

wal   den   three

the bud
to plant
is cheap
to buy   and yet

my love
to me
the bud
of life   and yet

my heart
is rich
in love
for her   and yet

not 'nuf
to pay
re pay
her love   and yet

her kiss
do part
do strip
my heart   and yet.........

a rose.........

Ross Flaven

Notice how the string of dots after the last "and yet" signals and sets us up for the other, more important, deviation from pattern. You may remember from Chapter 6 that this is one way of calling attention to the important point of the poem. You might have done it differently, but the poet clearly did it on purpose to emphasize his ending—an appropriate one for a poem starting with "the bud."

Here is how another student came out of an attack of pattern-doodling:

SCRABBLE, ANYONE?

```
w a r  m
   i
   r u n  s
        o
        w i  n  d i  n g
        h        n
        e        t o m o r  r o w s
        r        o             u
        e                      s
                               t h r o u g h
                               l          r e e d s
                               i          e
                               n          e
                               g          n

c  o  me
    e
    a
    n
    d o w n
    e  , i n t o
    r  n       u
    d     r e a s o n
             n
          d e s i r e
```

Patricia P. Wilson

This sort of thing, of course, takes time and effort, so don't do it unless you get fun out of it too. You might try your hand at using this or some similar typographical stunt as a model to follow. That way you can find out if it's fun for you or not.

EXPERIMENTATION WITH A FIXED FORM

Young poets have always studied patterns used by their predecessors and tried to put new poems into old forms. The sonnet for lyric poems, the ballad for narrative (story) poetry, the heroic couplet for almost anything, all are popular forms, in addition to the ones discussed in Chapter 5. Then there are dozens more, including the damnably difficult *pantoum,* which may be impossible in English. It is written in four-line metered stanzas, with the first and third lines having one rhyme, the second and fourth another. Then the second and fourth lines of each stanza must be used as the first and third of the next one, right down to the end, where the second and fourth lines of the last stanza are the first and third of stanza number one.

But what is probably more fun is making up your own pattern and seeing what you can do by sticking to it. You will remember from Mr. Ciardi's essay that Robert Frost did that in writing "Stopping by Woods on a Snowy Evening." Ross Flaven worked out his own pattern for "wal den three," and here is another student poem to demonstrate the point:

I Couldn't Come

I am a man	I am alone
I lie awake	I am alone
I speak with friends	I am alone
We pull and break	I am a man
I want the sky	to draw my breath
I need the wind	to draw my breath
I want your need	to draw my breath
The earth may mend	I want the sky

I couldn't come   I have to wait
I may be wrong   I have to wait
I may be weak   I have to wait
The day is long   I couldn't come

SHARING PERSONAL EXPERIENCE

Somewhat like wanting to tell a story is the desire to share with someone (the reader) some experience of your own that is laden with emotion, irony, humor ("a funny thing happened to me on the way . . ."), or philosophical insight that is worth passing on, and that can best be told in poetry. "Poem for My Son" in Chapter 7 is an excellent example, and here is another. The poet tells me that this was the second poem she ever wrote.

CATHIE AND I

Mitzi had twenty-seven colors or shades of colors in her coat.
We counted them one rainy afternoon—
Cathie and I.

Mitzi had beautiful kittens, mostly black ones.
We laughed when they fought over tangles of yellow yarn—
Cathie and I.

Mitzi used to chase green lizards, but never caught one.
We gave her extra milk on those days—
Cathie and I.

Mitzi hated it when she got wet on gray, rainy days.
We dried her off in front of the fire, then listened to her purr—
Cathie and I.

Mitzi screamed when she was hit. "It was a brown car," a
   neighbor said.
We were inside the house, but we heard her—
Cathie and I.

Mitzie was covered with her own deep red blood.
We wept while we buried her—
Cathie and I.

Maybelle R. Peverley

SHOWING A PHILOSOPHICAL TRUTH

Most of us think of philosophers as old men who write
long, impenetrable books with names like *Critique of Pure
Reason* or *Nicomachean Ethics*. But a lot of philosophical and
psychological principles that take a chapter to define and three
more to illustrate can be expressed more quickly and probably
as profoundly in poetry. Here is one that a student wrote:

UNTITLED I

The tremulous sea begs to kiss
the cliffs,
washing their feet
in momentary abandon, giving
little pause for relief.
Wilfully, she loves them long
and slowly eats them away,
eats them away . . .

Caroline Briscoe

LIGHT VERSE

Light verse is not so much a kind of poetry as a frame of
mind in which it is written. It may, in fact, spring from any one
of the sources shown above. Despite its name, it is by no means
always trivial, and it often makes as strong a point as serious
poetry. What it does have is an ironic, irreverent view of life,
and it is generally based on common, recognizable human
behavior, or on the operation of human institutions.

Light verse is almost always written in a close pattern, metered and with a set rhyme scheme. Ogden Nash, one of the best and most iconoclastic, broke all rules of meter and line length, but his poems always rhymed (and outrageously). One may say that whatever else he might be poking fun at, he was always poking fun at formal poetry (I think formal poetry is big enough to stand up under a little goodnatured joshing, and may possibly come out the better for it).

Besides adhering to form, light verse must be *clear* and not worry about being mistaken for advertising jingles. There is nothing flatter than a joke which has to be explained.

Light verse has been around for many centuries, but much of the older light verse has lost its impact. Humor doesn't keep as well as serious works, because the things it lampoons are frequently no longer around, often having been killed by the lampooning. We can still enjoy the works of Sir William S. Gilbert (of Gilbert and Sullivan) and Lewis Carroll, but not nearly so much as we could if we knew what it was they were knocking. Twentieth Century greats include Ogden Nash, Dorothy Parker, Richard Armour, and Ethel Jacobsen, among others. Felicia Lamport is one of many contemporary artists who write especially effective light verse.

Here is some light verse by students who might eventually join their ranks. The first is a commentary on my requirement that every bit of writing turned in had to have a title.

CURSES ON TITLES

I'm told a title's vital
And a last line is essential
But I sometimes find
The lines between
Are quite inconsequential.

Dorothy Burger

The next one gets its punch by a type of imagery comparing two kinds of artists usually considered not susceptible to comparison:

Role-Playing

The stripper and the poet
Each has his goal
One bares her body
The other bares his soul.

Kitty Harnish

And this last one is a sardonic comment on the fragility of the threads we use to weave friendships, love, and other human relationships:

Bus Stop

We're more alike than you think!

our hair is long
our teeth are strong
we both dig song

our feet are shod
our clothes are mod
we bathe the bod

we both like books
cosy nooks
look askance at sneaky crooks

golly there's lots that's going for us
so many things we should discuss—
oh no—you ride a different bus?

We're not too much alike I think

Elizabeth Petersen

CHAPTER 9
WHERE DO WE GO FROM HERE?

Now that you have written some poetry, what do you do with it? Let's say that you have already shown or read it to all your friends except that clod Elmer Gantz, who is too dumb to understand poetry anyhow. You may have gone further and made up a notebook for all your really notebookworthy poems and are keeping it on the bookshelf right between the Bible and the Hummell Dolls. If you write any more, you are going to have to start looking through the thrift shops for a good used trunk, or at least a footlocker.

A trunk was the solution used by one of the great American poets, the late Emily Dickinson. No more than two or three of her poems were published during her rather brief lifetime. (Hey! Don't be alarmed because I've mentioned several poets who died young. There's nothing toxic about poetry: Long-fellow died at seventy-five, Emerson at seventy-nine, and Wordsworth lived to be eighty.) But her heirs kept finding more trunks containing poems in her attic until almost fifty years after her death.

But maybe you have more realization of the value of your poems than Miss Dickinson did. If so, it would be a shame to have them moulder away, unread by anyone outside your creative writing class. What can you do to make your masterpieces available to a broader readership? How can you get them *published*? There are two possible motives for publishing poetry, both perfectly worthy so far as I am concerned: (1) personal satisfaction from seeing your writing in print, and (2) money.

PROFIT FROM GREETINGS

If you hope to get rich from writing poetry, I have bad news for you. Poetry is not only hard to sell to publishers, but it also brings low prices. Light verse is probably the most lucrative, but even light-verse writers generally have to be gainfully employed at something else to continue eating.

However, there is some money to be made from selling poetry. Probably chief among possible markets is the greeting card business. To find out who is in the market, look in the *latest* copy of *Writer's Market,* which is to be found in most libraries among the reference materials. There, listed under "Greeting Card Publishers," you will find names and addresses of companies, followed by a little squib describing roughly what sort of thing each wants. If any company looks promising, try to find some of its published cards on sale in the nearest drugstore or supermarket and see what the squib meant by what it said. This is called "researching the market." Always wash your hands first, so the store manager won't make you buy everything you have touched.

Perhaps after pawing through the birthday and get-well-quick departments, you will find that nothing you have written seems to fill the bill, and that you don't seem to have any ideas for poems or smart cracks that will. Besides, greeting cards don't carry a byline, so no one will know what is your work unless you tell him. It's no way to make your name a household word, certainly. So now where?

FILLERS AND STUFF

The next best bet is for what are called *fillers* because they are used to stuff into the crannies of a magazine or newspaper when the other reading matter and the advertising don't quite come out even on a page. Since such blank spaces are generally small, editors will usually favor shorter poems. So save that fifteen page epic for something else. Many general-interest magazines use poetry fillers, and so do a few special-interest and trade journals. Since the readership is different for each, so will their requirements vary. You should not send the same kind of poem to *Good Housekeeping* that you would to *Vegetable Growers Messenger,* and *Humpty Dumpty's Magazine* would want something different from either. So it will save you a lot of postage if you read two or three issues of the magazine before you submit. If you can't find one on the newsstand, write to the publisher, requesting copies.

Some newspapers, including Sunday supplements, use filler poetry too, and a small local paper might even prefer to publish poems by a local person. Whether and how much they will pay you is another matter. And before you publish, it would be a good idea to find out if the publication will be covered by a copyright. If it isn't, the poem will thereafter be in "public domain"—anyone can republish it without payment or even permission.*

CONTESTS

There is one more chance. A number of poetry contests are held every year. Some of the biggest are listed in *Writer's Market*; others may be advertised on your instructor's bulletin board or through the mail. There is even a *Contest Magazine* devoted to telling about contests, with helpful hints on how to win.

---

* You as author can copyright your own work to protect it. Several copyright guides are listed below.

Poetry contests vary in their requirements, from "write a last line for this limerick" on up through a prize for the best *book* of poems on the theme of objective relativism. Some want light verse, others demand serious poetry. Be sure to read the requirements on format and submission very carefully.

All these money-markets, except for a few of the contests, have one thing in common: they call for poems tailored to *their* requirements rather than to yours. Thus much of your very best work—best in the sense that it reveals your emotions—is not really very promising material for the publishers concerned. Unless, of course, you are lucky enough to feel like a greeting card sender or a vegetable grower.

PUBLISHING FOR PERSONAL SATISFACTION

But what should you do with your truly "good" poetry—the poems which no one but you could have written because the sensibility to experience is uniquely yours? Suppose they don't even fit any contest requirements. Are there markets for these poems too?

Yes, there are. There are in existence several possible outlets for such poetry, and the way to recognition if you happen to be highly talented is probably through one or another of them.

The first is the *poetry magazines*. Be sure to look in the very latest *Writer's Market* for their listing, for many of them are operated on a frail financial shoestring and their lifetimes may be short. Poetry magazines have a couple of drawbacks. First, they pay nothing or next to nothing. Payment is frequently made by sending you one or more copies of their magazine which you can show to George down at the bowling alley or send to Aunt Kizzie in Delaware. A few pay a nominal amount of money; some automatically enter each contribution in their own private contest, with prizes to the winners. Some won't even send you a free copy of the magazine, so you would have to subscribe to be sure of seeing your own poem in print!

Second, because the editors are in many cases publishing

the magazine for love rather than money, they tend to hold jobs as spot welders or shoe salesmen and to read submissions in their spare time, if any. That means it may be months before they are able to get around to accepting or rejecting yours. No use writing them irate letters; they are behind in their correspondence, too.

Poetry magazines also have a point in their favor: the more prestigious of them are read by book publishers and their representatives. If they should be taken with two or three of your poems, they might even write you on the subject of producing enough for the traditional "slim volume of verse."

Still more likely to catch a publisher's eye are poems included in one of the *literary magazines.* This is a rather loose term which includes standard "quality" magazines like *Harper's* and *Atlantic Monthly* and then goes on to cover quarterly magazines published by university presses and the so-called "little" magazines. A listing is included in that valuable book *Writer's Market* under the heading "Quarterly, Literary, and 'Little' Magazines." Publication in one of those is a feather in any poet's hat, not to mention a way to bolster the reputation and build up the ego.

However, in submitting to these as well as the other kinds of publications, it pays to have looked over the magazines, so that you will know which one to send it to first, and which one second.

Another specialized market is the *underground press,* a comparatively recent kind of newspaper business generally associated with radical or liberal social movements. Most of the comments I have made about poetry magazines applies to them also.

HOW TO SUBMIT

All poetry (like all other kinds of writing) should be submitted on white bond paper, typewritten double-spaced on a typewriter with clean type and a fresh black ribbon (not necessarily brand new, but at least readable by someone with no better than normal vision under dim light). Do not use one of those nice easy-erase papers. As an editor warned me, it "is great for fixing errors, but it is slippery and it drives compositors [typesetters] wild. We don't need any wild compositors. . . ."

Use a separate page for each poem, no matter how short it is. This enables an editor to accept some and reject others. Besides, I once submitted half a dozen brief untitled poems, all on one page. Eight months later, after I had forgotten all about them, they came back with the comment, "Some stanzas show promise, but the whole poem lacks unity."

Speaking of getting them back, you should take a few precautions:

(1) *Keep a copy, carbon or duplicated.* It is entirely possible for any submission to get lost. I still am missing the manuscript of a novelette I sent out more than fifteen years ago.

(2) *Enclose an envelope* big enough to hold the manuscript (you may have to fold the envelope) addressed to yourself, with stamps for return postage either pasted on or attached with a paper clip. The advantage of just clipping the stamps to the envelope is that the publisher can use them for a happier purpose, like sending you an acceptance notice on his own letterhead stationery.

(3) *Make sure your name is on the upper left-hand corner of every page.*

A cover letter is nice, but not necessary. It is generally quite clear why you submitted your poems. The whole thing should be put into an envelope large enough to take the pages flat if there are five or more of them. Fewer than five may be folded into a legal size envelope. Hold everything together with a paper clip, not a staple. If you are mailing the pages flat, it is a good idea to use cardboard backing so the corners won't get rumpled on the first trip to an editor. (If you don't intend to send it out again after it comes back once, you might as well give up in the first place and hunt up that trunk.)

The amount of material of any kind that is accepted the first time out is infinitesimal, at least until you have gained a reputation. If you feel sure it is a good poem, don't start getting discouraged before it comes back at least the twentieth time.

SELF-PUBLICATION

Perhaps the most ingenious way to get a poem into print was a system said to have been used by poet Gelett Burgess when he was still a boy. He wrote to the "Letters to the Editor" section of the local newspaper, using an assumed name and inquiring if any other reader could tell him the title and author of a poem which ended with a certain last line. Two days later he wrote a letter of reply, quoting the entire poem and giving the name of the author—Gelett Burgess.

If your ambitions are greater than this, if you have a considerable body of verse that you think is publishable but can't find a publisher for, there is the possibility of publishing it as a book at your own expense. There are at least two ways to go about this.

The first is to have it done by what is known as a *vanity press* publishing house, which specializes in printing books that have not made the grade with standard paying publishers. Instead of their paying you, you pay them. If you have more money than time, they must be your best bet, since for a specified amount of money they will produce a specific number of copies of your book. The cost per book will go down as the number you order goes up, since the bulk of the expense is in setting type and getting ready to go.

Do not worry about where to find these publishers. They generally run advertisements in magazines for writers, such as *The Writer* and *Writer's Digest*. Furthermore, if your name becomes known through the grapevine as an eager but not entirely successful writer, they will probably bombard you with brochures.

The nice thing about doing business with one of them is that after you have completed your negotiations (I would recommend getting bids from more than one) and submitted your manuscript, they will take care of all the details like selecting the right paper, type-face, binding, and so on. When they get your money, they will be able to deliver the agreed-upon number of copies of a well-constructed, professional-looking volume, suitable for storage in your garage or basement.

The only thing the vanity press cannot do is sell the copies of your book for you. It is not that they are unwilling to do that, but book stores are understandably loath to order books that no commercial publisher would take a chance on. They feel that most of the products of a vanity press are bound to be junk, and if they can be convinced that this book is an exception, *you* are going to have to do the convincing.

If you decide against vanity press publication, your next best bet will be to become your own publisher. This is substantially cheaper, but will require you to take care of every detail yourself. You have to find a printer.° Offset printing is probably the cheapest way to do a really nice job, and that choice will make it possible for you to be your own compositor by typing the pages yourself and having them photographically reduced to conceal any minor irregularities of the type. This is a nice thing about poetry—you don't have to worry about keeping the right margin even. If you are a sloppy typist, you should probably splurge and have the typing done professionally.

In any event, you will find yourself in long serious conversations with your printer over details like weight of paper and page size and number. Pages are traditionally bound in little bundles called "signatures," and there are specific numbers of pages that can economically be put into each signature. You may have to leave out a poem or two, or write more to make things fit.

° Get acquainted with R. R. Bowker's annual directory of the publishing world, *Literary Market Place*, described later in this book.

Before you give your printer the go-ahead, you should find a book-binder and discuss with him advantages and disadvantages of paperback and hard cover, pricewise and otherwise. Some of the things he tells you may affect decisions you and the printer have to make. Or perhaps you should explore a new plastic binding technique, which enables one to bind individual sheets instead of signatures. In some places you can even rent a table-top do-it-yourself binding machine and do your own plastic binding—another money-saver.

When it's all done, you will know all the wrong ways to go about publishing a book and some of the right ones. You will have saved considerable money, but the volumes may look a little more home-made than ones the vanity press would have produced. And, as before, you may have a garageful of books. Autographed, they make dandy Christmas presents (for one Christmas), and some of your friends and classmates may even buy copies. But eventually, even if you have a lot of friends, you are going to need the space in the garage, perhaps for the car, and something will have to be done with the books. This will be the case no matter which way you went about getting the book published.

A friend of mine published a book of poems herself, then put a few in the back of her car and went around to various book stores, asking them to accept half a dozen copies on consignment (to be paid for only if sold). She was a persuasive young woman, and she had a lot of friends, some of whom, I suspect, made phone calls to bookstores inquiring about the book before she arrived. She was also lucky in that she lived in a large metropolitan area with many bookstores. Over a period of a few years, I believe she disposed of almost the entire printing of five hundred.

If you publish your own book, by all means copyright it. The process is not difficult, but it does require some advance planning. You can find instructions in *A Copyright Guide* by Harriet Pilpel or *Writer's Market* or *The World Almanac*. And write to the Copyright Office, Library of Congress, Washington, D. C. 20540, for application blanks and detailed instructions.

There really isn't much money in poetry, and unfortunately, fame seems hard to come by, too. Nevertheless, you *can* have your poems published.

Part III

FICTION

Chapter 10
What is Fiction?

All writing is divided into two parts: prose and poetry. We have already defined poetry somewhat inadequately as writing with an uneven right margin, then gone on and attributed all sorts of other characteristics to it in Chapters 5 and 6. Prose, then, is everything except poetry. In general it is writing in which we try, within the limitations of our tools (handwriting, typewriter, linotype, etc.), to keep the right margin even except for vertical lists or the ends of paragraphs. To go further, let's say that it would be unusual to find rhyming prose; that rhythm will probably be less strongly marked than in poetry, and that prose comes in paragraphs instead of stanzas. Just about all the other hallmarks of poetry *may* be found in good prose, and often are, although less frequently than in good poetry. Most of us may be intrigued, like the man in the story, to find that we have been speaking prose all our lives.

NON-FICTION

Prose, then, includes a letter to the library explaining how you lost that book, directions for re-lighting the pilot light on

the water heater, and Anthony Burgess' *The Clockwork Orange.*
Now all we have to do is separate prose into fiction and non-
fiction. Of the three examples given above, we can clearly place
the pilot light instructions in the non-fiction category, *The
Clockwork Orange* in the fiction bin, and reserve judgment on
the letter to the library. *Non-fiction* includes all attempts to
convey fact, at least insofar as the writer knows it, or to ex-
pound an opinion based on fact as the writer perceives it.
Essays that you have written for English composition classes,
articles in magazines or books, Army field manuals, and books
like St. Augustine's *City of God* or Alvin Toffler's *Future Shock*
are all classified as non-fiction. Each of these works is probably
written with a writer's bias of some kind or other, but each
purports to give facts with the assurance of the writer that they
are true—or, if he goes into flights of imagination, he is obliged
to label them clearly so that they will not entrap the reader into
believing that they are guaranteed to be true. These types of
writing are important, but they are not part of the subject
matter of this book.

FICTION

Fiction may attempt to persuade the reader to accept the
writer's beliefs, and it may contain a number of facts, either in
minor details like the number of flutings on a pillar of the
Parthenon or in psychological fact concerning the way people
behave, but the author, by labeling his work as fiction, gives
clear notice to the reader that most of the specifics he is about
to read are imaginary and not reliable evidence for settling bets
on matters of fact. Indeed, it is common for novels to print a
specific disclaimer stating that the characters are not based on
"any person, living or dead," especially if they really are to
some extent. Even "historical" novels and stories follow actual
events only loosely, and the author may make up and put into
the mouths of real people, long since dead, speeches that were
probably not made at all, and that certainly cannot be verified.
Fiction writers sometimes even make minor alterations in

sequence of historical events, making act B precede act A in order to make a more orderly story. In a history book (non-fiction), this would be a reprehensible lie, and the writer would assuredly be drummed out of the profession of historian. In fiction, however, it is art, and if it is successful, the writer will be congratulated.

Fiction writing in general makes use of three basic techniques in creating a story: narration, description, and dialogue.

NARRATION

Narration is perhaps the most important of the three. It is possible to write all of a moderately brief story by use of narration alone. Narration is telling what happened. None of the characters speak, or if they do, their exact words are not used and we are told only the general sense of what was said. Thus, if we wanted to put the following dialogue into narration

> "You're a liar!"
> "Not as big a one as you!"
> "Bigger. You've had more practice."
> "Everybody in your family's liars. Your mother's a liar, your father's a liar, your grandmother's a liar—"
> "My grandmother is dead, you liar."

we might simply say: The two boys questioned each other's veracity and exchanged heated insults.

Obviously, narration is quicker than dialogue. Much more action can be covered in the same number of words. On the other hand, narration is not likely to be as dramatic, nor does it give the reader the feeling of being *there* as well as good dialogue does. However, since going in detail through very many conversations like the one above would soon get wearisome, it is handy to change the pace by encapsulating some of it into narration. Similarly, narration does not include detailed description of either the persons involved in the story or the place where it is going on. Such descriptions are often invaluable in giving tone and emotion to the story, but like dialogue, description can easily be overdone, and the sweep of narration can often carry the reader past a lot of unnecessary descriptive minutiae. Since narration is the basic ingredient of a story, we tend to think of stories primarily in narrative terms, and most beginning writers have the least difficulty in handling it.

DESCRIPTION

Description is like the background music in a movie or television program: much of the time you aren't even aware of it, but you immediately notice when it is missing, as it provides emotional tone, believability, and other story values. Sometimes description lets us decide whether to love or hate a character before he even performs any meaningful action in the story.

The most successful description is done by the use of details rather than by concentrating on the big obvious elements. And sometimes not too many details are needed. The great Russian writer Anton Chekhov has a character in his play *The Seagull* describe the artistry of a writer: "He would just mention the neck of a broken bottle glistening on the dam and the black shadow of a mill-wheel—and there you'd have a moonlit night."

Edgar Allan Poe, in "The Fall of the House of Usher," uses little more actual detail in his description of the Usher mansion:

> I looked upon the scene before me—upon the mere house, and the simple landscape features of the domain—upon the bleak walls—upon the vacant eye-like windows—upon a few rank sedges—and upon a few white trunks of decaying trees—with an utter depression of soul which I can compare to no earthly sensation more properly than to the afterdream of the reveler upon opium—the bitter lapse into everyday life—the hideous dropping off of the veil.

You will note that we know very little about the specifications of the house. How many stories high was it? Was it red brick, gray weatherbeaten shingles, or cinder block? Why were the windows "vacant and eyelike"? Mr. Poe did not give us these obvious facts because he wasn't interested in selling us the house; he wanted us to share his feeling of horror which he describes at more length than the appearance of the building. So he uses *only* those details which lead us to that feeling.

Another approach to description still makes use of details but with a heavier hand, in such volume that they look like a list or catalogue. Take the following description written by a student [H. A. Pazienza, in a sketch entitled "Three Meals a Day, a Roof Over Your Head, a Ration of Tobacco and Rolling Papers"], which reads, in part:

The sawdust sprinkled over the floor had covered most of his wet shoes by now, and he could feel the little chips of wood working forward from the holes in his heel to settle between his toes. Just in front of him stood a large wooden barrel and a sign tacked to it reading "Old Fashion Dill Pickles." From one side of the barrel hung a pair of metal tongs, and attached to the other side was a holder containing little waxed paper bags. The top of the barrel was plastic and hinged so as to allow customers to reach in with the tongs and select the biggest and best pickles. He did just that and held an enormous one before his eyes. He drew it closer, and it hung perilously over his tongue. His mouth watered. Quickly he released the pickle and watched it fall back into the vinegar and spicy brine.

As he walked on, he felt prisoner of the lines and lines of titillating foods. There were tins of sardines, imported from far-away places like Norway and Portugal, and oysters from France, and tiny clams in olive oil and natural juices. He saw cheeses of all kinds, including Camembert, several Swiss', Liederkranz, one of his favorites, from upstate New York—a horrible smelling but delicious tasting cheese, and speckled Blue Cheese from Germany, Cheddar, and American. On the next aisle, neatly lined and with seals unbroken, were a variety of crackers and cookies, and opposite them were the cereals, the cold brands and the stick-to-your-ribs oatmeal and wheats that he loved so much sprinkled with cinnamon, some brown sugar, and a patty of fresh butter. But all this was beyond his reach—beyond his means—and he thought of ending his torment and leaving.

When I tell you that this is only about a third of the complete passage, you can see that this kind of description can have the effect of overwhelming the reader—which is what the author intended. The effect is called "supermarket daze," well known to poor young housewives and to any small child standing in a candy store with a single nickel.

Descriptions may be either objective or slanted. Slanted descriptions are those which, like the example given from "The Fall of the House of Usher," try to impose the writer's attitude toward the thing described on the reader. Slanting is done partially by choosing which details to use (the delightful weathered gray of the clapboards, or the fact that they are warped and the remaining paint is peeling away), and partly by the use of descriptive words (Is the girl's hair "golden" or "bleached"? Is she "popular" or "promiscuous"?). If you look over the student's description, you will see that it is also slanted, though more subtly.

DIALOGUE

Dialogue is merely the use of what the grammar books call "direct quotation," the use of the exact words of characters to tell part of the story. As has been noted, dialogue lends realism and dramatic effect to a story. It also helps us to understand characters, since what they say and how they say it are very much a part of their personalities.

There are several problems in dialogue, but the first is to make the characters say what you want them to say and still sound like themselves. It would not do, for example to have a normal two-year-old child say, "I have severe contusions of the left hip and an abrasion on my left knee from having tripped on the edge of the rug." If you catch yourself perpetrating something like that, the only thing to do is listen to a two-year-old (you won't have to wait long until he trips). Probably it will sound more like this:

> "Waaaaaaaaah! Mommy, mommy! Waaaaaah-snf-waaaah!"
> "What's the trouble, Bobby?"
> "Waaaaah-snf vadow. Waaaaaaaaah!
> "Just try to stop crying, so I can understand and do something about it. Did you get hurt when you fell down?"
> "Waaaaaaaaah-uh—yah."
> "Oh, that's too bad. Poor Bobby got hurt. Can you tell Mommy where you hurt?"
> "Snf. Hurt right here-uh. Waaah. Get me Band-Aid?"

The same is true of any character you choose. If your character is an itinerant fruit-picker, don't have him talk like a psychiatrist—or vice versa.

NARRATION EXAMPLES

Since it's hard to talk about narration in the abstract, let's look at a couple of student efforts to write narration with no more than a minimum of contamination with description or dialogue. "Pure" narration is hard to write, since some description is usually necessary because action has to take place somewhere. And occasional dramatic points seem to cry out for dialogue.

DRUNK ROLL

How I Very Nearly Entered Penal Servitude in my Youth in Minneapolis

It must have seemed like an explosion, from the outside looking in. I'd been sitting and drinking most of the evening in the Green Goiter, and buying drinks for a little tail in a red dress who worked there. She was a B-girl, working in the Green Goiter for a percentage on the drinks she conned. I was aware of this, but that winter was lonely. The rest of the harvesting crew had gone back South, but I had opted to stay in Minneapolis, planning to enroll at the University there in the Spring. I had drunk myself dull and the duller I got, the less important little Red's occupational status seemed. It was naive of me, but I really believed that the plans that we were making for after closing would follow.

> *In the first line of the piece, the word* explosion *acts as what is called a "story hook": it promises that something exciting is going to happen and keeps the reader reading to find out what—by which time, we hope, he is interested in something more.*
> *Notice also that there is no description of the bar other than its name, and only enough of the girl to identify her and explain any actions she might take.*

The explosion occurred when I spent my last fifteen dollars on the last phony champagne split that little red tail would get from me. She asked me to buy her another drink, and I told her that gee, I was broke now and would she mind if I just waited for her? She signaled the bartender, and he inquired if I would like another drink. Again, I replied that I was just waiting for little Red. He nodded, and as little Red moved on to another fish, two burly bouncer-types grabbed the slobbering kid and ran him out the door. That was the explosion.

> *The story continues and explains about the explosion. At this point you are expected to be interested enough in what is happening to go on. Are you? What did the writer do right (or wrong) to bring you to your opinion? Did you have trouble identifying the slobbering kid as the narrator of the story? If so, what should have been done to improve the situation?*

I hit the sidewalk on my feet and stayed on my feet through the kind offices of a convenient parking meter.

It took several minutes for psyche to catch soul, and then I realized just how drunk I really was. There was a nut-shriveling wind, and the plows had banked the snow half-way up the parking meters. As a matter of fact, I was standing with one un-galoshed foot twisted into the pile of slush at the curb. I cursed; and when I was through cursing, I swore. And when I was through with that I got down to elemental things like muthers', and bastards, and sons of bitches, and they can't do that to me.

If you were wondering what it means for psyche to catch soul, I will join you. I believe the two words are synonyms, and my dictionary agrees.
There is some description here, of the snowy street and the weather. Notice that it is spare, and that we probably need it to explain future actions.

I was by then firmly convinced that red tail had meant to come with me but first I had to have more of the magic of money. They had broken me in the Green Goiter, and to no profitable end, or rather tail-end. In my confusion and growing anger I decided to acquire funds, and the best, the inspired course of action, would be to roll a drunk!

This paragraph takes place mostly in the mind of the narrator, but it still qualifies as narration. It is necessary to explain the rather remarkable frame of mind that the rest of the action requires—set a drunk to roll a drunk.

I hit fist into palm in delight, and shambled around the corner into the alley alongside the bar. Committed to my course of action, it occurred to me that the more dignified gent who had sat down the bar from me had been flashing a sizable roll all evening. As I recalled, he had been a rather wispy man, tall, with a pencil-moustache, wearing a coat with a fur collar, and deriving great pleasure from stroking the bulging knee of a fat little bar girl. I resolved to relieve him of any sum which the inhabitants of the Green Goiter left him.

By then the cold was beginning to penetrate my drunk; and it was cold, colder than a witch's tit. I stamped my feet into the packed snow in the alley and hammered my gloved fists

against the brick wall. Boy, was I ready for action. All I had to
do was wait for my mark and leap out behind him with a brutal
clubbing blow to the head. One good belt and he would be mine
for the cleaning. One mighty smash up along the ear would be
all that would be needed.

There was a puffy gust of warmth and sound from the
Goiter. I leaned forward, and ducked my head around the
corner to look. Two young men, muscular working types, were
leaving, heading my way. Prudently I decided to stay my
mighty arm, and as I ducked back they passed me unnoticed in
the shadows. Again, I mulled my scheme, smug and self-sat-
isfied; secure in the knowledge that wow, boy, would I make a
pack on this and then we'll see how little red tail acts.

> *Notice that again we have short descriptions of persons: the*
> *affluent but "wispy" man he picked for his mark and the two*
> *muscular working types he avoided. And again, we needed the*
> *information to understand our hero's attitudes toward them.*

A yellow cab pulled up to the bar and reluctantly released
an older man, a wealthy looking older man, and I damned my
luck that the cab was able to deliver him directly to the door. If
he had passed my alley I'd've had him.

I waited again; it seemed an interminable time, and then I
heard the clicky-clack of little heels on the cleared sidewalk. I
ducked my fattening head around the corner again and my
lecherous eye fell upon a sweet young thing passing the Green
Goiter in my direction. Thinking rapidly, I realized that a
whole loaf was better than the no loaf that I had had thus far; so
stepping around the corner with a leer, I said, "Hi ya babe."
The frost was more severe than the inclemency of the weather,
and I stepped back into my alley.

Almost immediately I heard again the sounds of revelry as
the door to the Green Goiter opened. Looking swiftly, I saw my
prey, walking rapidly, briskly, in the opposite direction!
Enraged, I leaped out to pursue. It was a fruitless chase, for I
had no sooner started than he arrived at and entered his car

parked at the far corner. Yielding to ill-fated circumstances, I re-entered my alley, determined to smite and mug the very next passer-by viciously, whoever he might be.

Once more I waited, until I heard the clop of a man approaching in galoshes. With my mighty arm, Excalibur, raised high, I joined battle; to confusedly scratch my head and ask the beat patrolman directions to my boarding house.

Knudson

The final paragraph here has a couple of faults: first, the mock-heroism is over-done—calling his arm Excalibur *after King Arthur's sword is going a little far, as is the term* joined battle. *Second, the last sentence goes by so quickly that a careless reader might miss the kicker—that in his enthusiasm he had almost committed the social error of attacking a policeman, presumably cold sober.*

"Drunk Roll" is an anecdote—the type of tale a person might tell on himself in the company of friends. The next example is a more sophisticated piece of work with a complete plot—or rather two plots which come together at the climax, just before the end. It could be classed as a short-short story.

Electric Ice-Box

Something happened when I was ten years old that made me feel so warm and good inside that I cried. Yet it became an evil thing.

What happened was that I found fifty dollars. Well, I didn't actually find it. I was rummaging around in my Mom's dresser and there it was. The drawer was lined with old newspaper and the money was under. I knew it wasn't Mom's money. In the first place, we were poor and had never had fifty dollars. Second, we had only lived there for two months, and the faded newspaper had been in that drawer for a long time. That's how I knew the money had been forgotten by a previous tenant—now long gone.

The first brief paragraph does two things. It is a story hook,
promising something interesting, and it does something a little
more subtle, called foreshadowing. That means not telling us what
is going to happen, which would be fatal to this story, but setting
us up so that when it does happen, we can look back and say, "So
that's what it meant!" We are now ready for it when it comes.
The small amount of description of the dresser drawers is essential
to make the narrator's conclusion seem valid.

Though my father was a laborer and poorly paid, we
always had a roof over our heads, plain but plentiful food on the
table, and, come Christmas, presents for us kids. Compared
with the McCarthys, who lived above us, we were fortunate.
Mr. McCarthy was a loafer and, worse, a drunkard who beat
and abused his wife something awful. Once my father had to go
up there and knock Mr. McCarthy out. They had three kids,
twin girls about my sister's age, and the baby, Shawn. Shawn
was sickly and, the doctor said, sure to die. Mrs. McCarthy did
laundry and housework for rich folks. I felt sorry for Mrs.
McCarthy.

This paragraph is background information and doesn't seem very
fascinating, but it contains essential information, including a
whole new plot element. This was a good place for it, because we
already want to know what the narrator is going to do with the
fifty dollars, and are willing to keep reading for awhile to find out.
Which we do, forthwith.

The instant I found the money, I knew exactly what it was
for. My mother always wanted one of those electric ice-boxes,
but of course that was over our head. Even in those days a new
one cost a lot of money. But then again, fifty bucks was not to be
sneezed at. As luck would have it, I found a real nice, modern
electric ice-box in a second-hand store, but it was fifty-five
dollars. I put on a sad face and, showing the man my fifty
dollars, explained it was a gift for my Mom. He not only let it go
for the fifty, he threw in free delivery to boot.

To make things even better, Mom's birthday was only a
few days off. It almost drove me nuts to wait, but we held up

delivery for her birthday. If I live to be a hundred, I'll never forget when that man brought the present. It was all gleaming white, with a red ribbon wrapped around and tied in a bow. It was lovely! The old Jew had pasted a little paper to the door which read, "Happy birthday, with love from Robert." I felt so good I bawled.

I think we must forgive the author for lapsing into a brief description of the refrigerator (notice how the time frame of the story is set by the term electric ice-box, *which ceased to be generally used in the mid-thirties).*

Mom hugged me and kissed me something fierce. Her face all wet with tears. In the warm afternoon of that summer day we cried together, my Mom and me. I, with the faint flush of tenderness that comes with generosity, and she for the man that I might be.

I did not tell my mother where I got the money, only that I found it and came by it honestly. She trusted me.

Another short paragraph to remind us that the story isn't over yet, and the evil thing *is still to come.*

We pushed the old ice-box onto the back porch, and, for all I know, it's still there. At first the shiny, white, new one seemed odd sitting there, but after while we quit looking at it so much. My Dad liked it all right, but he muttered that the money could be spent better than that. My sister got all stony-faced when she learned that it was my present to Mom, and said nothing.

One week later, in the morning, Shawn died. "Poor Mrs. McCarthy," all the people said. "She don't have enough troubles, and now the Lord has taken her little baby." Even her husband sobered up, and went around with a long face.

Now we pick up the second plot element, which we had temporarily forgotten, but we can now recall because the groundwork was laid for it near the beginning. The quotation may be a violation of the "pure narrative" rule, but it certainly lends realism to the situation.

It was that afternoon that I felt the touch of evil. For some reason I went into my folks' bedroom, and found Mom tearing through the dresser drawers. Things had been thrown all around, and her face was pale, like a person in shock. "What's the matter, Mom?" I asked, but cold shivers had told me the answer.

Distraught, my mother cried, "I can't find the money I hid for Mrs. McCarthy—so Shawn won't have a pauper's grave."

L. J. Scott

Here is the point at which the two plot elements come together, and their convergence makes the climax, the highest interest point in the story. Many stories have a "resolution" after the climax, in which all conflicts are taken care of one way or another. In this story, would it have been better to have gone on and told what the detailed outcome was? Why?

DESCRIPTION EXAMPLES

Talking about description (describing it) is much harder than showing it. The same is true about writing description. It is easier to *show* the reader a scene than to tell him about it—to lay out carefully selected details and let him see for himself. Sometimes, though, we would rather tell him about it, as when we are describing something through the eyes of a character, so that we get some insight on the character as well as the scene. The first of the two sketches to follow is shown through the eyes of a character. Each sketch is intended to portray a place with a person in it.

ADAGIO

It was early. Class wouldn't begin for almost an hour, so she would have the practice room all to herself. She pushed the scarred street door open and climbed the worn, creaky stairs, automatically skipping the wobbly third step. She climbed to the rhythm running through her mind, the "Rose Adagio," the ballet she would perform tonight. She climbed easily—her well-shaped, muscular legs carrying her lightly as she hummed to herself. Reaching the top of the stairs, she glanced into the small cluttered office. It was a musty little room, full of memories. Faded pictures crowded the walls, pictures of Madame's former triumphs—images of a young and lovely dancer at the peak of her career. Books overflowed a rickety corner bookcase and leaned in drunken stacks against one wall. They were not new, shiny, plastic coated books, but old friends—often read and well-loved. An antique mahogany desk took up most of the room and it, too, was cluttered with books, papers, photographs, an empty tea cup, and a neat pile of orange peelings. She smiled as she went by the empty room— never really empty because the beloved Madame's presence was always felt there.

> *Notice the use of intimate detail, such as* the wobbly *third* step *and* a *neat* pile of orange peelings. *These little specifics are more effective than the books and pictures, which are more generalized. Note also that the narrative of action is necessary to both describe the character and to move her eyes to where we can see through them.*

She remembered her first meeting with Madame Ruloff. She had been very young, very nervous, and had clung to her mother's hand as they stood before the mahogany desk. Now, eight years later, she remembered clearly the fear and excitement of being accepted into the school, of being a "new girl." She remembered her first class and how, in her shyness, she had wanted to hide behind the other dancers—away from Madame's eagle eye. She remembered how, gradually, her new life had become so important that her home and family had receded into the background. Now her whole life was bound up in the world of ballet and nothing else mattered.

The bit of "backflash" narration here is part of the mood of the description.

As she walked down the hall to the dressing room she tried to see the school as it would appear to an "outsider." The walls were a dull utilitarian gray, as were all the walls in the school. A spider web decorated one dark corner. No one could be bothered with cleaning corners when all one's heart and energy were needed for dancing. Scribbled on the wall by the dressing room door were the words "Diana loves Tchaikovsky" and the smudgy fingerprints on the door itself were mute evidence of the hundreds of sweaty hands that had pushed on the door after a hard class. Upon entering the room a newcomer would probably be slightly overwhelmed by the odor—not the delicate scent of cologne and rose petals—but rather the musty smell of unwashed tights, the wet-dog odor of damp woolens, and an over-all, sweet-sour, sweaty smell. A grimy window at one end of the room overlooked the roof tops and ventilating pipes of the old office building behind the ballet school. Someone had put a potted geranium on the window sill and it was loved and nursed by almost all the dancers, who hadn't time to love anything or anybody else. In one corner of the room was a shower stall constructed mainly of cracked tile and tin. It never offered anything but cold water and cockroaches, so it was shunned by all but the very brave. Along one wall of the dressing room were three make-up mirrors, each with a shelf and drawer underneath. A long clothes rack stood in the center of the room and was strung with old costumes, practice clothes, and damp tights hung up to dry. A long window seat built against one wall was stuffed full of unmatched shoes, tights with runs, cast-off sweaters, and other odds and ends. Two benches and a wash basin completed the decor of the room with a brown, wrinkled apple core and three hairpins presenting a still-life on the edge of the basin. The faucet was dripping, as usual, and had made a rusty smudge on the porcelain.

Notice that seeing a place through someone's eyes can have a disadvantage, particularly when that character is so familiar with it that he no longer really sees it. The author here resorted to the device of having the character try to see the school as it would appear to an outsider. *Can you think of other ways it could have been managed? Also note that most of the details of the description are distinctly non-glamorous. In fact they portray the place as being permanently the way you wish your home wouldn't get every time your back is turned. What effect does this have on your opinion of the fairyland world of ballet?*

She changed her clothes, noticing with a grimace that a run had started in her tights. Her leotard was still slightly damp, but she must save the sleeveless one for the afternoon rehearsal. Pulling on her soft, slightly tattered old ballet shoes, she picked up her point shoes and, throwing a towel over her shoulder, walked down the hall to the ballet studio. It was a large, high ceilinged room, with many windows. One whole wall was mirrored and the other three had practice barres attached to them. A big old grand piano stood in one corner and a droopy potted palm showed that at one time someone had tried to "beautify" the room a little. In the opposite corner was a rosin box. She went to the box now, crunched a small rock of rosin with her heel, and rubbed each foot in the powder. She walked over and stood appraisingly in front of the mirror. She saw a slender, wiry girl, a little taller than average, with muscular legs, slim hips, and very little bust. She was strong and supple, with the stamina of a workhorse, but graceful and fragile looking. She smiled as she remembered the little girl she had been: the braces on the teeth, the knobby knees, the tight braids of hair. She remembered also the homesickness, the aching muscles, the blisters, and the utter discouragement she had often felt. She was a soloist now. She still felt discouraged sometimes, especially when very tired, and, like all good dancers, was never completely satisfied with a performance, but it was her life. She loved the discipline, the challenge, the constant effort to be better. With one last glance at the dancer in the mirror she moved toward the barre to begin the tedious, necessary, daily warm-up exercises.

Trina Greig

*The device of having your point-of-view character look into a
mirror to describe himself is so good that it is rather worn-out by
now. Certainly in a room with this many mirrors it might seem
natural enough, but it is hard to believe that she would see herself
with so objective an eye. Most women look into a mirror to find
flaws that they may be able to correct—a blackhead to squeeze, a
raveling to cut off, or a loose curl to comb.*

The sketch above got its best effect from the use of detail,
mostly familiar if slightly unpleasant, that seems to strip the
mystique from the world of ballet, showing us the inner, or
seamy, side. It makes us feel better for knowing that dancers are
really human, and probably makes us more sympathetic toward
dancers too.

Now let us take a look at another description and the still
stronger ironic effect of the contrast between the scene itself
and the persons in it.

Anachronism

The name of the retirement home, Shady Knoll, is a mis-
nomer. The building squats in a slight depression of the ground,
and the scant shadows cast by the transplanted saplings shade
only ants, industriously creating havoc in the newly re-seeded
lawn. The building itself is stuccoed a rosy pink, the color of
hopefilled dawns, of the cheeks of little girls jumping rope, of
the clenched buds of sweetheart roses, of the luminescence of a
baby's toes.

A long shallow patio extends the length of the street front-
age on the east, just deep enough for a single row of aluminum
and plastic webbing chairs. Later on in the morning, these will
be occupied, one by one, by bundles of brittle bone and sinew,
held together loosely by a covering of mottled skin. But now the
day is still too young, the warmth of the sun still impotent
against the lingering damp of the night, and the chairs are
empty.

The general ironic tone of this description is set by the opening description of Shady Knoll as contrasted sharply to its name. And, perhaps even more forcefully for being a little separated and not being specifically commented on, is the contrast between the connotations made by the pink of the building and the blunt description of its occupants. All the descriptions of the pink shade are carefully selected and heavily slanted. The description is superficially objective, but the author definitely knows what she wants us to think.

This morning, as usual, Carrie is up long before any of the others. Each day, when the clatter of breakfast preparation begins in the kitchen, Carrie is walking along the brick paths ringing Shady Knoll, as if she still needed to fetch in kindling from the woodshed to start the day's fire in the old black range. A lifelong habit is not ended with the snapping shut of a suitcase.

Over her starched housedress she wears a heavy knitted sweater, fashioned in a haphazard design of many colors of yarn. The soft blue was left over from the snowsuit she had made for her grandson, the scarlet from the remnants of countless mittens (mittens should always be of scarlet yarn, so they can be found easily when abandoned in a snowbank), the navy blue worsted from a sailor's watch cap. Carrie's sweater is her memory book.

Notice the somewhat unusual device of Carrie's sweater to point up the fact that she has little but memories to sustain her. Does it work? Do you feel that it is overly sentimental?

Her gnarled fingers keep pace with her thoughts as she weighs the merits of fried potatoes, ham, and basted eggs against hot cakes, sausages and oatmeal as breakfast for the hay crew. She is vicariously stripping the skins from last night's boiled potatoes when the chimes sound discreetly. Carrie longs once again to hear that honest bellow, "Come and get it, or I'll feed it to the hogs," and she fights down the desire to run searching for the place where they've hidden the triangle gong.

We might question the use of the word honest *to describe the old standard farm call to meals (I don't think the cook really expects much of that breakfast to go into the pig-trough), but it is certainly more vital than the discreet sound of the chimes. See how the decor described in the following paragraph compares with the probable appearance of the farmhouse.*

The dining room is furnished in chrome, plastic, and formica, all looking as if it had been bought in a drug store. The small tables, set for four people, are centered with rigid bouquets of scentless sweet peas in improbable paint-box colors, ultramarine, magenta, and fuschia. Instead of the fried potatoes and ham that Carrie had decided on, she is served a small bird-bath dish of farina with skim milk and a rubbery boiled egg, prepared by a cook who hasn't yet learned to tell time. The coffee is Postum, Carrie is sure, and she wonders if her chipped blue enameled coffee pot would make it taste more like coffee. *In which box have they packed it away?* An old lady across the table spills farina down the front of her dress, and Carrie thinks *how sad to grow old* and hides her own quivering hands in her lap beneath the tablecloth.

After breakfast, most of Shady Knoll's residents move into the sitting room, which overlooks the rear of the property through ceiling-high glass sliding doors. The knot around the television set divides itself peevishly into soap-opera and quiz-show factions, and little quarrels about the volume of sound spring up. Along one wall, card tables are set up under hanging bubble lamps, and checker boards and decks of cards are stacked on the bottom shelf of a bookcase. Several copies of the morning paper are splayed on a low table for those who still have enough eyesight or interest in the world outside of Shady Knoll. Beyond the glass doors the sprinklers are already watering the birds-of-paradise and hibiscus bushes. A pair of sparrows ignore the brimming cement saucer held by green-capped gnomes, and elect to take a shower, tossing off the shining drops with rapid flicks of their wings. Carrie watches them, wondering where she will find space for her tomato plants, a few hills of cucumbers, and a couple of rows of snap beans. *There should be enough fruit jars in the cellar.* The television set screams a commercial for better-than-bright laundry, and Carrie is snatched back to Shady Knoll, with not even a smudge of loamy earth left under her fingernails.

As the sun gathers strength, the chairs on the front patio begin to fill up, one by one. Some are rocking and some are still, waiting. Waiting for lunch, waiting for the mailman, waiting for the sun to go down, or simply waiting. Carrie, her shoulders snug in her many-colored sweater, lowers herself gingerly onto the plastic and aluminum and settles back to wait, too.

Anita Jones

This descriptive sketch contains quite a bit of what is apparent narration, yet is still description, since the action only helps portray the place and the people and has no significance of its own. It is definitely not a story, as "Electric Ice-Box" was, because nothing has happened—at least nothing that will change things, nothing that will not happen tomorrow and the day after *ad infinitum.* That is precisely the point—that nothing ever will happen.

The use of the present tense throughout is one of the techniques for making us feel it—that it is going on again now, even as we read it. (Present tense is a hard one to handle. We generally think of stories happening in past tense, and a writer starting out in present has to be eternally watchful, or he will find himself drifting back into past tense.)

At any rate, even the most progressive and up-to-the-minute reader can hardly miss the pathos behind this study of the old (and presumably solid and real) fighting a foredoomed delaying action against the new, the shiny, and the ersatz.

DIALOGUE EXAMPLES

Dialogue has been saved for last because more students seem to find it hard. So now that you are beginning to get confidence in your own ability, let's take a look at some examples. But first, consider one of the problems: how do you make clear who is speaking? Of course if the two speakers use different language levels or have materially different points of view, there is no real problem. Just start a new paragraph each time you change speakers, start out with quotation marks, and go at it (see "A Quickie," the second dialogue example following, or Hemingway's "A Clean, Well-Lighted Place").

But if the speakers sound pretty much the same, at least in print, there have to be some hints. The simplest is "I said" just before or after the quotation, or even in the middle of it to slow down and punctuate the conversation. And don't be afraid of the word "said." It can be repeated almost an infinite number of times without getting tiresome. Or substitute "asked" or "replied" now and then, if appropriate. But stay away from "she screamed" or "he snarled." If you try too hard for variety, the reader stops looking at what is said because he's so fascinated by your word choice that he doesn't want to miss a single "she sighed." Let what is said indicate how it would have been said. Also, if you need variety, you might try, instead of a "he said," having him perform some small action, so it will be evident who said it:

> He struck a match and sucked the flame into his pipe-bowl. "I don't think so." He shook the match out and laid it on the ashtray.

This makes a welcome break in the dialogue, too. Incidentally, cigarettes may be harmful to health, but they are handy to keep a character busy, tapping, lighting, and leaning forward to get rid of the ash. And if you use a pipe, the possibilities are endless.

THE DROPOUT

Being a grandmother has many compensations; it is an education within itself; if there are several grandchildren, it is good training for the Diplomatic Corps. Several months ago, I accepted a dinner invitation at the home of a daughter, the mother of several small youngsters. I was greeted by a noisy babble of welcome and the news that five year old Michael was confined to his room. He was being punished. I knew that there could be myriad reasons for this, and a few minutes later, I slipped away down the hall to his bedroom.

This clearly is not part of the dialogue. How much—if any—of it is necessary? Why?

The small figure was sprawled face down on the bed.
"Michael."
"I got a whipping today," in a muffled voice.
"Oh, your teacher spank you?"
"No."
"Who?"
"Mommy."
"Why? What did you do?"
"Nothing."
"Michael!" I said, with just enough question in my voice to let him know I didn't believe him. I looked down at him and waited. Presently, one eye half-opened and with a lopsided grin, he said, "I played hookey today."

All my training as an English teacher causes me to revolt against the sight of two quotations from different characters in the same paragraph, and in general it's a good precept to follow. However, as I heard senior officer state during my sojourn in the army, "Regulations are made for damn' fools and second lieutenants." The writer of this piece falls into neither category.

"You did," I said, with a slight touch of amazement.
"Yes, Grandmother."
"Why?"
"Billy and I wanted to play."
"You have plenty of time to play, Honey."
"I wanted to play this morning."
"Don't you think the other little boys and girls missed you?"

"No."

"Wonder who sat in your seat?"

"I don't know. I guess nobody."

"What a lonesome little desk. I'll bet it cried."

He rolled completely over and looked up at me. "Desks don't cry, Grandmother."

"You don't think so? Bet they do."

He continued to look at me, not quite sure whether I was serious, or just laughing at him. It was an effort not to grin at him, but I waited; then he said, "Desks don't cry, do they, Grandmother?"

"No, Darling, but I'll bet your teacher missed you."

"No." Then hesitantly, "I guess she did; she likes me." He rolled over again on his tummy and pretended to be asleep. Then, "I had fun, Grandmother."

"Yes, Mike, but don't you have fun at school?"

"Sometimes."

"Well?"

"But I wanted to play." There was a hint of tears, but he muffled them in the pillow. I held his hand while he sobbed, offering what sympathy I could.

Then, exploding with all the fury of a little boy who feels he has been wronged, he said, "I hate Billy."

"Why, Michael? Billy is a nice little boy."

"He is not!"

"All right. He's not a nice little boy, but why do you hate him?"

"He told on me. I hate him."

"That wasn't a bit nice, was it? Why did he tell on you?"

"I don't know."

"Are you sure?"

Then quietly he said, "He told on me—because—because I hit him."

"Why did you hit him, Mike? That wasn't nice either."

"I know, but he took my ball and wouldn't give it back to me." He shrugged his shoulder. "So—I hit him." Perfectly logical!

We sat in companionable silence for another few minutes; then he looked up at me still with a hint of tears in his eyes and his voice. "Grandmother, I'm not a dropout, am I?"

"Where did you get an idea like that?"

"That's what Donald and Diane called me and I heard Mommy tell Daddy that she had a kindergarten dropout. I'm not, am I?"

"I don't think so, Honey."

Then, very seriously, he asked, "Grandmother, what is a dropout?"

"A dropout is someone who quits school before he graduates."

"Grandmother, I'm not a dropout. I'm going back to school."

"No more playing hookey?"

"No. I don't like being called names."

"Good."

He sat up then and reached for me. As I held him close to me he whispered, "I love you, Grandmother."

Then Mommy appeared in the doorway to tell us we would both be accepted at the dinner table if we cared to join them. So, hand in hand, my five year old Michael—my kindergarten dropout—and I walked down the hallway to join the family.

Esther Curry

Notice that although there are signposts now and then along the way in the example above, the levels of speech and points of view of the two characters are so different that there is little danger of getting them confused. And what did you think of Michael's conversation? Did it sound like a five-year-old speaking? How was it accomplished?

Now take a look at the second dialogue example, which takes place between speakers about the same ages and speech levels, but with nothing to indicate who is speaking but the speech itself. Do you have any problem in keeping them straight?

A QUICKIE

I don't care what kind of food these nature freaks eat, but
there's only so much a man can stand.

"Would anyone like anything to eat?"

"Sure."

"Yeah."

"Me too."

"What are you having?"

*Note that the question got four responses, apparently from four
different characters.*

"?? Why, we're having spaghetti with meat sauce."

"Oh definitely not! I stay away from meat."

"Well, is there something else I could offer you?"

"A nice green salad would be fine."

"OK."

"Wait a minute. Are the lettuce and tomatoes organic? I
don't eat lettuce and tomatoes unless they're organic."

"I bought it at Food Bas . . . . "

"No, I couldn't eat that. Do you know they spray plants
with poison?"

"Whatever for?"

"DDT's. They're poison. They use them on all the vege-
tables in the supermarkets."

"Oh, I see."

"I would like something to drink, though."

"Really? What would you like?"

"What have you got?"

"We've got Doctor Pepper, Pepsi-Cola, Seven . . . . "

"No thanks, I don't drink sodas."

"We've got Hi-C, vegetable juice . . . . "

"Canned?"

"Yes."

"No, I don't drink canned juices. Lead poisoning."

"There's beer, wine, and I think a little whiskey."

"No, not any alcohol."

"Canned orange, milk . . . . "

"Raw?"

"Homogenized."

"No. Homogenized milk contains as many toxins as most meats, did you know that?"

"I didn't know that. A glass of water?"

"Is your water chlorinated?"

"Yes."

"No."

"Are you sure you don't want something? You'll be hungry."

"No, I'm all right. It's one of my quirks."

"But you should eat something."

"Look, it's just something I believe, and I really think you should respect my right to believe as I wish."

"Oh, no, don't misunderstand. I'm not forcing anything . . . . "

"I'm sorry, I really didn't mean to sound ungrateful."

"Think nothing of it; everyone's entitled to believe what he wants to believe."

"You're perfectly right."

"Well, dinner's ready. I'm going to sit down and eat now."

At this point, it is apparent from the use of the word I'm *that there are only two people still present. What happened to the other three who answered affirmatively to the original invitation to eat? Try to avoid having questions like this come up in your writing.*

"Go right ahead; I'll just sit here."

"mmmchmm. mmch. mmmmch. mmchm."

"Did I ever tell you about how many people have heart attacks because they eat meat?"

Thom Eisley

If you would like further examples of dialogue by someone who knows how, read almost any of Hemingway's short stories ("A Clean, Well-Lighted Place" or "The Killers" would be fine), or Dorothy Parker's "You were Perfectly Fine" or "Here We Are." J. D. Salinger is an expert on children's dialogue. See "A Perfect Day for Bananafish" and "For Esme, With Love and Squalor."

MIXING THEM UP

In doing the exercises for this chapter, one can't help noticing how hard it is to write using *only* narrative, *only* description, or *only* dialogue. I suspect it is like the story of the horse who was being trained to eat an ever-increasing percentage of sawdust in his oats—just when they got him to eat *all* sawdust, he died. And so will most stories done without a combination of ingredients. How much of each depends on the story and the author's own taste and style, and most of us combine them without really thinking about it. However, if what you write dissatisfies you (or your critics), it may be that your mix is out of balance. Here are some clues that may help you with your problem:

(Clue 1). The language is beautiful, with occasional bright, fresh figures of speech, but the story seems to drag.

Look to see if there is too much description. If you are good at writing description, if you are proud of the way sparkling imagery rolls from your fingers to the page, you are luckier than most of us. However, description, like fire, is a good servant but a hard master. Try drawing a line through all that isn't really necessary to tell the story or gain your effect. This may mean chopping out some of your most deathless prose, but it will be in a good cause. If you can't bear to destroy it, clip it out and paste it into a scrap-book to use in a different piece.

(Clue 2).   The story plunges ahead rapidly, going from a plane crash at sea to a week on a life-raft before the hero is washed up on an island where there are adventures with cannibals; rescued by a helicopter from an aircraft carrier; and returned to Los Angeles, where he falls in with a strange hippie cult who are robbing a bank—all in four thousand words.

Clearly there is too much narration. What you have written is not a short story, but a narrative outline for a novel, or perhaps a series of novels. Sort out any one of the sequences, add enough detailed description and lively dialogue for us to see in a more leisurely fashion what kind of people the characters are and what kind of places they are doing their thing in. If necessary, add more narration of minor supporting actions, too. This sort of thing takes patience, but you will find that it is worth the effort.

(Clue 3.)   The characters are believable, the dialogue is clever and realistic, the story is lifelike—but interminable. It seems to take forever and fifteen minutes for anything to happen.

Check your dialogue. If there is quite a bit, you have probably let yourself record verbatim conversation which would be better summarized in narration or perhaps even omitted completely. This is an unfortunate symptom of the writer who is vain of his ability to write credible dialogue. If your story is too long for its purpose, there is no easier way to condense than to eliminate or summarize dialogue.

CHAPTER 11
BASIC ELEMENTS OF FICTION

In the last chapter we discussed the three techniques of fiction: Narration, description, and dialogue. In this chapter we take up the three *elements* of fiction: *character, plot,* and *theme.*

CHARACTERIZATION

Characters in fiction have been categorized by many critics into two-dimensional characters and three-dimensional ones, or as E. M. Forster refers to them in *Aspects of the Novel,* "flat" and "round" characters. Flat, or two-dimensional, characters are the ones who are easy to understand. They have simple motives or sets of motives, and once we are well acquainted with them, we can pretty well tell, if not precisely *what* one will do under a given set of circumstances, at least *why* he will do it. Flat characters do not usually change their motivations during a story: if one is pictured as greedy at the beginning, he will continue to be greedy; if one is the image of loyalty, he will still be loyal at the finish, although he may have changed the cause or person he is loyal to.

Three-dimensional (round) characters are less predictable and more like real people. Their motivations are confused, and sometimes they will be greedy, at other times self-sacrificing. They are capable of changing their attitudes when confronted with new sets of circumstances.

Round characters require a lot of time to develop—generally more than is possible in a short story. Heroes of short stories frequently get flashes of insight at the ends of the stories, but we rarely get to see them in action for long enough after that to know what effect the discovery will have on their future actions. Even in a novel, it would be unwise to have more than one or two of the characters be completely three-dimensional, since one of the qualities of fiction is that it imposes some sort of logical order on events, and we cannot see the logical order unless most of the characters move in set patterns that won't upset the plot and get everyone as confused as most of us are in real life. (If you want to be confused, why read a novel?)

So most of our characters will be of the flat variety. That certainly doesn't mean that they don't have to be characterized, and thoroughly. To begin with, we have to give each character some kind of individual trait, other than a name, so the reader can keep track. This is sometimes called a "tag." One of your characters may always wear her dresses too tight because she intends to take off fifteen pounds. Another may crack his knuckles when under stress. A third may be constantly rummaging through her purse in search of her partial plates, which she took out because they don't quite fit. These may seem superficial, but they bring out a uniqueness that each of your characters—particularly the minor ones—must have to make us keep them straight. Then we add any other traits they may have: tact, stubbornness, generosity, secretiveness, or integrity.

How do we apprise the reader of this? The simplest way, of course, is just to tell him.

> Polly got A's in high school, and everyone expected her to get A's in college. Certainly she was not going to be distracted by romance. The fire-scarred face and mis-set twisted leg from the automobile accident which had killed her father when she was ten almost precluded that.

And there is nothing wrong with this method, either, if Polly is a minor character and that's all we need to know about her. But it won't do for a truly comprehensive characterization. To get that, we have to go into some indirect means.

One of these is by dialogue. What a person says, the way that he says it, and what other people say to or about him all serve to characterize him. If he gives an eye-witness account of a lynching with relish, and punctuates it with guffaws at the more imaginative parts, we will get a far different opinion of him than if he had recounted the same episode with indignation and repugnance, and particularly if he had dwelt on the suffering of the victim's family rather than on the ingenuity of the lynchers. And if acquaintances of the guffawer refer to him as a "good old boy," we also get an idea of his position in the society where he lives, and of its moral standards. We learn, in short, how he got that way.

Another of the ways we can characterize a person— perhaps the most vivid of all—is by his actions. It used to be standard to introduce the villain by having him gratuitously kick a dog. (O. Henry gave that tradition an interesting twist by convicting a man who was unusually solicitous toward dogs on the grounds that such men are invariably cruel to women and children.) This is overly simple, of course, but we are inclined to make judgments based on whatever actions we have seen a character take.

A more subtle means of accomplishing characterization is to use both dialogue and action. They may be used to reinforce each other, as when our villain says, "I hate dawgs," and then proceeds to kick one. Or they may be used to contrast with each other. If, for example, the man who guffawed about the lynching is later found to be anonymously financing the lynchee's son in going through Yale Law School, we have a more complicated character than we had expected—possibly one with noble instincts (or a guilt complex) who is afraid to openly oppose the establishment into which he was born. Or there may be a contrast between the speech and actions of a man who declares that there is no generation gap today—all that is needed is to talk things over with young people as equals—and then withholds his son's allowance until he gets a haircut with white sidewalls. Contrasts such as these lend *irony* to your work, and irony is the backbone of fiction.

Another means of characterization which is used less today than in the past is the use of names. Some of them (Mrs. Malaprop, for instance) have been added to the language as lower-case words. I would not suggest the use of names of some real people I have known (Wiley Wisdom and A'Noble Ladd are a couple), because they wouldn't be believed anyhow. But I should also avoid having a dentist named Shoemaker in the same story as a cobbler named Mantooth. If it tickles your fancy to name the stingiest woman in town "Lucy," or your ninety-six pound weakling "Harry Armstrong," go ahead. Try to avoid names that are *too* contrived, however.

Two bits of caution while we are on the subject of names. First, unless you are writing an item about the Mafia or the Chinatown tong wars, avoid giving all your villains (or all your good guys) names of specific ethnic origin. Such self-restraint will result in better author-reader relations. In case of doubt, British and other northwestern European names are common enough in the United States to use for both good and evil folk.

Second, when you choose a name, make sure that it is not one which can be confused with any other you may use. Names with the same first letter or ones that rhyme are the worst, but not the only pitfalls. A friend of mine started a novel once with two major characters named Andy and Hank. Although at first glance these sound different enough, two names of four letters each, half of which are "an" caused all sorts of confusion. Eventually she had to go all the way through changing one of them—a truly Herculean job.

PLOT

A plot is essentially the recounting of a struggle. The struggle may be between two individuals, between two groups, or between two facets of one individual's nature. Or it may be

between one or more people and some great natural force—
wind, fire, flood, or even God Himself. It arises as the result of
two (or more) irreconcilable desires or drives of the two forces
involved. What is the nature of the drives? Among human
characters, three motivating forces are commonly involved:
Death, Love (Sex), and the Quest. Death is fairly obvious; it is
the only great event inevitable to us all, and we really don't
know much about it, except that almost every living individual
dreads it instinctively. And the biological reason for death,
ironically, is sex. Amoebae and other sexless one-celled beings
which multiply by dividing do not appear to get old and die;
they simply do or do not divide into two other amoebae, each of
which is of the same age as the other, and as the parent. Sexual
reproduction means the procreation of a separate new individual, and room for him must eventually be made by the
death of his ancestors. So although sex and its result, procreation, seem to be the opposite of death, they are really in-
terlinked. Still, literature's two great divisions, comedy and
tragedy, are closely tied with sex and death, respectively. One
can always recognize a Shakespearian comedy by the loving
couples lined up in the last scene waiting to be married. In one
of his tragedies, the stage would be littered with corpses instead.

The Quest is a little easier to understand, but harder to
define. The quest may be for the Holy Grail, or for a billion
dollars. Dorothy wandering through Oz looking for the Wizard,
who can get her back to Kansas; Ulysses sailing the wine-dark
sea, he hoped toward home; and Huck Finn looking for Cairo,
Illinois, are all part of the tradition of the quest.

The plot is composed of a series of events or situations
which arise from attempts of the characters to attain their
goals, which may be resisted either by other characters or
forces whose goals are in conflict with them, or merely by forces
or laws of nature, as in the quest of an inventor seeking to
develop a flexible potato chip. The events should be believable
within the context of the story: that is, what might be incredible
in a realistic story set in the 1930's could be perfectly believable

in a science fiction story set in 2062. Note that the fact that a sequence of events *actually happened* in real life does not necessarily make it credible enough for a work of fiction. A writer is expected to make occurrences happen as the logical results of prior events—not necessarily predicatable, but at least logical. Nature, unfortunately, recognizes no such requirement. The cause-effect relationships in fiction are usually more obvious than in real life. That is why truth is stranger than fiction, and why fiction writing is an art.

At any particular point in a story, the reader must have at least one unresolved question before him. Will Fearless Fred be in time to save Mildred from falling over the cliff? Who killed Aubrey Limoges? Will Wilma's husband find George hidden in the closet and jump to what we know is an erroneous conclusion? Some of these questions may be answered before the climax of the story, but if so, others must replace them before the reader has time to lay the book down and turn on the TV.

The *dramatic tension* which results from the unanswered questions must get tighter and tighter as the story progresses. This rise in tension is not usually a smooth curve, so that we can say that at the half-way mark the reader will be perspiring exactly fifty percent as much as he will at the climax, but generally undulates in a series of minor crises, each followed by a slight (never complete) relaxation of tension, only to be swept up to the next climax, a little higher than the last. We may breathe a sigh of relief when Henrietta does not step on the crocodile, mistaking it for a log, but we still have to worry about her getting caught in the quicksand before she emerges from the swamp to where the land mines are planted.

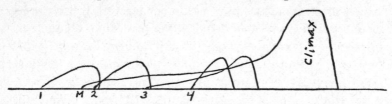

Figure 1. A graph of a plot.

The plot questions are introduced into the story at the points where the numbers are placed, and the one marked M is the main plot question. (Who did it? or Will Chet win Maggie's hand?) Even when it is not urgent, it remains to bolster the interest while each of the others is resolved. In this particular graph, the main question is not even introduced until the reader's interest has already been caught by something more trivial.

The highest point of interest is called the *climax*. Notice that at the point of the main climax, the graph levels off. This is what the writer of a story should do. Make sure that the climax lasts long enough so that nobody can read by without noticing it. You have done a lot of work leading the balky reader up to this point. Make sure he has to suffer for it. Draw out the suspense for as long as the length of the overall work, the ability of the author, and the patience of the average reader will permit. Make the reader sweat.

Right after the climax comes the *resolution* or *denouement*. In it the problem is finally solved (or the decision made that it is insoluble). It should include some irreversible action, so that the situation can never return to that of the beginning of the story.* It should include some lesson, explicit or implied, that is learned by either the reader or the principal character. The resolution, unlike the climax, should be as brief as possible without leaving too many loose ends. There is no point in prolonging the resolution—all the tension has now gone out of your story, and it is collapsing like a tired balloon. Let it collapse as quickly as possible and fold it up.

THEME

Every good story has a theme. The theme is a moral principle or a truth about human nature brought out for the edification of the reader. It need not be anything bold or new. Unlike clichés, themes seem to be reusable an infinite number

---

* Except in cases wherein the *theme* of the story is that we relive all our mistakes again and again, so that there is no beginning or end, only a closed circle.

of times. So don't be afraid to *show* (not *say*) that women are fickle, that straight shooters always win, or, conversely, that nice guys come in last.

But don't worry too much about theme. The chances are that your story will have one without your knowing that you put one there. Everyone has moral principles, and one or more of them will show up somewhere in everything that he writes —even if it is that there are no viable moral principles, and that honest men and cheats win in about equal percentages of the time.

Chapter 12
Who's Telling This, Anyhow?

Point of View is a fearsome term for something which is important enough to merit a fearsome term. It involves how the story will be presented—through what size and kind of peephole the reader will be allowed to watch the show you are putting on for him. How many choices there are depends upon which authority one believes. Here are my versions.

FIRST PERSON

The first person point of view is the one in which a character in the story tells in his own words what he saw of the action or heard from others about what he missed:

> "As I was reaching for the skillet, I remembered that George had told me that my new employer had once rubbed his overdone eggs in the hair of the erring cook."

Because he is a person with prejudices and interests in what is going on, the narrator will generally give a biased version of the story, which the reader may accept or reject just as a jury can accept or reject the testimony of a witness. The status of the first person narrator varies. He may be the main character of the story who will be able to recount the most important action of the story because he has been closely involved, a minor character who may be able to give an account with less bias and broader vision because he is less heavily involved, or merely a bystander who accidentally happened by just in time to observe the action with no background knowledge about the character or circumstances. He will understand fewer of the reasons for the action, but will usually have a cooler and more disinterested attitude.

Whatever the status of the first person narrator, there are some advantages which almost always apply to first person narration. First, you are right at the scene, with everything surrounding you in full stereo, rather than standing back and observing it as if it were on a stage or TV picture tube. Second, by the use of vernacular speech of the p.v. (point-of-view) character, and by the imposition of his biases and attitudes on the story, the reader is given a fresh and unique "angle" on the story—one which he could easily have overlooked if he were merely given objective facts. The reader's acceptance of this angle will, of course, depend on his acceptance of the character himself. If the reader considers the p.v. character to be a hypocrite, a liar, or a fool, he will be less inclined to accept his opinions and more likely to look for clues among the facts that the character is recounting (and misconstruing) in order to form his own opinion. Or if the p.v. character is shrewd, sensitive, and honest, the reader may be willing to accept his opinion whole and undigested.

Finally, the reader is immediately given a character to identify with, someone who will act as his proxy throughout the story. How much he will take advantage of the opportunity will depend, of course, on whether or not he likes the p.v. character and feels comfortable inside his skin. If the p.v. character is a stranger to the events of the story, like the anonymous narrators at the beginnings of *Wuthering Heights* and *Ethan Frome*, who start off really knowing no more than the reader does, the narrator can be used to ask some of the same questions that the reader would ask, and get desired responses. (I say *some* of the same questions, because the writer can always muzzle his p.v. character to keep him from asking some questions prematurely and thereby blowing the suspense. Or the p.v. character may ask the right questions and run into a strange reticence on the part of the local citizenry to give a direct answer. This, of course, produces all sorts of suspense.)

On the other hand, there are pretty severe limitations on the first person point-of-view. First, a p.v. character has only one set of eyes and other sensory apparatus, and they can be in only one place at any one time. So if you want to tell what happened "meanwhile, back at the ranch," you will be limited to hearsay evidence that may be told to the p.v. character later, and which loses all immediacy because of its second-hand feeling.

Also, any peculiarities of speech may get pretty tiresome by page 20, and you are more or less stuck with them. Besides, if your narrator's dialect is really thick, you may make your story so hard to read that everyone except amateur cryptographers will give up on it. And if he has a limited vocabulary, you are limited by it and may find it impossible to make any very complicated comments. A skillful writer can get by with this by letting up on the illegible dialect or the unduly small vocabulary so gradually that the reader is not aware of it.

One variation in technique that is frequently used in first person p.v. is the *first person innocent*. In it the narrator is a person of no great sophistication—generally a child (Huckleberry Finn) or a stupid person (The narrator in Ring Lardner's short story "Haircut"). William Faulkner went the limit in *The Sound and the Fury* by having as one of his narrators Benjie, the family idiot. This permits marvelous ironic overtones when the narrator draws ingenuous conclusions from the same information which the reader reads far differently. Huckleberry Finn's reiteration of his own essential wickedness for trying to help a black slave escape is a much more damning commentary on the institution of slavery than any abolitionist tract could ever have been.

Conversely, some good work has been done with what might be called the *first person guilty*. In it the p.v. character constantly justifies (unsuccessfully) his stomach-turning villany and duplicity, and seems much the worse for adding hypocrisy to all his other sins. Jerome Wiedeman's two novels *I Can Get It for You Wholesale* and *What's in It for Me?* are outstanding examples of this technique. We are tempted to crawl bodily into the book and throttle the hero with our bare hands.

SECOND PERSON

It is possible to write a story in the second person:

> "As you reach for the skillet, you remember that George has told you that your new employer once rubbed his overdone eggs in the hair of the erring cook."

However, since the only possible advantage of this point of view is to increase the reader's sense of identity and immediacy, it usually needs to be done in the present tense (a bugaboo in its own right, by the way).

> "You are running, running through the dark, silent streets. The footsteps behind you recede, draw closer and suddenly . . . "

Don't you do it—particularly for anything longer than a couple of pages. It is hard, uphill work, and when you get through, you have nothing that wouldn't have been easier and probably better in first person. The longest example that I know of is Rex Stout's *How Like a God,* a novel written before Mr. Stout had found himself as a great detective novelist.

THIRD PERSON

Most fiction is written in the third person:

> "As Joanne reached for the skillet, she remembered that George had told her that her new employer had once rubbed his overdone eggs in the hair of the erring cook."

But there are so many varieties of third person point of view that it will be useful to consider the most common of them separately to see the advantages and disadvantages of each.

THIRD PERSON OBJECTIVE

This p.v. is like watching a stage play or a film. We see people doing things, acting and reacting, but with no outside comment from the writer or any of the characters as to why they do them, or, indeed, any of their thoughts except as they may be expressed in their speech or gestures. Probably it is even harder to understand a work of fiction than a play, since a competent actor can convey a lot by tone of voice or body movement that a fiction writer cannot. The scope of observation is wider than in first person, for the writer can shift from one time and place to another at will, but it puts a heavy burden on the reader to interpret what he is shown, and only a very skillful writer can select his detail and words so that the reader can do the necessary interpretation. Ernest Hemingway made considerable use of the technique. His short story "Hills Like White Elephants" illustrates the technique well.

THIRD PERSON AS A CAMERA

In an experimental movie entitled *The Lady in the Lake,* produced in 1946, the viewer never sees the face of the leading character, Robert Montgomery, because all the picture is being taken by a camera mounted on his shoulder. What we see, then, is everything he sees, including, as I recall, the sight of an approaching fist that smashes the lens of the camera, to spectacular effect. I do not know how much the shattered lens cost.

A story told in the *third person as a camera* p.v. is much like this. We see what the p.v. character sees, and sometimes can see what he is thinking. If you think this sounds rather similar to a first person story, you are right. It has pretty much the same limitations, except perhaps the dialect problem, and some of the same advantages.

THIRD PERSON OMNISCIENT

This is by far the most flexible of the points of view. It permits the writer to tell what is going on without any limitations as to time or place. If you want to have a science fiction story take place on a planet of Proxima Centauri with occasional jumps to Space Control Center back on Earth, feel free. And since the author is permitted to know (and tell) everything, it is possible to climb into everyone's skull and see what he is thinking (except for the Proxima Centaurs, who have no skulls, but carry their brains in the bases of their tails).

Since this method is so flexible and handy, it is widely used by novelists. It is also dangerous, for getting from one person's mind to another's is unhandy at best, and terribly confusing at worst. Readers have been known to develop split personalities from darting from mind to mind too rapidly. Consequently, this omniscient point of view is rarely used in short stories, and even novelists find it important to use all sorts of devices to tag the thoughts as belonging to a specific character. One such device, which can be used in conjunction with dialogue, is to show what the character says (in quotation marks) and follow it immediately with what he is thinking, either in plain print without quotation marks, or in *italics* (done on a typewriter by underlining). This makes an excellent opportunity for irony by showing the difference between what is said and what is thought:

> "Oh, Mr. Graham, what a nice surprise! Do come in and sit down." *Now what would my father-in-law be doing here at nine o'goddam clock in the lousy morning? No good, that's for sure.*
>
> "Why, thank you, Millie." *She must feel guilty about something, or she wouldn't be this affable.*
>
> "I just dropped by to see if Killy might be home." *He's here all right. It would take a hydrogen bomb to get him out of bed this early.*
>
> "Oh, that's a shame, Mr. Graham. Killy had a job interview scheduled for nine this morning." *Well, I haven't had to lie yet. The old snoop needn't know that he's all spaced out in the*

bedroom. Unless, of course, Killy comes bounding out here, all full of sweetness and love. God, I hate it when he's on a "loving" acid trip. "Would you care for a cup of coffee?" *If he says yes, I swear I'll put prussic acid in it. If I had any prussic acid. I wonder how much LSD it takes for a lethal dose?*

"No, thank you, my dear," *I wouldn't trust her to boil water without scorching it. She does lie rather well, though. But she needn't think she has me fooled. I'll see if he's here!* "I must be getting along. Tell Killy I was here, will you? But one thing—may I use your bathroom before I go?"

Not without a search warrant, you won't! "Oh, this is so embarrassing, Father Graham. You see, the toilet is all stopped up. We have more trouble with that thing! I'm expecting the plumber any minute. Matter of fact, I thought maybe it was him when you rang."

"Oh, I see." *And I see right through you—and your shortie nightgown. So that's the way you greet plumbers—not wearing enough to flag a handcar.*

Another device, which doesn't require dialogue, is to have your character doing something, then to show his thoughts exactly as you would if they were spoken, but leaving off the quotation marks:

He pushed the tree-branch aside. Now I've got her, he thought. As soon as she steps out the back door, she'll be in the sights of my rifle.

As a general rule, a writer should avoid shifting p.v. from one person's mind to another's any more often than is necessary.

THIRD PERSON LIMITED OMNISCIENT

The third person limited omniscient is the p.v. most often used for short stories. It has the same leeway for shifting time and place as the full omniscient, insofar as telling what is happening is concerned, but it only goes inside the mind of *one* character. Other things equal, it is not advisable in a short story to go into more than one character's mind. The limited omniscient p.v. is also used for novels, to an outstanding degree by

James Gould Cozzens in *By Love Possessed* and others of his later novels. Cozzens' p.v. character is always a person of tremendous insight and sensibility, who is able to make such shrewd guesses as to the motivations and probable actions of others that his method approaches the scope of the completely omniscient point of view.

ALTERNATING POINT OF VIEW

Many novels and occasional short stories are told by using different points of view in different parts of the work. One chapter or group of chapters in a novel may be told in the first person with one p.v. character, and the next section, still in the first person, with a different p.v. character. This makes for more depth in the story, since we get a different angle on what is going on from each narrator.

Or the story may be told partly in first person and partly in third person, as a camera, omniscient, or limited omniscient. Hemingway's novel *To Have and Have Not,* originally printed as a series of short stories in *Cosmopolitan* magazine, uses both first and third person, but with the same p.v. character.

Here are two examples of the same situation being told from the points of view of different participants. The first is told in first person using thoughts and dialogue, first by one character, then by the other, covering identical events.

PART ONE: MARSHA SMITH

Oh, dear, this is the day for Marsi to see Dr. Roberts. . . . Eight o'clock appointment too. I wish I could have gotten a later appointment for her. . . . Would have made my day a bit easier. Oh, well, I guess it's better to get it over with. . . . The poor baby is so afraid of doctors. . . . Good, I hear Sid coming. . . . Let me see; yes, everything is ready.

"Good morning, dear.

"Your breakfast is all ready.

"Is Marsi up? Oh, I think I hear her now.

"Marsi, is that you?

"You're up bright and early this morning.

"Why? Don't you feel well?

"Oh. Well, you'll probably feel better once you're awake. You'd better get dressed now. We have to leave early, you know.

"It's a shame she is so frightened of doctors.

"Yes, I know, it's as much the idea of facing a new situation as anything.

"I suppose you *are* right. She will probably grow out of it. . . . Marsi, your breakfast is getting cold! Better hurry.

"Hello, darling. Sit down and eat.

"Better eat something anyway, or you'll be hungry before lunch time.

"Yes, you have to.

"Now, Marsi! At least drink your juice."

Sid is so good with her. . . . She seems to face new situations so much easier with her daddy there. Oh, well, it'll work out. . . . Oh, dear, look at the time!

"It's seven-thirty, Sid. . . . Marsi, finish eating, dear; you have to brush your teeth before we go.

"What did you say, Sid?

"Yes, dear, I'll call you as soon as we get home. You don't think the doctor will find anything seriously wrong, do you?

"I hope not too; I'll try not to, and don't worry too much either. Goodbye, dear. Have a nice day."

Oh, dear God, don't let there be anything seriously wrong with our little girl! . . . Let's see. . . . Yes, I'm all ready. Hair looks O.K. Just a dab of lipstick and that's it.

"Marsi, dear, hurry up. It's time to go. . . . Well, here's my girl. All ready? Did you go to the bathroom?

"You look very nice.

"Nevertheless, you look nice. And you'll feel better this afternoon.

"Well, for goodness sakes, hurry up and go."

That child, every time she gets a little nervous or excited she has to go a dozen times before we can leave.

"Hurry up, dear! It's getting late."

I really shouldn't scold her for stalling; she's upset enough, but if she doesn't hurry. . . .

"Come along, dear. Let's get in the car. . . . Did you close your door tight and lock it? . . . Don't forget your seat belt.

"Here, let me help you. . . . There now, all set."

Traffic sure is heavy this morning. . . . Watch out, mister. This is a four-way stop, you know! . . . All right, make up your mind. Which way are you going to turn. . . . Well, finally.

"Yes, Marsi?

"Well, dear I guess that's because when you're having fun, you don't think about the time, so it seems to go faster."

Almost there, thank goodness. Now if I can just find a place to park, within walking distance, that is. Well, will you look at that, there's one right in front of the office. Will wonders never cease?

"Well, if we aren't lucky today.

"Just a minute, dear. I have to put some money in the meter. There. Let's go in. . . . Marsi, you go up and tell the receptionist that you're here.

"No, dear, it's time you learned to do these things for yourself.

"All right, dear. Why don't you read a magazine while you're waiting?"

"Let's see. . . . Name. . . Marsi Lynn Smith. Address 1414 North Elm. . . Phone 121-3456. . . Father's name. . . Father's occupation. . . . My gosh! . . . They sure want to know everything. . . . Funny they don't want to know the color of the dirt under her toenails. . . . There, that's all done. . . Well, they're ready for us already.

"Yes, dear, of course I'm coming too. Go along now.

"Isn't it nice we didn't have to wait very long? Here's your paper. Hurry along."

"Oh, my poor child! The look on your face . . . the way you walk . . . you are so frightened. . . . I wish there was some way I could help you.

"Good morning, Doctor Roberts. It's nice of you to see Marsi on such short notice."

PART TWO: MARSI

If I just lay here and don't move . . . if I don't make any noise . . . maybe Mama won't remember. Maybe she'll even forget to wake me up and it'll get too late to go. . . . I'll just lay real still and keep my eyes closed tight. . . . My toes are getting warm . . . wonder how come. . . . If I open my eyes . . . just a crack. . . . Oh! Sure, the sun . . . feels nice . . . looks pretty . . . makes a bright spot on my quilt . . . pretty and fuzzy looking. Mama says that the fuzzies you can see in the sun are dust and lint. . . . Looks too pretty to be just old dust and lint. . . . Gee! . . now I gotta go to the bathroom. Maybe if I can wait long enough. . . . Oh, gee! I can't wait! . . . Now if I can just sneak back to bed without Mama or Daddy hearing me. . . . Oh, dear!

"Yes, Mama, it's me.

"If it's early, can I go back to bed?

"No! I'm not sick!

"I'm just . . . I'm just tired, that's all.

"O.K. I'll get dressed."

Gee, she sure has good ears. I wonder how come Mamas have such good ears. Gee, why couldn't she forget? . . . She put out my pink dress . . . my favorite school dress. . . . I'm not sure I want to wear my favorite dress to see any ol' doctor. . . . Maybe if I put on my play clothes instead . . . I could say that I forgot. . . . Then I'd have to change and that would take time and maybe it would be too late to go. . . . No, better not. . . . That'd make Mama mad. . . . Besides, it would be a lie. . . . Better get dressed, like she said.

"Almost. . . . O.K. I'll be down in a minute."

Don't know why I have to go to a new doctor anyway. I like my old doctor.... Don't know why I can't go to Dr. Davies like always.... This new doctor probably gives lots of shots.

"Yes, Mama. I'm coming.... Hi.

"I'm not really very hungry this morning.

"Do I have to?

"I might throw up!

"All right, I'll drink my juice, but I don't like grape juice much.

"Hi, Daddy.

"I'm fine, I guess.

"I . . . I just don't feel like going to the doctor.

"Yes, Mama explained that to me, but why can't Dr. Davies take care of me? He always has before.

"O.K. Daddy, I promise. I won't be any trouble.

"Yes, Mama, I'm finished.... O.K., I'll go brush them now.... Bye, Daddy."

I still don't see why I can't just go to Dr. Davies. He could study up on whatever it is.... Then I wouldn't have to go to any new doctors.... Gee, it can't be time to go already.

"I'm coming.

"Yes, I'm all ready. Yes, I went.

"Well, I sure don't feel nice.

"Mama, I gotta go to the bathroom again!

Gee, I sure wish I didn't have to go to any old doctor.

"Yes, Mama. I'm hurrying.

"Yes, it's closed.... I locked it.... I can't get my seat belt out ... it's stuck."

Man, Mamas sure do things fast. I'd rather done it myself ... takes longer.

"Mama?

"How come when you don't want them to, things go fast?

"Oh."

She didn't know what I meant, 'cause I'm sure not having

fun now and things are sure going fast. . . . Gee, we're almost there. . . . Maybe there won't be a place to park. . . . Gee, there's one right in front. . . . Maybe someone will get there first.

"Sure was lucky."

It was luck, all right . . . bad luck. Maybe the door won't open. . . .

"Oh, Mama, do I have to? Can't you tell her for me?"

"O.K. . . . Mama, the lady said for you to fill out this paper and give it to the nurse when we go in to see the doctor."

Funky magazines! . . . Nothing here for kids to read . . . whole place is funky. . . . Bet the doctor's funky too. . . . Gee, already!

"You're comin' too, aren't you, Mama?"

"Just great, Mama."

That's for sure! . . . We didn't have to wait long enough. . . . I'd liked to wait forever. I don't want to see this doctor. I bet he's mean. . . . There he is, waiting for us. . . . He sure looks mean! I bet he just loves to give shots to little kids and hear them scream. I don't want to see this doctor. I don't want to! I WANNA GO HOME!

"Hello, Doctor. . . . I'm just fine, thank you."

Jeaneen A. Campbell

Notice that the half-dialogue in the first part fits perfectly with that in the second. Would the piece have worked better if the two halves had been told simultaneously? Why?

The second example, "Craftsman," has a more complex structure. Set in third person limited omniscient, it alternates rather rapidly between Juan and Tom as p.v. characters. Note that a change in time, place, or point of view is indicated by a little extra space between paragraphs. This is simply done on a typewriter; just throw the carriage as you normally would, then reach up to the knob at the end of the platen and turn it one more click.

CRAFTSMAN

In El Paso, summer is hell, and late summer is the devil's delight. All day the sun pours its fire into the ground, and at night the earth gives its heat back to the air. Every moment you feel as if the air is about to blister the skin. But life moves on despite the heat, though much slower. And this September of 1931 was even hotter than usual.

Juan Estardo lazed under the cover of the cottonwoods. He didn't have to move until dark and was enjoying the measure of coolness that was there. Until then he would watch the crazy gringos, and especially for those *cabrones,* the Border Patrol. Perhaps if he were lucky, he would be able to shoot one tonight. He felt a warm thrill and smiled at the thought.

El Paso is skirted on two sides by the Rio Grande. Across the river is Old Mexico. Cordoba Island, formed by a shift in the river channel, is no man's land. Trails led through its thick-growing cottonwoods and willows. By day children play on these trails, but at night men use these trails for more serious games.

Prohibition gave impetus to the grand and glorious profession of smuggling, for the Americans were thirsty. Narcotics were soon more popular because of the small bulk and high sale value. The men who carried and guarded these shipments were real *chollos,* tough and spiny as the cactus they were named for. Every man paid his way in blood—another's or his own. Juan had gained his fame in Mexico City, killing a man in a bar with a knife. A series of robberies resulted in two more dead men. Juan discovered that he enjoyed holding a man's life in his hands, to end or not as he chose.

Tom Simmons was passing the time until he was to go on shift at 6 P.M. An hour to wait seemed to be a long time. He decided to spend it caring for his tools. An oil can, rag, and bore brush were brought out. He set to work, whistling under his breath.

Tom had a single line of work in his life. Raised on a ranch, he enlisted in the army at the start of World War I by saying he was two years older than his 16. He soon gained sergeant's stripes, two scars, and a reputation as a tough and *sabe* fighting man. The war's end gave him a chance to dislike the tedium of garrison life. The next best thing was a deputy sheriff's job in Arizona. When the Border Patrol gave him a chance for action again, he jumped at the chance. A gun felt as natural to his hand as boots to his feet. He made a career of his gun, for it was a tool to be used well, when and as needed.

Dark had brought relief from the sun, but the heat still prickled the skin. Juan had left the cottonwoods and was wandering about the adobe and board shacks that lined the border in El Paso. He was now watching for all signs of police or Border Patrol activities. He had left the trees when the rest of the *contrabandistas* had joined him. He and Roberto had cautiously left and crossed the border. The crossing was definite, but first there must be a check of the enemies' activities.

By 11:30 most houses' lights were out. A guitar was being strummed, accompanied by a slightly drunken voice. Juan was leaning in the corner formed by two walls. Deep shadow kept him hidden from all eyes. All that had been seen were normal police activities. He would now stay here until the shipment came across and was distributed for hiding and sale. The moon was well below the horizon; it was a perfect night to carry a shipment over. But until the job was over, Juan would keep alert. When it was over, he would take his six dollars and go to the cantina in Juarez. Some cold tequila and a warm woman would be welcome.

Tom leaned back in the seat of the sedan. His partner was driving, and they both kept on the alert for any unnatural activity. The car cruised very quietly through the streets. A number of cats fled from its approach, and a few drunks stared stupidly in the glare of its headlights. A gleam in the cottonwoods drew the driver's attention. "Over there." The driver pointed with his chin.

Tom looked out of the corner of his eyes. "O.K., Let's have a look-see."

Juan was only a little concerned. The car had passed and gone on without slowing. Perhaps this was a wasted night. He took out his nickeled revolver and idly toyed with it. It was time, and Roberto walked out into the open. He lit a cigarette. Even though there was no wind, it took three matches. Then he threw the cigarette away. Soon cautious movings told of men coming. Then a small file of men appeared, all armed and all hard looking. There were six of them, three carrying small bags over their shoulders. They walked as does a dog entering another dog's domain, stiff-legged and ready either to fight or run.

After turning back, Tom and his partner walked from the car. Finally, above the point where the reflection of the headlights had alerted them, they split up. Tom went down a narrow alley, his partner going down an ill-lit dirt street. Tom unsnapped the retaining strap on his holster and eased the well-cared-for bulk of steel. The partner carried a shotgun. When he was about 40 yards from where he was to take position, he released the safety catch, and gripped the gun tighter in his sweating hands.

Tom saw the men coming from the island as he neared the end of the alley. He bent and swiftly pulled off his boots. His mouth was dry, and he felt a strong urge to urinate. He ignored these signs of fear and padded ahead blending into the night.

Juan saw a glimmer in motion. He froze and looked carefully; then he saw the man. The man was tall and lean, and moved very silently and easily. A broad brimmed hat hid his face, but the gleam of starlight struck from the badge on his chest, telling what he was. Juan smiled. This was his fortunate night, for he would kill a Border Patrolman. From now on he would get as much as $14 for a trip. How wonderful this pistol was; he would never get close enough with his knife. But he would miss the feeling of the jerk of the body as the life left it. Slowly raising the gun, squeezing on the trigger, he tried to picture the look on the man's face as the shock of the bullet ripped the life from his body. The gun flashed and bucked in the dark. The tall man rolled forward from the hip. Again the gun flashed its word of death. The tall man jerked. Juan smiled a very happy smile, but he could not explain this squeeze in his chest. It was as if he had been the one who had been shot. Then he saw the blossom of flame in the tall man's hand. He lived and was shooting at him. Juan tried to laugh, but a thick salty wetness filled his throat. This was all a bad dream, and soon *Mamá* would wake him. The bed felt as hard as a packed dirt alley.

Tom saw the muzzle flash of the shot even as the bullet tugged at his shirt sleeve. As the sound of the shot registered he was bending forward, pulling the gun from his holster. He swore at himself for not having it in his hand already. The second bullet laid a groove along his left side, jarring him. He thrust his Smith & Wesson .44 out at shoulder height and triggered off two fast shots at the other gun's flash. As he stepped forward and to the left he fired twice more. His own muzzle flash showed his target crumpling. A soft thudding noise told of its stop.

Surprise was gone. Tom ran forward, pulling the empty cases from the gun. As he stopped he fed four fresh shells into the cylinder. The *contrabandistas* were running forward, abandoning all hope for stealth. Tom took aim and fired four shots at the two men in the lead. One dropped, obviously dead. The other stumbled and crawled for cover, hurt, but firing all the same. The night was alive with the flame of firing guns, the sound of shots, and the screams of ricocheting bullets and hurt men.

Then the welcome thump of a shotgun joined and dominated the melee. Two more men fell. One lay there and moaned in a falsetto whine. One man dropped his package and ran, firing over his shoulder. A final blast from the shotgun lifted him from his feet and dropped him, a tattered bundle empty of life. The sixth man dropped his gun and raised his hands. Too many had died too fast for him to buck the odds. His eyes were empty from shock.

Roberto crept from hiding and went over to Juan. Juan lay on his side, curled as does a small sleeping boy. But his sleep was to be a long one. *Mamá* would never be able to wake him. Roberto crossed himself and whispered, *"vaya con diós, Chico."* He slipped the six dollars from Juan's pocket and faded into the night.

Police and Border Patrol cars were all around. The lights gave a false life and gaiety to the night. A middle-aged man was in charge. He took reports and gave orders. As he did, he walked around the scene. He knelt and checked the contents of one of the bags. Then he spoke to Tom. "Four dead, two wounded, and one scared so bad that he wet his pants. You boys had yourselves one hell of a party. Any get away?"

Tom sat, smoking a cigarette as a man bandaged his side. "Not that I saw," he drawled. "Maybe a lookout or two, but I couldn't say for sure."

A policeman spoke from the alley. "Hey, look at this one. Plugged four times, and he's smiling." Tom's cigarette tasted bitter. He threw it away with a convulsive movement. The older man looked at him quizzically.

Tom spoke: "The coyote jumped me in the alley, gave me this," indicating his side. "I don't know how he didn't finish me."

A stretcher came out of the alley, bearing a limp, covered form. Tom drew the sheet off. A cheap, shiny revolver caught his eye. When he picked it up, its loose parts rattled. "A toy," the older man grunted. Tom held it for a moment, and then threw it down beside the still form. He looked at his ambusher, avoiding the ugly holes and the blood. Only a boy, probably only seventeen. He spoke. "A toy. . . ?" He felt tired, and his head ached from the heat.

In El Paso, summer is hell. . . .

You may wish to try your hand at point-of-view Exercise S in Appendix B.

Chapter 13
How Long Should I Make It?

Every work of fiction is in a way different from every other, but it is human nature to try to put everything into pigeon-holes so that we will all be talking about more or less the same thing. Here we will discuss the *sketch,* the *short story,* and the *novel.* Note that these are discussions and descriptions of the different types rather than rigid definitions, which would be impossible to make, since there are so many varying opinions. Mine, I hope, are about mid-road, but what is one man's novelette is another's "full length novel," and still another's long sketch.

THE SKETCH

Sketches are short works of fiction. They usually run from as few as 300 to as many as three or four thousand words. Short sketches, up to about five hundred words, are sometimes called *vignettes,* a name also given to stories of similar length. A sketch differs from a *story* in that it lacks a completely developed plot with an action twist at the end which precludes life ever being the same again for the persons involved.

Sketches may be descriptive, like "Adagio" or "Anachronism" in Chapter 10. Or they may be character sketches, intended to portray (or describe) a person. The "My Most Unforgettable Character" series in *Reader's Digest* are character sketches, although not technically fiction.

Another common type of sketch is the *slice of life.* "Anachronism" would qualify as a brief slice of life sketch, since it shows a sort of sample or specimen by which to judge a whole phase of life as it is being lived. There is a beginning and an end, of course, but one feels that both points were arbitrarily chosen, and that some other segment of time would have done equally well. In a plotted story, on the other hand, the precise time it begins, and particularly the exact time it ends, must be selected with great care, as are the exact events between.

Don't get the idea that sketches are in some way inferior to stories. They also require artistry and technical skill. The details to be included have to be picked out carefully to lead to the effect the writer desires and the handling of words must be even more careful than in a story, where the reader will overlook more because of his fascination with the plot.

Sketches are becoming more popular than in the past, probably in reaction against the "surprise ending" stories first popularized by O. Henry about the turn of the century and imitated by lesser writers ever since. Many magazines publish sketches in preference to short stories, and frequently call them short stories when they do. Before sending one of your works to a magazine, it is always a good idea to look over a couple of recent issues to make sure whether they want stories or sketches.

THE SHORT STORY

A short story is, as the name would indicate, a story, and a brief one. The top length is going to vary with the whim of the writer or the editor, but generally it will be seven thousand words or less. A story vignette will be five hundred or less, and stories from five to fifteen hundred words are generally designated as short-short stories. In general, the shorter they are, the harder they are to write, since all the elements of fiction—characterization, plot, and theme—must be compacted into the smaller scope. And the short-short or the vignette is not simply a dehydrated short story with the details knocked out; it is a complete story idea that fits into the smaller frame. No well-written short story contains enough details to permit miniaturization.

As I mentioned in Chapter 11, characterization in a short story is pretty well limited to flat (two-dimensional) persons. The length limitations really do not permit more, although at the end of some great short stories such as Daniel Wilbur Steele's "How Beautiful With Shoes" we find the leading character struggling with an insight which will, we assume, change her forever into at least a bas-relief character. But we don't stay with her long enough to see it happen.

An important quality of the short story is that it has one single character on whom the reader's major interest is focussed. No matter if it has a cast of thousands (although that is really too many) if either the writer or the reader cannot tell instantly whom the story is "about," the story needs rewriting until they both can. I once wrote a short story in the first person, using a minor character as the narrator. Apparently I put in too much of the p.v. character's personality, for when it was discussed in the class for which I wrote it, there were wrangles as to who was the leading character. I had to rewrite it several times, once in third person limited omniscient with the hero as p.v. character, once in first person with the hero as p.v. character, and finally, having exhausted all the possible wrong ways, in third person limited onmiscient with the minor character as p.v. character. By focussing more of the narrator's attention on the hero, I got the effect we wanted at last.

As we saw in Chapter 12, the point of view in a short story is almost always limited in permitting access to only one mind. This sometimes makes for trouble; it almost precludes telling a first person story in which the narrator gets killed at the end because one wonders how he told the story posthumously. (The great Japanese tale "Rashomon" gets around this by having a medium recall a soul from death to testify. But then "Rashomon" breaks all the rules about short stories, by having the same incidents recounted by a number of first-person narrators and leaving you to wonder which, if any, was telling the truth (like a juror or a member of a Congressional investigating committee).

A modern short story must have some kind of conflict situation—enough to grab the reader's attention—on the very first page. Preferably in the first paragraph. If you can do it in the first sentence, that would be even better. Remember, you are competing against television, and if the reader picks up your story during a commercial, you must have him hooked by the time the commercial is over. It doesn't pay to play fair.

Your story hook does not necessarily have to be the real main issue of the story. It rarely will be, in anything longer than a short-short. But the story hook problem should not be resolved until the main issue *is* introduced and the reader's interest is firmly involved. (See the plot graph in Chapter 10.) *Never* leave the reader enough breathing space to walk away, even if you have to make up false crises to hold him until time comes for the main one.

Do not waste words in a short story. Keep it lean and compact. If you find on reviewing it that you have put in words or phrases *only* because they are beautiful, cut them out ruthlessly, just as ruthlessly as you would in the work of another. Unless the words advance the plot, aid in the characterization, help create the proper emotional state, or develop the theme (preferably two or three of these things together), they are useless decoration and will serve only to catch on things and impede the progress of the story.

Another point on economy. Start the story at as late a point as possible. Of course you must start it early enough to include all the action necessary to explain the ending, but if you are writing a story of young love, it is rarely necessary to include the birth and early childhood of either party. If it should be necessary to reach into the remote past, it can always be done by the technique called the flashback:

> She closed her eyes and for a moment could almost hear the whinnies of the horses being led from their stalls and the slap and jingle of the harness. She was walking into the kitchen—how long ago? Twelve years! Oh, no. Day before yesterday. But there was no time to think about that, because this was the Day, the day she was to get on the train and go away from the farm, away from her friends, away from Mamma and Papa and Jerry, the hired man, away to the vast unknown of college.

But be sure we are interested in something more immediate before going back.

THE NOVEL AND LIKE THAT

Somewhere between a long short story and a brief novel, most authorities place another category called the *novelette* or *novella*. Some even separate them into two categories, the novella being somewhat shorter than the novelette. This whole situation is in a state of flux, because the magazines may advertise a "book-length novel, complete in this issue" that runs to perhaps ten thousand words, whereas Mark Twain's posthumously published masterpiece "The Mysterious Stranger," some thirty-five thousand words long, is generally classified as a short story! If you pointed a pistol at my head and demanded that I assign a length to the novelette or novella, I would say from seven thousand words to perhaps thirty thousand, with everything longer than that deserving to be categorized as a novel. The whole discussion is silly anyhow, because all the things I will say about novels will apply to novelettes unless they are quite short, in which case what has been said about short stories will probably apply better.

The rules for writing novels are less stringent than those about short stories because there is more room in one of them, and one is almost tempted to start and finish with Henry James' dictum that the main responsibility of a novelist is to be interesting. That is certainly the most important thing to remember, but I believe more detail than that is indicated.

A novel should contain all the elements of fiction: plot, characterization, and theme. You may occasionally read a novel, as I have, which did not seem to have a plot visible to the naked eye. In most cases you will find on close scrutiny that one is there, but it is a subtle one, and so overlaid with heavy characterization as to be overlooked.

Plot in a novel is usually more complex than in a short story; again, there is more room for things to happen. Often there are one or more sub-plots spun by the actions of minor characters and having only incidental effect on the main plot.

In the so-called picaresque novel, the novel of quest and adventure in which the hero moves from place to place and exploit to exploit, like *Don Quixote, Tom Jones, Huckleberry Finn*, or any of Edgar Rice Burroughs' Tarzan books, there is almost a new plot for every chapter, with only occasional reminders of the main plot question so that the reader will not forget it.

In other novels of more complex weave like James Gould Cozzens' *Guard of Honor* and *By Love Possessed* or Herman Wouk's *The Winds of War* several characters seem always to be doing their own thing and creating their own plots, each of which effects in some manner the main characters and the primary plot. Juggling this many balls at once is a terrific chore, and it is rarely possible to wind them all up neatly at the same time without leaving a lot of loose ends trailing. I recommend that, in your first novel, at least, you give your major effort to the main plot and keep the minor ones subdued. For a horrible example of what can happen to even a seasoned novelist, get a copy of Mark Twain's novel *Pudd'nhead Wilson*. Generally included in the same volume is his humorous light novelette, *The Extraordinary Twins*. In between is his rueful account of how he happened to write the novel when he thought he was doing the novelette, and what he had to do to lay all the ghosts he had raised. Read it and be warned.

The immediate "story hook" is not so urgent as in the short story, but it should not be neglected. Today we cannot devote the entire first chapter to a masterful and brilliant description of the London fog "within and without," as Dickens did in *Bleak House*, nor, as Victor Hugo did in *Les Miserables*, can we spend the first fourteen chapters telling about a man who really is not a character in the novel. Nowadays readers expect to be entertained, whether they deserve it or not, beginning right away. And since there are many other sources of entertainment, we have to give them what they expect. So pose a dramatic question, at least in the first two pages, and then flash back if necessary to give all the background information that may be needed.

A novel can afford a few more flights of flashy fancy and passages of purple prose than a short story, since it is longer, but even a novel cannot carry much excess baggage. So check for excessive description and unnecessary dialogue before you type your final draft.

How can you tell if dialogue is excessive? One way is to see if each speech makes progress. If you listen carefully to people speaking as they *really* speak, you will find that around 65% of what they say is redundant or irrelevant—what a computer programmer might call pure garbage.

> "Hi, Joe, how are things?"
> "Great. And with you?"
> "Can't complain. How's the family?"
> "Just fine. And yours?"
> "Fine too. Heard the news?"
> "What news?"
> "Gertrude's in the hospital."
> "Gertrude? Gertrude who?"
> "Gertrude. My wife, Gertrude."
> "Oh, my God! No, I hadn't heard. Anything serious?"

Now I submit to you that this is real dialogue. Idiotic, yes, but genuine. But it's not good dialogue, because, although it doesn't bother us to hear it (who listens?), seen on the page, it is dull, dull, dull. Try rewriting the passage to see how much you can cut out of it and still give the effect of the spoken voice and produce all the vital information—that Gertrude is in the hospital. Cut down, it will be *realistic* (as opposed to *real*) dialogue.

Characterization is vital to a novel, even more so than to a short story. The men, women, and children who people your book must seem real enough to the reader that he loves one, hates another, feels contempt for a third, is sorry for a fourth. He cares what happens to them. And that is important, because if he doesn't care, why will he bother to read and find out?

How does a writer go about making a character real enough for a reader to become emotionally involved with him? Probably the first way is to make sure that the character himself has strong emotions. It is hard to feel sorry for someone who gives no indication of feeling pain, and it is almost impossible to love anyone who is himself incapable of loving.

Some writers who are personally inclined to be poker-faced and ashamed of their own emotions may have trouble in making their characters emote visibly. If you have been taught, as my mother was, never to scream when in danger "because it scares the horses," it may be hard for you to have your heroine scream as the rapist tries to drag her into his car. If it is necessary to have someone get the word and come running to the rescue, you'll just have to rise above your principles and have her scream. If the scream isn't necessary to the story, you have another out. Let her struggle in silence, if you must, but tell us at least what she is thinking. Even the most self-contained, outwardly composed person is usually aseethe with emotions inside, and these inside feelings are what the reader wants, so he can feel the same way (or possibly the opposite way). And the secrets of a character's hidden emotions are unlocked by the skillful use of point of view.

Many fine novels have been written in the first person or the limited omniscient point of view. But if you choose one of these, you must remember that only one character, your p.v. person, can have his secret inner emotions told, unless the p.v. character can read minds. All the other characters must either tell what they are feeling or demonstrate it by their actions. (If your heroine, seeing the approach of the hero, runs to him, wraps all four limbs around him, and kisses him on all exposed parts, we will be justified in believing that she holds him in affectionate regard.) If you like your characters to behave in a more reserved manner, then you will do better to use the complete omniscient point of view, so that the thoughts and feelings of any character may be revealed if the need arises. But remember that breaking and entering into too many minds makes the reader lose track of who thought what and when, so rapid shifts of point of view must be heavily tagged to keep them straight.

In the novel you will find enough scope to describe even a three-dimensional character—one who learns from experience, and who occasionally breaks his standard pattern of actions to do something unexpected. But even with this leeway, avoid making more than a couple of your characters round, at the very most. Flat characters should occupy most of the slots, because flat characters behave according to program, and we have to have someone the reader can depend upon for contrast to the round one(s).

Don't think because a character is flat that he cannot have emotions or grab the sympathy of the reader. Dickens, probably the most successful, if not the greatest, English novelist, never developed more than two round characters in all his novels, yet more tears have probably been shed over one or another of his flat but unforgettable characters than over those of any other writer in the English language. Try it yourself.

HOW A NOVEL HAPPENS TO A WRITER

Two questions I have often been asked are: (1) How can I tell how long a story to write based on the idea I have? and (2) How does anyone ever work up enough courage to attempt a complete novel? I think the two questions can best be answered together.

Until you have had some experience with story ideas, it is

often hard to tell how long they will take. The only answer seems to be to write until it is finished. I once started out to write a ten-thousand word science fiction novelette. It turned out to take twenty-five thousand. Another time I sat down to dash off in a couple of pages an entertaining wartime anecdote. When I was finished, it was a 2,500 word short story—my first to be published.

As to writing a novel, I believe the best way to begin the first, or even the second, is to back into it. A novel is really easier to write than a short story, because there are fewer limitations—length, point of view, characterization, etc. It's just that there is so much of it that it terrifies anyone who hasn't been through it.

Here is what I mean by "back into it." While writing *Spacehead*, that ten thousand word novelette I was telling you about, the one that ran to twenty-five thousand, I got a picture in my mind of a highly interesting sequence of events for my characters to go through in the same general milieu, but at a later date than the action in the first novelette. I decided that I should write it as a sort of sequel to the first. Also at some later date, such as when I could find time. And when I finally got around to it, it had become clear that there was too much of a gap between the two, and something (a 25,000 word novelette, for instance) had to be written to account for the change in situation between the first and third. Are you still with me? Well, by the time the second and third were finished, the first novelette, *Spacehead*, had been bouncing from publisher to publisher for so long that I could tell it wasn't going to sell in its present form, so I put in a few transitions and nailed the whole thing together into a novel of some 90,000 words, which still occupies a trunk in my storage shed. That is an unhappy ending, but it at least proved to me that a novel is not too long to consider writing, and that writing one is invaluable experience. So if you have an idea that really won't fit into short story length, no matter how you trim the fat off, don't panic. Keep on writing until it's finished. And remember, a novel is really easier to write than a short story.

Chapter 14
Ideas and Inspiration

Probably the biggest difference between a successful writer and an unsuccessful one is persistence. Persistence in writing until a piece is completed and polished, persistence until it is published. Perhaps the second biggest difference is in knowing what to write about. Most amateur writers either can't think up subject matter for a story, or they can think of so much that they don't know which to use.

Almost everyone has, or at least thinks he has, material enough for one book. Only a comparative few ever get around to writing it, but most of those who do seem to be able to find enough for more. There have been a few great one-book authors, as attested by Emily Bronte's *Wuthering Heights,* Margaret Mitchell's *Gone With the Wind,* and Harper Lee's *To Kill a Mocking Bird.* (Ms. Lee is still young enough to produce many more, but she has had a long dry spell.) But probably the first story is the one you are interested in right now. Stories are generally written one at a time, and the second idea can wait.

PERSONAL EXPERIENCE

The first and biggest source for good story material is the writer's own past life. You may think that yours has been pretty uneventful, but you've probably been around more than the Bronte sisters, and I'm sure something has happened to you—or almost happened to you—that is story-worthy. At the very least you will have the advantage of knowing what you are writing about as no one else can, and you can certainly describe how at least one of the characters feels. Technical details should be no problem, but even more important, you can put in those little personal touches of detail that add so much to a story. How does a welding mask feel as you pull it down over your face? How can you tell when bread dough has been kneaded enough? What do machine gun tracers look like from behind the gun? All these details give verisimilitude to your story. Verisimilitude is an invaluable quality, especially if you are going to expect your reader to accept some incredible situations later on.

If you don't have any experiences of your own to write about, try borrowing one from a friend. You at least have heard someone telling about that funny thing which happened to him on the way to the swimming pool. A borrowed experience may not be quite so vivid, but if your friend has a background similar to yours, you should be able to imagine yourself in his slacks.

There are some precautions to take in writing from personal experience, however. To begin with, when you show it to your friends, do they giggle uproariously and say, "Man, I can just see you doing that"? If so, stop and think a minute. Will it be equally amusing (or interesting) to anyone who *can't* "see you doing that"—anybody who doesn't know you personally? If not, you may have to spend some time in describing or explaining just what kind of person is "doing that." It just doesn't work to say, "Well, then Ann—you know how Ann is—went to pick up the frisbee, and found the crab . . ." unless the reader *does* know how Ann is and how a crab would probably affect her. The groundwork must be carefully laid in advance for such a scene to be effective.

Then you must learn what happened that should *not* be included in the story. A sculptor is said to "see" the figure of what he intends inside the piece of marble. Then all he has to do is chisel off all the stone he doesn't want. Your problem is similar. If and when you can see the story you want inside the tremendous mass of incidents which surround it, you have a good start. Then be careful to omit any details which might serve to contradict the impression you want to make or confuse the reader about what is important and what isn't. (If you can recall in detail everything that happened, there is bound to be something contradictory or confusing. Real life is like that.) Now that you have caught all those things, look again. Is there anything which, although it might not be contradictory or confusing, is unnecessary? Now, before you decide that it is unnecessary, make sure that it does not (1) advance the story; (2) characterize an important character by showing some trait that we might otherwise never learn or fully remember, or (3) give us some background detail needed to understand the story. If it does none of these things, either cut it out completely or modify it so that it *will* do one or more of the things mentioned.

Another problem you may run into when writing from personal experience is *perspective*. This means that you, the author, must be able to stand far enough away from the "you" in the story to see yourself objectively. Even if you're writing in first person, and putting in all your own feelings and emotions, it is important to see yourself in the story as an outsider will. Otherwise, how can you possibly know what to put in and what to leave out? If you write about an unhappy love affair, for instance, when you're in the throes of recovering from one, you probably won't have this perspective. What you write, therefore, may be excellent catharsis, but lousy literature. Your character is likely to appear maudlin, rather than sympathetic. Go ahead and write it, however. The act of writing itself may help you gain the necessary perspective (and incidentally recover). You can always rewrite it later, when you do have the perspective, and still retain all the little memories that, when properly used, make your story immediate and lifelike.

Each one of us knows a good many things that are not

common knowledge. Many of these things we have known for so long that we tend to forget that there was ever a time when we had to learn them. Here are a few that I know which might fall into that category:

(1) Precut lumber to make boxes or crates is called *shook.*
(2) The term *"case in"* means to pack something into a box, or case.
(3) To guide workers in assembling coats or pants in a garment factory, each piece has a tag sewn or stapled onto it to show size, lot number, etc. These tags are called "jokers" and removing them is an arduous chore.
(4) A French 75 millimeter gun has an eccentric-screw breechblock.

Of course there are millions of people who know each of these facts, but each of them is sufficiently esoteric to make me feel that I would owe the reader a short explanation before using it as in important point in a story. In case of doubt, risk insulting your reader's intelligence rather than letting him miss anything important. Of course what needs explanation will vary with your audience. If you are writing for *Apparel Manufacturer Magazine,* you probably won't have to explain about joker-tags. If your story is going to *Ladies Home Journal,* you really should.

The term "fiction," as I mentioned in Chapter 10, implies that what is told is not necessarily true. A beginning writer sometimes forgets this fact, and tries to tell a personal experience just as it really happened. Sometimes it makes a good story that way, but often it lacks just a little of being as good as it might be. For instance, you may be telling about the time you locked your keys inside your father's car. What really happened was that a nice young man from the drug store on the corner came out with a wire coat hanger and helped you get the window down and the door open. You thanked him; he blushed, stammered, and retreated to the drug store. You have never seen him since. Exciting? Not very. But suppose your rescuer was on probation for a car theft conviction, and just as he was sliding his hand through the three-inch space at the top of the window, a police car rounded the corner and stopped beside you.

Isn't that better? But, you protest, that wasn't the way it happened! Well, perhaps it wasn't, but it should have been. George Washington may have gotten plaudits for his inability to tell a lie, but he never would have made it writing fiction. Never hesitate for a single second to alter, shade, or omit the facts if you will get a better story that way. If the reader wants dull facts, let him read an encyclopedia.

CROSS-FERTILIZATION

Next to personal experience, the biggest source of story material is probably your reading, television viewing, studying, and the like. This does *not* mean you should take that beautiful Rod Sterling TV piece and rewrite it in your own words, changing the names slightly. This is called *plagiarism,* which is a nasty word in the writing profession, and could result in successful lawsuits—against you. What it does mean is that watching it may start ideas churning around in your head. Author William Golding read a novel entitled *Coral Island,* in which a group of English boys who are shipwrecked on a desert island (what would fiction be without desert islands?), create a microcosm of England: orderly, law-abiding, and inventive. Golding, who was a schoolteacher well acquainted with boys of that age, snorted scornfully. He knew what boys would do without supervision! So he wrote another story of shipwrecked boys: *Lord of the Flies.*

Of course all your story ideas need not come from reading or watching fiction. Newscasts and newspaper stories often carry the germs of ideas. I have often suspected that anyone who followed one of the better-known advice columns, such as "Dear Abby" or "Ann Landers," would pick up a confessions story plot at least once a week. (I am told, however, that you should not use these nationally syndicated sources. Too many other writers see them, and the one who is quickest and nearest to the magazine office will beat you to the draw. If you have a local love-lorn column, though, watch it for potential story material.) And a work like Toffler's *Future Shock* contains basic ideas from which a hundred science fiction stories might spring. All you have to do is answer the question "What if. . . ?"

If you do confine your idea reading to fiction, do not despair. There are plenty of non-plagiarizing ways to use what you read. One thing would be to take the *theme* of a story you have read or seen and use a new plot and characters to prove it. This is certainly not a criminal offense, since there aren't very many themes available, and you aren't likely to find a virginal one anyhow.

Probably a better and easier scheme of maneuver would be to take a plot idea and give it a new twist, as Golding did to write *Lord of the Flies*. It is amazing how differently a story will turn out with a change of only one character. How would *The Catcher in the Rye* have worked out if Holden Caulfield had been a girl? Or what would *Treasure Island* have been like if the first person narrator had been Long John Silver? Or try the *Don Quixote* story with Sir John Falstaff heavy in the hero's saddle.

Another way to re-use someone else's plot would be to make a change in a fortuitous set of circumstances. What if the U.S. Cavalry, riding to the rescue, takes the wrong turn and ends up so lost and confused in the badlands that it takes them until after dark to get there? This actually happened to a third of Custer's command at the Battle of the Little Big Horn. Or what if Sherlock Holmes, a known user of cocaine, turned out to be stoned when his services were most needed, and Dr. Watson had to take over the investigation? Of course you wouldn't use the real names of the Conan Doyle characters, but you could develop similar ones of your own, characters with different tags (Holmes could be named Rourke, be pudgy, smoke only a certain brand of cigars, and wear a bowler hat).

So far as that's concerned, you could lift a whole cast from someone else and put them into an entirely different plot position. By the time you changed their names and "tag" traits, put them in a different kind of situation, then did a good rewrite job, the chances are that no one would ever know, since by then your own stamp would be on the people as well as the story.

YOUR OWN IMAGINATION

I suppose that most stories that people sit down and dream up out of their own minds are bound in the long run to be nourished to some extent or other by either your own past experience or your reading. But the original story idea, apparently at least, springs only from the recesses of your own mind, triggered by something you experience or imagine, then worked out to a logical conclusion (plotted).

William Faulkner claimed to have once gotten a mental image he couldn't get rid of. It was of a little girl up in a tree. As is the case with most tree-climbing little girls, her underpants were showing, and on them was a spot of mud. By the time Mr. Faulkner finished exploring the ramifications of how his dream girl had gotten mud on her drawers, he had the entire story of *The Sound and the Fury.*

Not all of us are Faulkners, but all of us have, if we are to be successful writers, some imagination and some curiosity. And the way to make them work for you is to let them wander a little, once you have found a starting point. And the starting point might be almost anywhere. Perhaps you might start with a good title—there are worse places than that to start. Take the opus I have repeatedly referred to in Chapter 13: *Spacehead*. It started out as a title. I had once attended an Army school in which the tactics of an airhead had been discussed.

The word *airhead* was rather recently coined, created as an extrapolation from older military terms; *bridgehead,* the area on the far side of a river that an assaulting force must seize and hold so that a bridge can be built to bring supplies and reinforcements across, and *beachhead,* the area of a beach and inland from it that an amphibious landing force must hold to enable supplies and reinforcements to be landed on the beach with minimum interference. In the Normandy landings in 1944, a beachhead was made simultaneously with an *airhead* further inland, created by the landings by parachute and glider of two airborne divisions. An airhead is a precarious place to be, since all supplies and reinforcements must be flown in until a link-up is made with ground-fighting troops.

But suppose one were to launch an attack on a hostile planet? Then what you would have to hold would be a *spacehead*. Despite the fact that such invasions are made all the time in science fiction stories, from a practical military stand-point it would be a fiendishly difficult operation. The logistical problems would be terrific. So I set about developing solutions for all possible problems and ignoring the impossible ones. Then, to lend human interest, I created a character, a stupid soldier, and nicknamed him Spacehead, on the grounds that space was all his contained. (Eventually I had to change his name because, since he was a minor character who got dropped fairly early in the story, his name was unnecessarily confusing.)

Anyhow, the point is that, although much of the working out of the story was based on my own military background and still more on my prior reading of science fiction, the basic situation was my own, and so was the (unsuccessful) story which developed out of it. We are not all Faulkners.

For another specific example of a simple combination of words triggering a story, see Harry Kemelman's short story "The Ten Mile Walk," almost purely imaginative.

Sometimes a story whose genesis is from personal experience will require considerable of an imaginative kick to complete it. When my wife was in college she wrote a short story entitled "Green Popsickles" about a self-conscious and maladroit ten-year-old girl. Most readers identified easily, because they had all been ten, and most of them had been, or at least felt, clumsy. And most of them had, like the heroine, had problems in communicating with their mothers. So far, so good. Then somebody suggested that there might be material for a novel. So my wife set off to write a novel with alternating chapters in the points of view of little girl and mother. Since she had not, as yet, had any experience as the mother of a ten-year-old, the mother's chapters had to be based primarily on imagination. Unfortunately, they turned out to lack the charm and authenticity of the daughter's. Imagination, in this case, did not quite fill the bill, so the author now has another five years to wait before she can do the job she intended.

But for developing any story, remember the magic question: "What if. . . ?"

Chapter 15
Breaking Into Print

Some people write only for their own self-fulfillment, for catharsis, or to amaze and amuse a few friends. These are all perfectly legitimate purposes. But frequently even these writers will produce something so good, so true, and so beautiful that the world really ought to have a chance to see it.

Then there are other writers whose main purpose in writing is to make money so that they can buy gasoline for a second car or even quit working on the assembly line of a widget factory or repairing automatic sprinkler systems for a living. In between the group with stars in their eyes and the ones with dollar signs are a lot of compromisers. But, for all kinds of writers, the problem is ultimately this: where can they find a publisher for their book?

FINDING A MARKET

There are two ways to approach the problem. Either find a market which seems closest to fitting your interest and abilities and then write what they seem to want, or write to suit yourself, then hunt for a market which wants it. There is really a third way: Find the market which pays the most and train yourself to write what they want. But this is the way only for the very hardy (and greedy), and besides, the methods for researching the market are the same as for the first above.

Maybe you already know of a magazine, underground newspaper, or book publisher who prints exactly the sort of thing you write. *Even if you do, read on anyhow.* You will need to know to whom to send it next, in case your first choice doesn't take it (and if you are betting that they will, you should demand pretty good odds).

The first step is known as *researching the market.* This is true of either the starry-eyed or the $-eyed group. It in turn is divided into what might be called sub-steps. Sub-step one is to look into a basic reference book to find out what you should research. Here are several basic reference books to be found in any well-stocked college or public library:

1. *Writer's Market.* Probably the most complete compendium of U.S. markets, divided into categories so that they are easy to find. Each of them has an accompanying brief blurb trying to say a little about the sort of thing they like to publish. The blurbs are not very thorough, but they should be enough to tell you whether to abandon that particular market or look at it in more depth. It does not include underground papers, although it does include a section called "Alternate and Radical Magazines." It also contains several helpful articles on format for submission, copyrights, and general advice on marketing.

2. *The Writer's Handbook.* Contains some excellent How-To articles by established writers. These take up most of the space, but there is information about markets in the back of the book.

3. *The Writers' and Artists' Yearbook.* Does for the British market about what *Writer's Market* does for the American. Don't downgrade the British market, either. Many a good American writer got his first publication—and recognition—in the United Kingdom.

4. *LMP.* (Stands for Literary Marketplace.) It contains, ac-

cording to the index on the front cover, information on "Agents, Artists & Art Services, Associations, Book Clubs, Book Publishers, Book Reviewers, Calendar of Trade Events, Columnists & Commentators, Courses for the Book Trade, Direct Mail & Promotion, Editorial Services, Employment Agencies, Exporters & Importers, Government Agencies, Literary Prizes and Awards, Magazines, Newspapers & News Services, Paper Mills—Suppliers, Photographers, Public Relations Services, Radio & Television, Sales Representatives, Services—Typing, Shipping, Translators, Wholesalers, & Writer's Conferences. Blurbs about what a publisher or editor may want are missing: instead you get the names of the president, vice-president, editor-in-chief, *et al,* which might be a great help if you were personally acquainted in the publishing field.

5. *Literary and Library Prizes.*   An historical and comprehensive rundown on all the major ongoing prizes and awards offered for the best this or that. Most of them seem to be for work already published, but there might be just exactly the right thing for you there.

In addition to these, there are magazines which can be found at most newsstands and many supermarkets. Some are:

6. *The Writer* (published by the same company as *The Writer's Handbook,* described above) and *Writer's Digest* (same publisher as *Writer's Market*) are monthlies with helpful hints on writing from established writers and some up-to-the-month information on marketing.

7. *Writer's Yearbook* comes out annually and also contains considerable marketing information and some How-To articles. It serves as sort of an extension to *Writer's Market* and is put out by the same people.

Now that you have searched the appropriate references and come up with a dozen or so names of, for example, magazines that might want your story, get at least one copy of each magazine and read it carefully before submitting a manuscript to it. Do not complain that this is expensive and time-consuming. So is wasting postage and time sending a story about bird-watching to a magazine published only in braille. Make sure by reading the magazine (preferably two or three issues) exactly what that blurb in *Writer's Market* meant. If you can't find a copy at a newsstand, write directly to the magazine for one.

HOW TO SUBMIT

As soon as you have narrowed your sights to a half-dozen or ten possibilities, buy some gummed labels just large enough for the typed address of a magazine. Type up, in advance, addresses of *all* the magazines you have selected. Tear off the first one and stick it on an envelope. Clip the rest to your retained carbon copy of the story. Then make sure your story is ready to go, using the format shown in Figure 2. Make sure you have used a reasonably new typewriter ribbon. Now place the story in your addressed envelope. If it's more than five pages, use a big envelope and mail it flat, with a paper clip holding it together. Five or fewer may be folded.

Now take another envelope, also big enough to hold the manuscript, and type your own address on it. Put it inside the first one with the manuscript, folding it if necessary. Do not seal the first envelope until you have taken it to the post office and found out how much the postage will be. Buy twice that many stamps, clip or stick the surplus to the inside envelope, put it back inside, seal and stamp the outside envelope, and mail it right away, before your courage fails you.

Suppose what you have written is a novel, 150 or 200 pages long. That really should be packed into a box or a book mailer. And it will require a lot of postage. And a lot of time for the readers and/or editors to read it—which means a lot of time before it is returned (as it likely will be). And what if it should be lost in the mail, or in the publisher's office? You have kept a

Mabel Mae Gantz
8458 Parkway Drive
La Mesa, California 92041
Phone: (714) 466-0501

Short Story
c. 3200 words

Sin, Sex and Satin

by

Perspicacity Smucker

The way to make up the first page of a story, Eva considered as she thoughtfully surveyed her shapely silken leg in the mirror, is to put one's name and address in the upper left corner of the sheet. She carefully straightened the seam of the nylon. Johnny Strong might be an evil old man, but he was a power in the publishing field, and a girl who was trying to break into print for the first time should be meticulous about her appearance, at least on their first date. What was it he had told her went in the upper right corner, opposite the name and address? Oh, yes. The kind of piece it was--short story, novella, article. And under it, the number of words. No need to be meticulous about that, though; he had said that it was all right to estimate the number of words to the nearest hundred, if you remembered to put the letter c. before it. That stood for--let's see now-- circa, meaning about or around.

Figure 2. A sample manuscript page.

S, S & S   Gantz 2

Eva lifted her arms above her head, admired for a moment the extra
uplift the gesture gave her bosom, and let the black satin frock slide
down her willowy frame. She had to tug a little to get it over her hips.
A girdle would have made her even more willowy, but all the girls said
Johnny Strong hated girdles, and she was anxious to get that first story
published.

What else went on the first page? The title, of course, centered and
nearly half-way down the page. Then, two lines below it, that single, beautiful word "by." And two more lines down, still centered, the author's
name. If you didn't want to use your own name, you could put your pen
name there. Probably a good idea. She blushed as she wondered what Ronald
would think if he knew she had written a story like "The Bawdy Broad." He
probably didn't think she knew all those words.

Another thing that was probably a good idea was not wearing a girdle.
The skirt would have been too short to cover it anyhow.

After the first page, it was easy. Just put the page number in the
upper left corner, with your name right before it if you were afraid of its
getting lost. And to be extra careful, she'd put the story title or an
abbreviation at the left end of the same line.

She glanced at the array of lipsticks on the dressing table, let her
hand hover for a moment over the Lovable Lilac, and finally settled on Flu-
orescent Flame. That would come closer to matching Johnny Strong's raw-
beefsteak complexion, so that he needn't be embarrassed to go home with
strange lipstick on his face. And a touch--just the merest touch--of
Exotic Erotic perfume on each ear-lobe. She mustn't arouse him too early

Figure 2 (continued).

copy, I hope, but it's a carbon copy, probably on onionskin or second sheets, and you'd never get around to typing it again. What alternatives have you?

Write what is known as a "Query Letter" stating that you have a novel and giving general subject matter. Ask if the editor is sufficiently interested to read the whole thing. Enclose a couple of sample chapters and an outline of the whole thing, divided into chapters. Place letter, sample chapters, and outline in an envelope, exactly as if you were submitting the whole thing—stamped, self-addressed envelope and all. If you get a favorable response on this, you can send the whole manuscript, knowing that it will at least be read. If you get a No, you have at least saved time and postage.

Now you have some time to wait until you get word about it. There is no use telling you to relax, I suppose, or to avoid making guesses as to what is happening back in the editorial offices. Some authors consider that a longer than usual wait means that it is being seriously considered, and that could be true. There are probably several people around who have the authority to say No on their own: readers, junior editors, *et al.* But a Yes comes only from the top, and it takes time to get the story there. However, an undue delay might mean only that the first reader has the mumps, or that your manuscript got put into the wrong stack by mistake. So the thing to do while waiting for the rejection slip is to try to concentrate on writing something else. Something even better. If you do this, you *may* be able to accept your first rejection in a preoccupied manner and not even notice much. In any event, pause long enough when it comes back to see if there is any specific criticism on the rejection slip or letter, and whether you think it has merit enough to justify making any changes. Then, after taking care of whatever is necessary, check the first and last pages to see if they are shopworn enough to need retyping. When all is done, stick the next pre-typed address onto another envelope and go through the same process again. It will come easier this time.

After the third or fourth time, you will be feeling numb enough so that it may not even hurt.

Do not give up. Re-write it if necessary, but don't stop sending it out until you have exhausted your list, and then see if you can't make up a new list. If it sells before the twelfth trip out, you can count yourself lucky as well as talented.

Is there any way that you can get an editor to say Yes? Well, if there were and I knew it, I probably would be using it instead of writing about it. But, so far as I know, no editor will make a practice of accepting manuscripts he doesn't think are "good" for his purpose, which is usually to sell magazines or books. I have never tried blackmail or seduction, but I would have no confidence in either method over the long haul. Editors who make consistent errors in judgment don't continue to be editors for very long. But you can get some ideas that might help at least to get your story seriously considered, if we take a look at how the average editorial office works.

Someone of considerable importance, maybe a mail clerk, opens the incoming envelopes and puts the manuscripts into the "slush pile" awaiting to be read by one or another of the first readers. The readers are sometimes specialists in one field or another, so the clerk may examine your manuscript hastily before deciding whom to give it to. If he is properly trained, the latest manuscript in will go on the bottom, not the top, of the pile, unless it is sent by a reputable literary agent, in which case it goes on top. (See discussion of agents below.)

When the first reader gets down to your manuscript, he will pick it up and take a quick look at page one. If what he sees is a mass of misspelled words, a lot of mangled and incoherent pseudo-sentences, a series of cliches looking for something to describe, or a lot of dim gray marks on a thumb-printed sheet of paper, he will clip on a rejection slip and hand it without delay to the mail clerk to be stuffed back into the stamped, self-addressed envelope and returned to you.

But of course yours won't look like that. It will be in your own lucid, masterful prose style, typed on clean white paper with a brand new black ribbon. Only one word will be misspelled, and that will have been your typewriter's fault. This being the case, the reader will really read page one, and possibly even page two.

Now he will be looking for a story hook, or something equally arresting, and you will, of course, have put one there. But he will probably also be looking for the *slant* that his editor wants. Each editor, or at least each publication, wants something pretty specific in each story. This is particularly true of formula stories, which will be discussed in Chapter 16, but it is also true to some extent of experimental and other nonpattern pieces. You should not, for example, write a story displaying in a sympathetic light an undercover narcotics agent (narc) and hope to sell it to the underground press. Most slants will not be this obvious, of course. They can be discovered only by careful perusal of the magazine (or similar books) previously issued by the same publisher. And if the slant is missing, back goes the story to the mail clerk for appropriate action, even if it is otherwise a brilliant story.

But suppose your first reader finds himself truly fascinated. (That will be the day! You wouldn't believe how blasé a person can get, after reading fiction all day for a living.) Then he will turn the whole thing over and look at the last page or two. If it looks as if it has a good tight ending, not as if you had just gotten tired and stopped, he will sigh. Now he may have to read the whole thing, and he is beginning to develop a headache. But first he will flip through, looking at random pages to see if your limpid prose holds up throughout. Now, unless his headache is getting worse, he will settle down and read the whole thing, or at least until he finds something he doesn't like. Remember, any time that headache gets too bad, he can quit. So what if he turns down the best story of the year? There are always other years. And plenty of manuscripts.

After he decides (let's assume) that your story is a sure-fire winner, he puts it at the bottom of a smaller slush-pile for the next person above him in the heirarchy, who will go through very much the same processes. This one will also be busy and harrassed. If the first reader passes too much on to him, he will chew the first reader out for not eliminating all the schlock (like your story?). He also can return anything he wants at the slightest whim.

How many of these poorly-paid hired hands a manuscript must go through before it reaches the person with authority to say Yes depends on how large a staff the publisher has. If it is a shoestring outfit, there may be only one reader plus the editor-in-chief. Does that mean quicker action? Not necessarily. It may just mean larger slush-piles. In any event, you can usually count on it taking *at least* three weeks to get a reply from most publishers. The reply may simply be the manuscript itself with a printed form rejection slip saying, more or less courteously, "Thanks, but no thanks." Some rejection slips contain a little list on which the reader or editor can indicate with a check-mark which of a dozen or so stock reasons for rejection applied most to yours. On slow days the reader may even take time to scrawl a few words on a scratch pad and enclose it. (That's a good sign—someone took at least momentary trouble with it.) If it is a book manuscript, you probably will get a real typewritten letter, especially if you wrote a cover letter when you submit-ted it. The letter will state some reason (which may or may not be the real one) for turning down your manuscript. If you get more than one comment with the same general complaint, you should consider some more re-writing.

Perhaps this is more than you really wanted to know about the functioning of an editorial office, but it should bring for-ward two points: (1) Make your manuscript as presentable as possible, especially the beginning and the end. And do *not* misspell the title, as did Daisy Ashford (age eight) in *The Young Visiters* or Jane Austen (age seventeen) in *Love and Freindship*. (2) It is very easy to get *re*jected, but don't get *de*jected. Keep it going out. Next time you may get a first reader who doesn't have a headache, or an editor who likes your slant.

AGENTS

Perhaps you ask, "Will my story get more consideration if I send it through an agent?" Yes, if he is a good agent who has a reputation among publishing houses. The reason is that he will already have read your story (or had it read for him) and adjudged it publishable before he sends it out. But he cannot sell a bad story, and if he knows what he is doing, he won't try. Sometimes it is as hard to get an agent as it is to sell a manuscript yourself.

What are the mechanical processes for getting an agent? The first step might be to go through the current edition of *LMP* or *Writer's Market,* each of which has a lengthy list of literary agents. Cull out of the list all those who specialize in some type of writing you aren't interested in at the moment, such as plays for production on Broadway or television scripts. Then, if possible, get hold of a copy of *LMP* or *Writer's Market* dating back four or five years, and see if the same person or firm was already in business then. If not, cross it off. You might lose some good ones that way, but you will also get rid of possible fly-by-nights. Now look through current copies of *The Writer* and *Writer's Digest* magazines; also *Writer's Yearbook* if you can find it. Thumb through the advertisements and see which agents are offering their wares there. Scratch them off your lists too. They may be all right, but usually *good* agents have as many clients as they can handle without advertising, just as good dentists do. There are two possible ways for an agent to make money: (1) by getting a percentage, generally about ten percent, of the author's royalty or other fees paid by the publisher, and (2) collecting fees for reading, editing, or other services paid for by the author *before* the manuscript is sold. Some of the agents who advertise get their money from the authors. Unscrupulous ones may even take money from authors whose works they know to be unsalable in any circumstances. Avoid any agents who give any appearance of making a living by other means than sales. (Some legitimate agents charge a nominal "reading fee" of up to about $1.00 per thousand words—not too nominal, really, if you have written a novel—and that is fair enough, but only if you cannot find one who will do it for free.)

Perhaps you would be interested in one of my own experiences with an agent which points up my caution about the tribe. On May 5, 1959, I sent the finished manuscript of *Spacehead* to Mr. X, enclosing a five dollar reading fee (pretty reasonable for a full length novel). On June 8 Mr. X. responded, saying the manuscript had some good characteristics, but that it also had sufficient weaknesses to keep it from selling. He also suggested that for a fee he could write up a complete blow-by-blow critique of the novel that should enable me to eliminate the weak points.

Since I had already suspected that it wasn't perfect, I took his bait, at least to the extent of saying that I would accept his proposition if it cost me no more than fifty dollars. (I was feeling wealthy at the time.) His next reply (June 22) accepted my offer, although he said that seventy-five was the normal price.

On October 6 Mr. X. sent me a fifteen page commentary on the novel. I will have to admit that whoever had read the manuscript and written the fifteen pages had probably earned the money, but despite the fact that the criticisms were, for the most part, valid, they were not anywhere nearly as specific as I had expected. (I was not a creative-writing teacher at that time and didn't really know much about commenting on a story.)

We exchanged a few more letters to try to coalesce our understanding, and I went into hibernation with the manuscript for nearly two years. (My job was pretty time-consuming about then.) By September 24, 1961, I had completed rewriting the whole manuscript—577 pages in its rewritten form—and mailed it back to Mr. X. On October 27 he got around to his horrified reply. How, he wanted to know, had I managed to get it so long? No science fiction book could be published with a length like that. However, he went on, he would send it out to a publisher or two to see if they would accept it tentatively, subject to substantial cutting.

The next missive was his letter of November 28, 1961. He said that there was no enthusiasm among publishers (no mention of names), but that the book might sell with considerable revision. He didn't think, judging from my record, that I was the guy to do it, but that he could. The service was called heavy editing, he said, and would give the manuscript about a 75% chance of selling for an advance payment against royalties of perhaps a thousand dollars. If I would retype the new manuscript myself, Mr. X could hold the fee for heavy editing down to five hundred dollars, *which would be refunded out of his commission when the book sold.*

About this time I started to do some arithmetic. The standard agent's commission is 10% of whatever royalties, etc. the author receives. At that rate my royalties would have to run up to five thousand dollars before Mr. X could figure on making more than he already had without selling the book at all! From what I had read about first books by unknown authors, this would be highly improbable. So I wrote him back (December 1) stating, truthfully, that I didn't have five hundred dollars. I suggested that, if he was so sure the book would sell after he got through, that he take the whole $500 fee out of the first royalty check I got and collect his agent's fee of 10% *in addition.* I pointed out that this would really bring him more money when he sold it, and the only risk was that of not selling it—a risk he was in a better position to take than I, since he controlled the selling effort.

We did some dickering after that, but it ended up by his returning the unedited manuscript on April 12, 1962, nearly three years after we started the correspondence. I do not *know* that Mr. X. was unethical, but I hate to see an agent make all his money from an author *before* he sells the manuscript. Please note: not all agents work the way X did.

Now that you have cut your list by removing all the newcomers, all those outside your field, and all the advertisers, you will still have quite a formidable number, and you need only one. Don't worry. They will eliminate themselves. What you must do now is write each one a letter (don't worry if it is the same letter—they probably won't compare notes) detailing your qualifications and asking if they would be interested in reading your manuscript with a view toward handling it for you. Enclose a sample of your work: a copy of something you have already had published, if any, or a few pages of your current manuscript. You may send out a letter to the first name on your list and wait for a reply, just as you would in sending out a manuscript; then, if you are turned down, write to the next one. That would take quite a while. Or you might send out letters to several agents simultaneously. That method risks having two or more say yes simultaneously, but the risk is not nearly so great as you think. Most agents already have quite a stable of writers as steady clients, some of them with reputations already. If you do get two yesses, try to stall one of them while you do business with the other, who may turn you down politely after he has seen your completed work.

Of course, if you have already published a best-seller, getting an agent will be easy.

This sounds like an awful amount of trouble. Is it worth it? What good is an agent, anyhow? We have already mentioned one advantage, that publishers pay more attention to manuscripts which have already been screened by an agent. A second is that your agent should know more about the markets than you do. He keeps track of what sort of slant each editor wants in his stories, and can tell which one most nearly matches your work. He knows what publishers already have more fiction than they can afford to publish and which ones are hungry. These are factors which are in constant change, like the river Mark Twain tells about in *Life on the Mississippi,* and the agent, like a river pilot, must keep track of it all.

A third is that an agent knows more about "rights" to a story, which are what you can sell. If he sells North American rights, that means he can sell the same story for you in Great Britain or New Zealand at the same time. He can give you advice about film or television rights, or recommend you to another that can. Actually these "subsidiary rights" could bring in more money than the original story. If you are interested in money.

But probably the best thing an agent can do for you is save you from the hideous trauma of getting a manuscript back every few weeks and then having to send it out again. He will do this for you, giving only occasional reports on progress if you insist on knowing.

And he *will* let you know when it sells.

Chapter 16
Writing to Formula

If you are one of the writers described in the preceding chapter as having stars in their eyes, or if you are primarily interested in writing the Great American Novel, this chapter is not really intended for you, and I suppose you might as well skip it and move on to Chapter 17. This chapter is intended only for writers with dollar signs in their eyes, the ones more interested in seeing their names on a check than in print. It is not necessarily devoted to hack writing, for there have been and will be stories in each of the genres to be discussed that have become masterpieces. As a matter of fact, they have frequently been masterpieces of such magnitude that they are still being imitated. And each of them fulfills some need or desire of readers which must be pretty fundamental, or the genre would not have lasted.

The genres we shall discuss here are not all-inclusive, and most of them include some writing that is non-standard in addition to the works that follow a disciplined and rigid plan. They are: confession stories, Gothic novels, mystery and suspense, men's adventure stories, western stories, sex fiction, science fiction and fantasy, and children's books.

MARKET ANALYSIS

In writing formula fiction, the first and primary rule is to analyze the market thoroughly *before* you start to write. Slant your story not only to the standards of the genre, but also to the whims of the magazine or publishing house which is to be your target. Before you write a Gothic, for example, visit a large bookstore or a public library which contains a lot of them. Choose a publisher who has put out a number by different authors. Read, with some care, and making notes as you go, at least a half-dozen, by three or four authors. See *what they all have in common.* That will be the publisher's slant. It could be almost anything. Are all the heroines blonde? If so, your heroine had better be too, even if you have to bleach her hair yourself. Does the villain first appear on the second page of Chapter 3? How large and what structure are the mansions that serve as the focus of action in each? These details may sound pretty trivial, but trivia are the cornerstone of a story slant. And they will be different for each genre and each publisher.

CONFESSIONS

The confession market is the field which has given a start to more writers, particularly though not exclusively women, than any other. How many we will never know, since confession stories are traditionally published anonymously to preserve the interesting old fiction that they are true stories told by the tortured young women they happened to rather than carefully contrived and plotted stories mostly written by middle-aged men and women, usually happily and uneventfully married or widowed. Probably the reason that confessions are such a good jump-off point is that they must be written with a lot of good honest emotion showing. Emphasize the word *honest.* One thing a confession writer must never do is let the reader think for a single second that he, the writer, feels superior to or condescending toward the main character or the reader. This is not the place to let your ironic instincts or your sense of humor get the best of you. When the heroine of a confession story suffers, her suffering has to be genuine and diaphragm-shaking, and the writer as well as the reader needs to feel compassion and sympathy.

The audience for confessions is not overly sophisticated; it is almost exclusively female and young—in the teens and twenties. Most of the readers will have a high school education or less—readers who are destined for college tend to change their reading habits when they matriculate, if not before. These readers are not looking for allusions to the works of Euripides or Petronius. They don't expect brilliant metaphor—a good, well-turned cliche will do—or even over-niceness in grammar. This does not mean that you or your point-of-view character should use "ain't" or "I seen him" habitually, but neither should she strain to use a subjunctive or to say "Am I not?" instead of Aren't I?" Saying "Would that it were not so" or "Tell is as it is" would be likely to turn some of your readers off.

On the other hand, the theme must be strong and clear. The plot must be tight, but not so slick as to appear contrived or "fictionalized." And if you ever borrow a plot from anywhere, make sure it isn't from a television soap opera, because it won't work. Soap operas, by their very nature, must never end, so there is always a loose end or two left dangling, and the plot can meander before getting to even a partial solution. A confession story, on the other hand, has a beginning, middle, climax, and end, with everything sewed up neatly when it is over. The characters in confessions and soap operas may be similar, but the plots just are not interchangeable.

The old conventional confession story is long—six to seven thousand words. It is told in the first person by a young woman or girl from a lower middle class family with a moderate or low income, no great educational pretensions, and a simplistic point of view. Her readers will have no trouble identifying with her, because she is probably one of them. In addition, she has strong ideas of her own and lots of spunk. She is *never* the submissive doormat type. She has a definite character flaw (who hasn't) which the reader can recognize early in the story: greed, jealousy, pride, over-possessiveness, recklessness, or you-take-it-from-there. The story, up to the climax, is like a classical Greek tragedy. The heroine's character flaw leads her into a violation of one of the canons of morality generally accepted by her audience. It has to be her own fault, not something that just happened by accident or was thrust upon her by another character.

The violation could be sexual: fornication, rape (as a victim, but due to her own actions—teasing or over-confidence) adultery, prostitution, premarital pregnancy, abortion, etc. Or it might be something more general: theft, embezzlement, reckless driving, drinking, drugs, defiance of parents. Anyhow, it must be a sin by her own code, and she has to suffer for it, either from her own conscience or because of social pressure. After the suffering, she ends the story either by vainly wishing that she could do it over differently or, better, by resolving to make the best of the situation and face life anew. By this point she must have recognized her own defect and, purged by her experience, resolved to overcome it to the extent that it will not lead her into error again. The solution to her problem, like the problem itself, must result from her own actions, not from those of friends, family, or a *deus ex machina.*

Nowadays, with a "new morality" making premarital sex and even pregnancy acceptable behavior in many circles, with abortion becoming legal in several states, and with filial disobedience commonplace, the confession story is shifting ground. Leading characters still suffer, but they do not always repent; they may occasionally decide that the principles they have broken are unimportant or incorrect. And the scope of the subject matter has enlarged. Once-taboo subjects like incest, venereal disease, and homosexuality are now seen in confessions. An occasional story may be wrapped into a crime mystery format. Quite a few have occult backgrounds (satanism, witchcraft, astrology, etc.). Story length is more elastic, including the "queen size" novelette and the story of less than six thousand words. An occasional story may be about the problem of someone besides the p.v. character, and some few are even told in a third person point of view. Occasionally a story with a boy as a leading character appears, sometimes even a sub-teen boy.

But these are still far-out experiments at the time this is written, and the situation may have stabilized or changed further by the time you read it. The only way to see for sure what is being done is to get current copies of several confession magazines and read them thoroughly yourself.

GOTHIC NOVELS

The gothic novel is another form with an ancient tradition, but instead of being like a tragedy, it is a melodrama. The necessary (or at least customary) ingredients are (1) an innocent young woman, long on sense of responsibility but short on the instinct of self-preservation. (I think it helps if she is somewhat feebleminded, but some of my friends who are *afficionados* of the gothic hotly deny this.) (2) A large old house with lots of atmosphere. (It originally required a castle, but castles are in short supply, especially in the United States. A colonial farmhouse will do; I've even seen it done with a boarding house.) (3) A man beyond his first youth and with a mystery in his past, and (4) a menace, not necessarily but frequently a younger and more winsome man who turns out to have very few scruples. All characters usually are flat, but should have strongly marked and memorable characteristics.

The novel is generally told from the point of view of the heroine, either in first person or third person as a camera. The plot, skeletonized, runs like this: The heroine, alone and a stranger, comes to a new locality, is impressed by The House and The Older Man. Frequently she finds herself actually living in the Mansion, together with the Older Man, but fully chaperoned by a flock of sinister-looking servants. She soon comes to realize that there is danger—to her and perhaps to others—and that there seems to be a diabolical conspiracy to make her (and possibly the reader) doubt her sanity. The Older Man is either the ringleader or another innocent victim, probably the former. About this time the Younger Man appears, looking at first like a white knight. More and more incomprehensible but dangerous events occur, until eventually the heroine, secretly and with the best intentions in the world, but against the advice of the Older Man and all canons of common sense, places herself into a Lois Lane-like position of great danger and vulnerability, preferably at night. Just as she realizes that the Younger Man is definitely the villain and that he is about to push her off the roof of the Mansion onto the crags below, she is rescued by the Older Man, who reveals to her the reason for the plot and the Secret of His Past, which turns out to be much less guilty than what she had guessed. And they live happily ever after.

This plot may sound silly. Do not worry—skeletonized plots tend to sound silly. And the actual episodes that fill it give plenty of scope for your imagination, especially in making it appear plausible that she would go alone up on the roof of the house or edge of the cliff, from which three persons have already fallen to their deaths, at two A.M. And some of the parts of the plot I have given you may be disguised, altered, or even omitted.

What the plot must have—and this makes the gothic a technical challenge to write—are the hints or clues that must be built into the action, so that although neither the reader nor the poor bemused heroine will probably figure out the mystery, when it is revealed they both should be able to say, "Of course!" as they look back on the clues in retrospect, where they are as visible as Burma-Shave signs. The reason they weren't noticed in the first place is that they were camouflaged in among the extraneous detail and probably given in such an inverted order that, having found "A," "B" has gone by so long ago that you have both forgotten about it.

Probably even more vital than the plot is the *atmosphere* of the book. It must be permeated from the first page by a sense of foreboding that soon escalates into terror. It need not build up evenly throughout the novel, a little release being necessary to make the next episode more effective, but it must never be forgotten entirely. For hints as to how to develop such atmosphere, read Poe's non-detective short stories.

And certainly before writing a gothic you ought to read at least a couple of the classics of the genre, say Charlotte Bronte's *Jane Eyre* and Daphne DuMaurier's *Rebecca*. Both these depart from the prototype that I gave, but not so far as one might think before scrutinizing them pretty intensely. And both are slower in starting than the contemporary trend, so it is well to look at recently published gothics by several authors, but put out by the same publisher, before submitting your work to that company. Some editors go for black magic or the occult as a device to create the atmosphere; others may adhere more closely to buried treasure or trickily-worded wills. All are capable of changing their opinions, so look at *recent* books.

MYSTERY AND SUSPENSE STORIES

This is a field in which it is hard to make generalizations, not so much because it has no formulas, but because there are so many varieties put under one roof. Suspense stories have many characteristics of the gothic novel, particularly regarding atmosphere, which must be either foreboding or actually thrilling all of the time, and the necessity for clues. Ira Levin's *Rosemary's Baby* is a suspense story that is at least half gothic and, at the same time, fantasy. Others, however, like Eric Ambler's *Journey Into Fear,* have a hero instead of a heroine in danger, against a totally different kind of background.

Here is a partial list of kinds of *suspense story,* enough to show how various they can be:

(1) *Occult and Macabre* (*Rosemary's Baby*, W. S. Jacobs' "The Monkey's Paw") These overlap the category of *Fantasy,* to be discussed later.

(2) *International Intrigue* (*Journey Into Fear,* Ian Fleming's *Dr. No,* etc.)

(3) *The Inhuman Monster* (*The Collector* by John Fowles)

(4) *The Damsel (Man) in Distress* (see preceding paragraph)

And overlapping into the suspense story, the mystery stories which may be categorized by type of detective:

(1) Police procedure (Ed McBain's Eighty-Seventh Precinct novels, or Dell Shannon's L.A.P.D. mysteries.)

(2) Private Eye (Ross MacDonald's Lew Archer)

(3) Amateur Detective (Dorothy Sayers' Lord Peter Wimsey, Agatha Christie's Miss Marple).

Included under either of the latter two categories is the almost separate genre of the "tough guy" detective—the hard drinking, rough-and-dirty fighting, hard-wenching, and hard-headed type developed by Raymond Chandler and Dashiell Hammett, imitated by Mickey Spillane, and currently holding his own as John D. MacDonald's Travis McGee.

Also included, and invaluable, if you can think of one, are the "novelty" detectives, like Gilbert Chesterton's Father Brown, John Ball's Vergil Tibbs, or Harry Kemelman's Rabbi Small.

Another method of categorizing mysteries would be by their approach:

(1) *The Puzzle.* The oldest of all, the one in which the mystery must be solved just because it is there (Poe's "The Murders of the Rue Morgue" and all the "locked room" mysteries that have followed it).

(2) *The Suspense Mystery*—Will they catch the killer before he can strike again?

(3) *The Character Mystery.*   The solving of the mystery is less interesting than what makes someone (frequently the criminal) tick. (Patricia Highsmith's *The Amazing Mr. Ripley*, which also fits into the next category).

(4) *The Backwards Mystery.*   The reader knows who did it and why; the only question is whether the authorities will catch him. It's like the silent thriller movies of my youth which had the audience shouting "Look behind you!" to the heroine.

Perhaps one of the two most essential characteristics that all mystery and suspense stories have is a mystery, which a character or characters manage to unravel, *using only clues also available to the reader* (like those in a gothic). Hell hath no fury like a cheated mystery or suspense buff who has had evidence withheld from him (as in Sir Arthur Conan Doyle's Sherlock Holmes short story "The Lion's Mane"). The other essential is a feeling of suspense right up to the concluding pages. In a suspense story the mystery may be solved before the climax, but only if the suspense can be maintained by some other dramatic question: Now that he knows the facts, will Bill Terrier be in time to warn the others and thwart the evil Mike Lassisohn? Can Joan maintain her cool while acting as bait to entrap Jack Spratte?

Another word of warning. If you are using professionals—policemen, licensed private eyes, or defense attorneys—as characters in your story, find someone with expertise who will advise you on the ethical standards, normal procedures, and limitations on the activities of the gentry concerned. Supreme Court decisions of recent years regarding search warrants, informing suspects of their constitutional rights before questioning them, wiretapping, etc. have severely restricted investigators, and if you are not careful you may allow your detective to solve the mystery without an iota of admissible evidence to take with him into court. Or he may risk being fired, having his license suspended, or being disbarred. (I'll never understand how Perry Mason managed to continue practicing law after all the breaking and entering he seemed to do.) Some mystery writers of the "police procedure" branch of the genre who appear to have done their homework are Ed McBain, Elizabeth Linington (who also writes as Dell Shannon) and John Creasy writing under the pseudonym of J. J. Marric. Since state laws vary, and so do police procedures, organizations, and titles of rank, it is well to place your action in areas you know about or to put them in some noncommittal Never-Never-Land, whence no one will rise up to call you on the protocol between police detectives and laboratory men.

I suppose that suspense stories of international spying and intrigue can afford to be a little looser. CIA agents are less likely than police officers to blow their cover and publicize their *modus operandi* by writing in, "I have been an espionage agent in Bhutan for the past seven years, and I feel I must point out that. . . ." However, if you happen to have a friend who has had experience as a secret agent, you might show him your manuscript for suggestions not inimical to the national interest. I suspect that there are better authorities than 007.

Again, as I have mentioned before, read before you submit, and make sure you are with the mainstream, unless you have a new wrinkle so novel that it is destined to sweep all before it and change the direction of thrillers forever.

BLOOD, BOSOMS, AND BICEPS

Men's adventure stories have heroes like the "tough-guy" detectives. They can take, and dish out, an amazing amount of punishment from other, but inferior, tough guys, wild beasts, and natural disasters. They usually are experts in one or several traditionally masculine athletic areas: football, wrestling, baseball, boxing, karate, ice-hockey, and/or plain rough-and-tumble fighting. Not only are they athletes on the playing fields and in barrooms, but also in the boudoirs of the scantily clad and fantastically beautiful nymphomaniacs who infest the stories.

The story plots are usually of the *quest* variety. The hero is after hidden treasure, lost civilizations, or his buddy, lost in a plane crash deep in the jungle. The action must be rapid, suspenseful, and written in clear, uncomplicated prose. The background locale is usually somewhere exotic; the Amazonian rain-forest, central Greenland, or a remote atoll in the South Pacific. Since World War II, the Korean War, Viet Nam, and the development of jet air travel, it is getting increasingly hard to find places that no one knows about. Subject matter is somewhat easier: war, crime (not mystery), sports (including hunting and fishing), hijacking, scuba diving. And usually lots of sex of the uninvolved love-'em-and-leave-'em category.

Men's adventure stories rarely have much theme, and the plot is not intricate, but a means for stringing together a series of picaresque adventures. If confessions are Greek tragedy, the first men's adventure story was the *Odyssey*.

Who reads the pulp paper magazines that contain these stories? I don't have the full details, but I suspect the average reader is a ninety-five pound (or possibly 295 pound) weakling who has a confining job as bookkeeper, bushelman, or high school student, and who is afraid to ask even the pimply mangle-operator at the laundry for a date for fear she will turn him down as all the other girls have. The stories are in short, escape fiction at its most basic, and they must be told in all sincerity, not with tongue in cheek. The readers may know better, but they *have* to believe that such adventures are possible, or they wouldn't be able to continue operating as they are until they get around to becoming adventurers themselves. Meanwhile, they live vicariously.

Again, if you want to write men's adventure stories, you must read them first. Read the men's pulp magazine that you hope to interest in your work. Then—lots of luck.

WESTERNS (COWBOY)

If your time is short, this is a good section to skip. At the time of writing, western magazine stories in the standard tradition are defunct, and novels are rare, probably having been killed off by the big television westerns. But since they may return, I'll give you a little background.

A western is basically a men's adventure story told with a limited locale: the western United States or Canada during the brief period between the pacification of the Indians and the arrival of civilization and barbed wire. The weaponry used is more limited too—revolvers (six-guns), occasional rifles, fists, or sometimes a chair used as a club. Sex is minimal, largely because women were a scarce commodity during the period. Horses may take their place as objects of casual affection, but more often they are only transportation.

Characterization in westerns varies greatly with the writer, but is generally more important than in other types of men's adventure stories. It is a good idea for a writer to know which side a horse is mounted from and how many times one can fire a six-shooter without reloading.

This type of western is not to be confused with the historical story with a western setting. They are not necessarily formula stories, and their background is, or should be, more carefully researched. (See, for instance, *The Man Who Loved Cat Dancing*, by Marilyn Durham.) Such books may have any type of plot, characterization, and theme.

SEX FICTION

This is also an inactive field at the time I am writing. Known by such varying names as *racy* (or *spicy*) *fiction, pornography, sex books,* or *smut,* it has always been a precarious field, attacked on the one hand by judicial decisions, postal regulations, local censorship, and vigilante book-burners and the other by heavy competition from the increasingly explicit handling of sex in much new standard fiction. Sex fiction is produced by a small group of publishers who have the further disadvantage of lacking the control of distribution channels enjoyed by the big general-interest publishers. Most of their sales are made through specialized porno bookstores (also precarious ventures) or by mail order via the plain brown wrapper route.

Fortunately writers are not subject to prosecution for writing sex fiction, but those who publish it are, and there is always the possibility that the publisher who had planned to use your book will be in jail, out of business, or under injunction to suspend publication by the time you have written it. As I write this, I understand that their presses are at a standstill. When or whether they will resume is not known.

Books of this kind are published anonymously or under pseudonyms, unless the authors request otherwise. Generally they are rapidly written and sold outright to the publisher for a lump sum, often less than a thousand dollars. Characterization is negligible—there is more interest in characters of both sexes as sex objects than as living, thinking, emotional people. Plotting varies considerably: the story may be a standard gothic, mystery, or men's adventure tale provided that at least 50% is devoted to a heavy-handed and explicit treatment of sex exploits. Or it may have only enough plot to string together a long series of bizarre erotic events.

The latter might almost be written by use of a check list. Write down all the conceivable ways a human being can achieve orgasm. (If, as is probable, your own imagination and experience are inadequate, a translation of Krafft-Ebing's encyclopedic work *Psychopathia Sexualis* or one of the Marquis de Sade's works might help.) Just make sure you use at least a dozen techniques in each chapter, and all of them before the book is finished. There is no reason to be afraid of four-letter words—your first page should have some of them used in describing or anticipating an explicit sex scene. But you had better have several longer synonyms, too. You will be needing to write about them enough that one term would speedily become monotonous.

Again, if this market returns and you should decide to try it out, read and research before you write. Editors in this field as well as others have specific "slant" requirements.

SCIENCE FICTION

It is unfair of me to suggest that science fiction is all written by formula; it varies perhaps as widely as all other literature put together. But there are problems which all science fiction writers share, and this is the best place to discuss them. But first let us examine some of the commoner species of the genre:

The Space Opera is a men's adventure story taking place in a super-exotic setting: a spacecraft, another planet, etc. Scientific gimmicks required to set the atmosphere are either ignored completely or brushed by with a casual comment on space-warp, force-field, etc., while the action goes on with ray-guns, atomic blasters, and big-busted babes from Betelgeuse VIII. (See books by A. E. Von Vogt, some later works of Robert Heinlein.) Juvenile space opera might be called a sub-genre here. It is essentially a boy's adventure story, with a teen-aged (or sometimes younger) hero, and it contains all the elements listed above, except for the big-busted babes.

The Anthro-Sociological Science Fiction. This type of story postulates a new scientific discovery (anti-gravity, for instance) and weaves a story around the impact the inventions springing from it will have upon human life. (Isaac Asimov, Robert Heinlein, Ray Bradbury) Or the story may be based on the discovery of another planet with a different intelligent life form and the effect of the meeting of two radically different cultures. (H. G. Wells, Bradbury, William Tenn, Murray Leinster) The actual amount of extrapolated "science" may vary considerably and may be treated exhaustively or brushed by.

The Engineering Story. These are rarer, because they require a good scientific and engineering background to write, plus the ability to put it into non-technical English. In it, an extrapolation is made from actual scientific knowledge of today, possibly plus some minor additions only guessed at, and a story is woven around the actual difficulties in performing some as-yet-undone feat of engineering. (Jules Verne, Arthur C. Clarke, early works of Heinlein)

In all of these types of science fiction, characterization, plot, and theme are necessary. Plot is usually more important than theme in space opera; theme usually overshadows plot in anthro-sociological science fiction, which is usually a veiled commentary on contemporary life. In the engineering story, characterization is most important. And there are exceptions to all these rules, plus many mixtures of the types described. Read a sampling from your magazine or publisher to find out what is wanted.

The common problem all science fiction faces results from the fact that it always takes place in a milieu unfamiliar to the reader. In a story set in a contemporary suburban area, a couple of swift sentences can get the reader's mind in gear with the story. Even an historical story need only specify the date and place to give the reader some preparation, though it may be necessary to refresh his memory as to whether the railroad was in use by then, or if it was the day of hoop-skirts or bustles. But a science fiction story has to start from scratch and tell the reader enough to let him understand and follow the action. Obviously the best time to do this is at the beginning. Equally obviously, the impatient science fiction reader is not going to plow through two chapters of dull facts before getting into the action. There are several devices for this, and the writer must select the one which works best for him and that particular story. First one must put in a little drama at the beginning: a personality clash, a threatened danger, or a maladroit and unsafe act by a character. This episode may have little to do with the story, but it gets things started and should maintain interest until a few facts about the time, locale, state of science, etc. can be imparted. Methods of feeding in the information once the reader is hooked include:

(1) Having a character doing something and explaining the procedure as he does it:

> Gunnar reached for the yellow switch, the one which would fire the retro-rockets and slow the full two hundred meters of the spacecraft into the proper speed for orbiting the planet below. He fixed his eyes on the apparent speed and gravity indicators and slowly depressed the switch until the two needles were almost pointing at each other. Holding his breath, he released the switch and reached for the micro-dial instead. Even after landings on a score of new planets, his hands always trembled as he made the final adjustments that would permit an orbit and a soft landing.

(2) Having a greenhorn present, one who asks enough dumb questions to wring from the old-timers all the information the reader needs. This method is a *real* test of the writer's ability to write convincing dialogue.

(3) Giving a straightforward account—writer to reader —but doing it in little dabs at a time, so that it soaks in instead of running off like a desert cloudburst.

(4) Using some standard, pre-defined science fiction terminology that all SF buffs understand: space warp, space station, force field, time travel, anti-grav, or Asimov's Laws of Robotics.

FANTASY

This genre is often classified with science fiction, and the line between them is a narrow one. Many writers (Ray Bradbury and Kurt Vonnegut, for instance) skate back and forth between with no noticeable effort. Some fantasy, particularly that intended for children, is primarily intended for entertainment, but much if not most of adult fantasy is intended as social commentary, like the anthro-sociological science fiction. Theme, therefore, is vital, as well as enough characterization and plot to maintain interest.

Some of the very best fantasy predicates only one important deviation from normal life as we know it. Ira Levin's *Rosemary's Baby* and *The Stepford Wives* owe much of their horror effect to the fact that in general everything is normal and recognizable except for the existence of the Satanists and Satan himself in the first novel and the only-partially-strange behavior of the housewives in the suburb of Stepford in the other. The problem of explaining the situation that exists in the science fiction story is at a minimum here. The oddity of the milieu tells itself along with the story.

Other fantasy stories, however, take place in a time and place so unfamiliar to us that the reader requires almost more briefing on the situation than there is story. Tolkien's *Lord of the Rings* trilogy uses every conceivable device to bring in background, and it is still coming in up to the very end of the book. Not only that, but he devotes a full half book to index with further background information.

CHILDREN'S FICTION

This also is so broad a field that it is hard to make any generalizations about it. There are books for pre-school children, books and magazines for beginning readers, older pre-teens, and adolescents. There are books and magazines slanted for girls and some slanted for boys.

The first thing to remember is that children, particularly young ones, have limited vocabularies. In fact, considerable research has been done and graded vocabulary lists are available at most public schools. If you are writing something for a specific age group, it would be well to select words that they know. This does not mean that you have to confine yourself *completely* to a list (how will they learn more words unless they are exposed to them?) but other words should not come more frequently than the reader can absorb.

Children's stories should be brief, to match their attention spans. Younger children's books must be heavily illustrated.

Pre-readers want more space taken up with pictures than with print. As the age group rises, the percentage of pages devoted to pictures diminishes and so does the size of the type. If you are an illustrator yourself, like Dr. Seuss or the Berenstains, that takes care of one worry. If you are not, contact your publisher about what to do. He may have his own staff illustrators, or he may expect you to find one. Also contact him about how to submit the drawings. Usually he will want them oversized, so that reducing them will take care of irregularities. It is usually best to type or print your copy on the page about where you think it should go and put in your own crude drawing to indicate the desired space it should take up and in general what it should show.

Very young children go for verse. They are less interested in plot line or characterization than in the silly sounds of the words. Theme, if any, should be slanted to the problems of the age group. (*Green Eggs and Ham* by Dr. Seuss is an excellent example of theme, as well as a number of other things.)

As children grow older, their attention span lengthens, and they will demand more plot and more characterization. They generally prefer lots of action, suspense (mild for the young, pretty tense for teen-agers), and characters they can identify with or (occasionally) admire. The hero may be a basketball star, but he has to have problems the reader can share. Avoid complex plots.

In writing complete books (like Baum's Oz books, for example), each chapter should be a story of its own, and the dramatic question for that chapter should be answered by the end. There may be a dramatic question for the whole book (Will Dorothy get back to Kansas?), but the problem of getting her out of the slumber-ridden poppy field must be solved right away. This is unlike the technique of adult fiction, in which each chapter should end with a cliff-hanger.

In children's fiction as much as any other, it pays to know what the market wants. Explore other works from the same publisher before you write and submit.

CONCLUSION

As I look back on this chapter which attempts to give generalized hints on writing routine or formula fiction to sell (probably the best reason for writing by formula), I see one comment made oftener than any other: Know your market. Read what the publisher has been putting out recently, see what slant the editor wants, and give it to him. I won't bother to say it again.

Chapter 17
Stars in Your Eyes:
Experimental Writing and
The Great American Novel

If you skipped Chapter 16, you may be disappointed to see how much shorter this one is. That is because it is much easier to describe formulas which already exist than the ones which haven't yet been created. For that is what experimental writing is: an attempt to create a new but effective way of communicating an artistic truth. If it is truly successful, it will be imitated. If it is supremely successful, it will be imitated again and again, until it establishes a new writing formula. For all formulas were first created by some experimental writer, just as all cliches were once striking and effective *bon mots,* or they would not have been reused until they wore out.

WHAT EXPERIMENTAL WRITING IS

James Joyce was a great experimental writer. Both *Ulysses* and *Finnegan's Wake* are studied like Holy Writ by Joyceans —and with the aid of commentaries and concordances almost as long. Certainly longer than the books themselves. Joyce was one of literature's foremost wits—puns and absurd juxtapositions of irrelevant allusions flash constantly from his pen, to be lost on all but the most erudite, who are familiar with the subject matter, or the student with the definitive commentary who can read two pages before he gets the joke—if he still wants it. But Joyce did write beautiful stream-of-consciousness sequences, so that he made stream-of-consciousness a tool available to every writer since his time. And it is often employed, though usually in a more comprehensible modification.

Hemingway was an innovator. He was the first person to write dialogue so that it really sounded like ordinary people talking. (Mark Twain sometimes came close, but not that close.) Nowadays more writers than ever before are making their dialogue sound like the real thing, because consciously or not they are imitating Hemingway.

Faulkner, he of the sesquipedelian sentences, was an innovator. His tortuous language forms a suitable counterpoint to his tortured characters and lends an aura of mystery to what otherwise might have seemed mundane events. He too has a wide circle of imitators.

Anthony Burgess is a more recent innovator, though it might be objected that he derived a good bit of the weird language his characters speak in *The Clockwork Orange* from both Joyce and George Orwell.

WHAT EXPERIMENTAL WRITING IS NOT

Experimental writing is *not* a slavish imitation of Joyce, Hemingway, Faulkner, Burgess, or any other of the great innovators. Anyone can, and probably will, borrow from them, and if it is done often enough, whole new genres may develop: Mississippi Gothic, Scholastic Fun-and-Games, the Newspeak Novella, etc. But none of this is experimental, because the ground has already been broken. The only way for you to write experimentally is to break your own ground and write as no one has before.

There is an old saw which says one must never tell an old story in an old manner, because it will be dull, nor a new story in a new manner, because it will be incomprehensible. This may be only partly true, but still it would be silly to expect anyone to write a story that is entirely experimental. The words you use will have to be standard ones, or at least, like those in *Finnegan's Wake,* derived from standard English. And even Joyce used an old plot for *Ulysses.* So everyone's writing is partially derived, partially experimental (even if the experimental part is only an individual style). When we talk about experimental writing, we mean writing that is at least 25% experimental. Almost invariably it will violate some—possibly all—of the precepts given in this book.

PERILS OF EXPERIMENTAL WRITING

Since I cannot tell you how to write experimentally—if I did, it would be my experiment, not yours—the least I can do is warn you about some of the problems you will encounter.

Experimental writing is like a biological mutation, a genetic accident which produces a living individual unlike any that has existed before. According to evolutionary theory, if the mutant has "survival characteristics" and is well fitted to live in its environment, it will thrive and have children with the same characteristics. But if the new traits the mutant has are undesirable and make it less able to survive, it will probably die young and leave no descendants. Almost all mutations are of the latter category.

So is most experimental writing. If we define success as being read by an audience that is substantial either in number or quality, about 99.44% of it is unsuccessful. Usually it will be too difficult for the reader to understand and follow, and he will give up in exasperation, as many readers have with Joyce, Faulkner, *et al.* The average reader is lazy; he wants to read things he can comprehend at once. If he can't follow what is happening, he has trouble getting emotionally involved in it, so he is inclined to give up and go to sleep instead. Much experimental writing compensates in part by an infusion of strongly emotional mood or zany humor which will carry the reader along past the hard parts.

The other serious danger in experimental writing is that the author himself may get lost in the morass and lose control of the characters, the plot (if any), and the theme, and end up doing a kind of automatic writing in which the hand is no longer guided by the brain. I have seen, for instance, writing which was done by a writer under the influence of marijuana or one of the stronger hallucinogens like LSD. The trouble with them is that they could be appreciated only by a reader who is on a trip himself, at which time almost anything looks good.

Another problem you will have is in getting adequate criticism. Writing is a lonely pursuit at best, and when you write something new and different, it will be hard for your classmates to comment on your work. There really aren't as many standards for experimental fiction as there are for traditional pieces. It is hard for someone to say "your climax came too early" or "your opening is too slow" when you have written in a plotless form. Nor is your instructor likely to be of much help. If you are lucky (and talented), you may draw a teacher who will confine himself to correcting your spelling and giving you words of encouragement. Advice for real changes is hard to make when there is no set of criteria, when no one knows what it *should* be like.

REWARDS OF EXPERIMENTAL WRITING

If a writer's chance of success is rated as low as 0.56%, why would anyone want to write experimentally? Well, there are several reasons for it.

First, there is always the chance that yours may belong to that lucky half of one percent that *does* work, that has talent glowing through it so clearly that you can find a publisher for it, and that enough readership will develop that you will have fan clubs like the Browning Societies of your great-grandmother's day, or the much more recent Tolkien Clubs. And your name will go into the hall of fame reserved for the great literary innovators. But don't expect big monetary rewards. You may get them, but you should be warned that the great Dutch experimental painter, Vincent Van Gogh, never sold a single painting during his lifetime.

Second, something there is that doesn't like a rule, and most of us have some of it. I know of at least one good instructor in creative writing who used to make up his own rules just as a challenge to his students. "The best stories always have a body of water in them," he would assert solemnly, "even if it is only a tiny stream." Or "Trying to write with an animal as point-of-view character always sounds phony." And at the next session he would pick up a bunch of stories told from the point of view of a camel in mid-Sahara. Experimental writing may be used to prove the teacher wrong.

Next, experimental writing is wonderful practice. It develops originality, stretches the imagination, and helps the writer in creating his style. It is my own opinion that a writer should really master the basics before he launches into new territory, that he should know how to write narration and how to characterize and plot, just as most art teachers feel that students of painting should learn to draw, using balance, perspective, light and shadow, etc. before they begin to do non-objective abstractions, and teachers of music theory want students to know the scales, the keys, and the principles of harmony before they begin to compose symphonies.

Once you have learned the rules of the game, however, it is a heady experience to test them out, to see how much you can get by with breaking them and still end up with something worthwhile. I do *not* believe that experiment should be used, as it often is, as a cover for shoddy work done by a student too lazy to learn the trade.

Finally, the last reason for doing experimental writing is for the sake of literature itself. The art speedily grows stale when there is no change. Had it not been for experiment, we would still be getting our kicks out of listening to bards singing epics and sagas about the heroes of the Civil War and their exploits or watching plays with only two actors and a chorus. All the types of fiction, all the poetic forms that we have studied, all the dramatic forms and devices that we will study in the next section have evolved at one time or another from experiments by someone. And all the great literary forms that we do not have because nobody has thought of them are still waiting to be discovered. Maybe you are the one with the combination to the lock.

THE GREAT AMERICAN NOVEL

The Great American Novel is a mythical title, of course. There never will be one, because one of the things that makes a novel seem particularly significant is its relevance to the American culture. And American culture never seems to stand still long enough to let literature catch up. The jokes being told about Poles today are the same ones that were told about the "two Irishmen named Pat and Mike" a century ago. The only difference is in the dialect, and the only reason for the change is that the Irish have now been with us so long that we have begun to realize that they are ordinary human beings whose ancestors were standing on their hind legs long before the invention of the wheelbarrow. Jokes about the penury of the Jew or the Scotsman, jokes about the "heathen Chinee" have come and gone, and jokes about the superstitious, watermelon-eating Black are retreating rapidly behind them. And good riddance to them all.

But the point is that novels tend to come and go, too, unless they are rooted in something more basic than the world or the nation as it is today. Perhaps it is significant that the three most often mentioned candidates for the title, *The Scarlet Letter, Moby Dick,* and *The Adventures of Huckleberry Finn,* were all written in the nineteenth century. At that time things were changing pretty fast, but not with the blinding speed of our own times. There have been great novelists in the twentieth century, of course, and they have written great novels, but only a few have really been suggested as candidates, and they in no more than a passing manner: *The Great Gatsby, A Farewell to Arms, Main Street, The Grapes of Wrath* (No novel of Faulkner's is included because, despite his stature, no one of his novels is considered his best by a clear majority of critics).

If you want to write *The* Great American Novel, then, you must write about people and attitudes that will be similar to real people and real attitudes of today—and, even more important, of tomorrow too. *Main Street,* for instance, lost out because it came out of a period—the 1920's—when self-confidence reigned and the small town was still the center of American life. Even the language was the slang of the 20's. In the 1970's it isn't applicable.

Let's take a look at the three novels that are still in the running, despite their age. What are their topics? *The Scarlet Letter* is about sex—and death. The other two are quest stories, although they contain considerable thought about death too.

The locale and time of *The Scarlet Letter* is New England during the early colonial period under the rigorous puritan moral code—a period which had been gone for well over a century at the time the book was published in 1850. *Moby Dick* is about the sailing-ship whaling industry, which was still extant at the time the book was written, but long gone by the time it had become a classic. *Huckleberry Finn* is about the Mississippi River as it had been a quarter-century earlier, and about slavery, which had been illegal for twenty years when the novel was published. So we cannot say that timeliness was a feature of any of them. Perhaps it is necessary to have some perspective before writing a Great Novel.

The plots are quite different: *The Scarlet Letter,* despite its Victorian tendency to meander and its unnecessary long prologue, is a short, tightly plotted novel. *Huckleberry Finn* has a typical picaresque plot, with a goal—to get Jim to free territory—that really is inoperative from Cairo on, and the episodes are strung together in a manner which suggests that they could have come in almost any sequence. *Moby Dick* is so slow-moving (like a stranded whale) that the plot seems less an adventure story than an excuse to tell us all about whaling and whalers—or to hang great curtains of allegory and metaphor over what is essentially a simple story about a man's obsession to destroy a *particular* whale, of no more commercial value than any other sperm whale.

The characters in each novel are strongly portrayed and memorable—and two-dimensional, with the possible exception of Hester Prynne, who is showing signs of developing into a bas-relief at the end of the novel. Captain Ahab and Huck Finn teach us a lot, but they never learn it themselves. Ishmael may have learned something, but we do not see that it has made him a different man.

All three novels have in common a strong sense of irony: that the man who must demand confession from Hester Prynne is the man who would be ruined if she did confess; that Ahab can destroy the whale only by destroying himself; that an innocent like Huck Finn is able to tell good from evil by instinct, but only when he turns his back on the morality he has been taught.

Two of the three, *Moby Dick* and *Huckleberry Finn,* are told in the first person point of view. And Huck Finn is clearly an innocent (not that he doesn't do anything dishonest—he always lies in preference to telling the truth); the story owes a lot of its power to the fact that he is innocent. Ishmael is somewhat more sophisticated than Huck, but his position as a minor character and onlooker gives the same aura of wonderment and fresh viewpoint.

The themes of *The Scarlet Letter* and *Huckleberry Finn* are strong indictments of the moral codes of the times in which they occurred, but in different manners. *The Scarlet Letter* suggests that too repressive a moral code makes criminals of those who might otherwise have been virtuous (perhaps foretelling the eras of prohibition of alcohol, and later, marijuana). *Huckleberry Finn* seems to be saying that human nature is essentially evil, and that the only way to avoid it is to "light out for the territory" where one can be alone with a sinless nature.

The theme of *Moby Dick*, like everything else in the book, is less obvious. But it is generally taken to mean that good and evil are inseparable parts of each other, like the yin and yang of oriental thought, and that one cannot be eradicated without destroying the other as well.

The indications are that the hallmarks of a great and timeless novel are: (1) that the time be far enough back that objectivity and irony are possible, but that features which date it firmly can be omitted; (2) that sex is not necessary for a great book, but that death apparently is; (3) that characters should be memorable, but not necessarily three-dimensional; (4) that the first person point of view can be effective and (5) that the theme be a comment on morals that has been valid for millenia and will presumably continue to be valid (unlike standards of dress and sexual conduct, which have always been changing, and we see continuing to change).

But, who knows? The next candidate for the position may be a science fiction novel.

Part IV

DRAMA

Chapter 18
Why Wright a Play?

Before you start this section, I should warn you that it covers only plays intended to be acted out upon a stage. The failure to include writing for film or television is not because I consider screen-writing unimportant—obviously it isn't—but because it requires knowledge of techniques and terminology outside the scope of such a generalized text as this. The fields of film and television both deserve full-length books of their own.

THE PLAYWRIGHT

Did you ever wonder why a person who writes plays is a *playwright* rather than a *playwrite*? It isn't a typographical error, as you might have supposed. A wright is someone who makes things. A wheelwright, for instance, makes wheels, selling them, presumably, to a cartwright, who makes carts, or a wainwright, who manufactures wagons (wains). And a playwright "makes" plays in a different way than a novelist writes a book, or a poet a poem. A play does not depend on words alone for its effect; reading a play is a poor substitute for seeing it. A playwright has to carry a stage around in his head all the time he is writing and test everything he puts down on paper by seeing it performed on that mental stage, for a play that cannot be performed is no play.

Perhaps that is the reason why playwrights, unlike poets, are comparatively late bloomers. There have been a few good plays made by youngsters, but most of the best plays are written by playwrights above thirty years of age.

Next to poetry, drama is the oldest form of creative literature. Its history reaches back into pre-writing times. The earliest known plays seem to have been religious rituals or extensions of rituals, in character quite like American Indian rain dances, war dances, and hunting dances. To take it even further back, it may be related to the courting rituals performed by many birds and mammals, or even to the pattern-flying done by a bee who has made a big find and wants to tell her colleagues where to go for it.

At any rate, the dramatic art was far advanced by the sixth century B.C., and we still have complete Greek plays from that period, some of them so viable that they are still being performed today. By that time, although their plots were based on Greek mythology and the gods' presence was felt throughout the action, plays had progressed well beyond the ceremonial stage and were about the struggles and sufferings of mortal human beings.

ADVANTAGES OF THE PLAYWRIGHT

Every kind of writing has its advantages and disadvantages, and it is a good thing to know them in advance. First let us see in what ways drama is a more effective means of communicating between the writer and the recipient (in this case, the audience, not the reader).

APPEAL TO TWO SENSES

A person reading a story is looking at a lot of small black marks on a sheet of paper, and his mind and imagination convert them into the sounds of a crash and tinkle, the sudden aroma of baking bread, and the sight of a broken kitchen window. Or he may be listening to another person reading the story aloud and transmuting the sounds into the same sensations. But he is using only a single sense—the rest of it goes on in his mind. The richness he experiences in the story depends as much on the reader's artistry as the writer's.

A play, on the other hand, is not usually intended to be read. In a play, a member of the audience actually witnesses what is going on. He *hears* the glass break. He *sees* the broken window. Technicians are still working on the smell of baking bread, but even that is only a question of time. The audience's imaginations may amplify what they see—in many plays they are required to—but the point is that they have a good headstart in the things which are going on right there in front of them, something which can be directly seen and heard together.

SOUND AND SPECTACLE

A musical background has become so much a part of film technique that we hardly notice it—unless it is not there. It probably got its genesis in the days of the silent films, when a piano player was hired to make enough noise to cover up the hum of the projector. The music was scored, hopefully, to fit the film. (I'll never be able to forget the sight of covered wagons lumbering over the skyline to the strains of the *Largo* from *New World Symphony*.) Music can be used on the stage too, in legitimate drama as well as musical comedy. And nothing, with the possible exception of smells, can invoke emotion more quickly than well-chosen music. Unfortunately, few novels come equipped with mood music.

Not only can music have impact on the senses and emotions, but so can scenery and costuming. A good stage setting can be overpowering. I remember once seeing a Renaissance throne room depicted on a stage, and a richly elegant one it was, too, done in gold and silver with touches of muted blue and lavender, carried out in the costumes of the court. And then, with a suitable musical fanfare, in swept a visiting princess—dressed in full-skirted crimson velvet. With the addition of a spotlight on her, there could be no question about who was the central character of that scene. Fiction has its trick effects too. But they are not so—well, not so *dramatic!*

CHARACTERIZATION

A fiction writer has several means for characterization. He can describe Genevieve; he can tell what she says, what she wears, what she does, and even what she thinks. But he cannot have us *experience* Genevieve. We can know a lot about her and think we understand her thoroughly after about a hundred pages. But a capable actress can make us better acquainted with Genevieve in five minutes. The presence of actors on the stage—living, breathing human beings—can do things that printed words on a page cannot, no matter how masterly the writing. Of course there may be a problem here, too. The actor may not portray the character the exact way that the playwright intended. The odds are that he will not. And the lines may not sound the same as they did in the playwright's imagination. But they will come closer to meaning the same thing to all the members of the audience than they would if the same people had only read the play, and the total reaction of the audience will be deepened and enriched by what the actors have done with the words the playwright has put on paper. Indeed, the fact that the playwright has the help of the actors in interpreting a play gives an additional dimension that never is there when a single artist is responsible for the entire production, as in fiction or poetry.

THE DIRECTOR

Another, and some say even more important, factor in adding depth to a play is the director. He is the person who takes the play the playwright has so hopefully wrought and fits it into the actual operating conditions. If he turns out to have a leading lady who cannot pronounce the letter *r,* he may send her lines back to the playwright to be changed to minimize her problem. (If you don't believe there is any such leading lady, you obviously have never done much work in amateur theatricals, at least not in a small town.) If he sees an opportunity to get an extra laugh—or sob—by a bit of action that the playwright hadn't thought of, he will throw it in. If he finds that a scene just will not "play" as it is, he will send it back to the playwright for revision, change it himself, or even drop it if it is not really necessary to make the whole play work. And throughout the rehearsals he will be interpreting and reinterpreting the meaning of the play as he goes along. By the time it all is ready to go before its first-night audience, there may be some doubt as to whose play it truly is.

Many playwrights get antsy, temperamental, or just plain mad at their directors and what they are doing to a beautiful piece of work. And sometimes they are entirely justified. But I have read scenes that have been chopped out of plays by such recognizable giants among playwrights as Anton Chekhov, Berthold Brecht, and Arthur Miller—sometimes over their violent protests—and I am inclined to believe in general that the legal axiom "The defendant who acts as his own attorney has a fool for a client" has some valid application in the playwright-director relationship. There have been notable exceptions: Noel Coward wrote, directed, and played the lead in his plays—but the feat is perhaps more memorable than the plays.

IMMEDIACY

Writing a piece of fiction in any tense but the past is a difficult chore. Fiction *feels* like something which has already happened, and this is as true even of science fiction set in the year 5492 A.D. as it is of a prehistorical novel taking place in 5492 B.C.

A play is different. A drama is *always* told in the *present tense*. When it is being played before an audience, it is going on right then as well as right there. The audience gets a sense of immediacy—of instant replay. It is much easier to get involved with something that is still happening. I recall seeing a play entitled *Camille in Roaring Camp* in my youth. It involved a traveling troupe of actors stranded in a gold camp in post–'49 California inhabited by characters right out of Bret Harte's stories. The troupe attempts to put on the play *Camille*, a tragic romance by Alexandre Dumas *fils*, in which the heroine, deserted by the last of her several lovers, dies of destitution and consumption. The assembled miners get so caught up in the plot and characters of the play that they swarm up on the stage brandishing firearms and hangman's ropes and require the hapless leading man to "make an honest woman" of the startled Lady of the Camellias. The play was not entirely convincing, even to my ten-year-old eyes (the amateur actors were hamming it up more than the playwright probably intended), but the moral is there. The magic of the theater *can* hold an audience so enthralled that they forget where they actually are and become participants in the imaginary life up there on the stage. Or, rather, right *here* on the stage.

DIRECT EMOTIONAL APPEAL

If you can write a short story which makes readers laugh, you have talent. If you can write one which makes them weep, you are probably even greater. If you can write one which has them laughing and crying at the same time, or even alternately, you may well be a genius.

But a playwright, backed by a competent director and cast, is *expected* to be able to do these things. And it is really easier. Why? Because when you actually see an actress on the stage racked with sobs, and you know why she is crying, there is bound to be a lump in your throat, unless you are the type that takes candy away from babies for the sake of hearing them scream.

Again in my youth, I saw a road show version of *Abie's Irish Rose*, a tremendous hit in its day (which is long since over). It probably wasn't an exceptional troupe, or they wouldn't have been barnstorming that deep into the boondocks, but they were professional. As the house lights went down, we could hear the sound of laughter: deep, genuine laughter that made your diaphragm ache. It kept coming, peal after peal, as the curtain went up, and by the time we could see the laugher, the whole audience was laughing as hard as he. And with that as a start, they kept us off balance and laughing for the entire play, except for the sentimental tear-jerking parts of Acts Two and Three, when there was not, to coin a cliché, a dry eye in the house.

One of the most pathetic scenes in drama, I suppose, is the end of Chekhov's *The Cherry Orchard*. After all the important but impotent characters have left their mansion forever, and as the sound of axes can be heard chopping down the trees in the largest cherry orchard in that part of Russia, in shuffles the doddering and faithful old servant, Firs, left behind by mistake. He moves around for a few minutes, fussily rearranging the furniture, then lies down on the sofa for what we know will be his last rest. On paper, it isn't exactly a rouser. On the stage, where you can actually see the octogenarian ex-serf, it is devastating.

PROBLEMS OF THE PLAYWRIGHT

If drama has all these advantages over fiction, why doesn't everyone go for it? The first reason is that books and magazines are more portable than stages and theaters (although home television is almost as convenient as a book). But in reality there are other disadvantages and limitations to compensate for all the immediacy of drama. There are limitations in time, in space, and in facilities, such as set design, properties, and actors.

TIME LIMITATIONS

I once had a student who wrote into his play a scene in which two characters sat down by a fireplace on stage and spent eight hours in tearing out the pages of books and tossing them into the flames. OK in fiction, where it can be covered in a short paragraph. Not so on the stage. Let us suppose that we have been able to square away the theater fire regulations and secured an inexhaustible supply of cheap books to use night after night. We could play the scene all night—but not with an audience. Since the advent of Theater of the Absurd and of audience participation shows like *Hair,* spectators have learned to put up with a lot, but not with being bored to death. Your heroine can't even sit by the telephone waiting for it to ring for three hours—unless something else is going on at the same time.

Of course there are ways to get the same effect. The late Will Rogers starred in a movie version of *A Connecticut Yankee* during a time when censorship regulations limited the length of time a kiss could be held before the eye of a viewer. Rogers and the actress playing the part of Morgan le Fay were shown kissing; then the camera went on to another scene for a few moments before turning back to the couple, who were still in a lip-lock. Back to the other action, then a return to the kissers, who were beginning to show signs of fatigue. Perhaps half a dozen such switches were made, until, with about ten seconds of actual kiss, we got the impression of a ten minute kiss—a record even for the silver screen. Maybe something similar could be worked out for your play. But the point is that *something* will have to be worked out.

SPACE LIMITATIONS

Imagine yourself in the eighteenth row of a packed theater. What can you see? Well, if that tall girl sitting in front of you will only put her head on her escort's shoulder, you will be able to see most of a little spot of floor which has been raised up higher than the rest and is partially concealed by a wall with a wide-open arch. When the arch is not covered by a drawn curtain, you can see the people and furniture on this piece of floor, which is called a stage. That is all. If an actor walks behind a tall bit of scenery or off into the wings, you cannot see him any more.

This is disconcerting if you are of a generation brought up

on cinema and television, whose cameras are put on dollies with wheels, so that they can chase the actors around corners, and which have lenses that will show tiny detail very clearly. A stage has none of these niceties. If you have one of your characters pick up a pin from the floor and show it to another, the pin had better be the size of a twenty-penny nail if the audience is expected to see it too. And do not have, as one of my former students did, a stage direction saying "A troop of cavalry is seen five miles away, galloping toward the town." This would be routine in a work of fiction, but not even the enormous stages at Oberammergau, Germany, or Takarasuka, Japan, would hold a troop of cavalry, including the horses, let alone give them five miles to gallop in. If you want horses, keep them off the stage and let some of your characters watch them through field glasses and give an animated account of what they are doing.

It will probably be helpful if, before you write your first play, you draw a plan of the stage to scale and draw in any furniture or other properties you may have in mind, also to scale. Then see if you have left enough room for the actors to get around. But most helpful of all is to remember your view from the eighteenth row. If you can see or hear it from there, go ahead. Let the nineteenth row take care of itself.

SET LIMITATIONS

A set is the arrangement of scenery, furniture, and other properties for a particular scene in a play. It may vary from the almost bare stage of Thornton Wilder's *Our Town* to the wildly elaborate scenery of a Hollywood extravaganza. But it has limitations. It has to go on the available stage. And it has to be capable of being set up quickly and, unless one set will do for the whole play, being taken down rapidly. Good set designers are usually pretty ingenious, so before deciding that your proposed set for a scene is unattainable, you might ask for advice from one. On the other hand, if you plan a short scene at the beginning of Act II that requires a pool full of live dolphins on stage, you had better explore the possibilities of omitting that scene and just having someone on stage later describe it.

ACTOR LIMITATIONS

We will not often be faced with the problem of a leading lady who cannot pronounce *r*, but there are some problems you can pretty well count on. Suppose you want to put on a science fiction play with creatures from outer space. Actors with five legs and three serpentine arms are hard to find these days, so you had better stick to more mundane variations on the human form. Even if you write a script which requires a giant, you may be in trouble. A star basketball player in elevator shoes might be the right size, but will he be able to act too? If he can, you are lucky. Now where can you get some performing midgets? (I am told that this problem is not absolutely prohibitive. It is said that, in the silent film days, when Mary Pickford and her husband, Douglas Fairbanks, Sr., were great, though undersized, stars, it was necessary to hire entire casts, including the extras for mob scenes, in ultra-small sizes to prevent their overshadowing the diminutive leads. But at that time Hollywood was jammed with people of all sizes and shapes looking for jobs.)

One last word of caution regarding actors. Do *not* include small children or domestic animals as key members of your cast. They are completely unreliable. You may think that you have Rover better trained than Rin-tin-tin, but you can never tell what he will do in front of an audience for the first time. Cats are even worse: dogs are at least anxious to please, but cats are only interested in doing their own thing. Horses—well, just make sure you have one which is completely housebroken. Sure you see them on film, but a film doesn't have to be right every time. Cameramen can re-take the bad scenes.

Children, if anything, are worst of all, possibly because we are apt to expect them to behave like human beings. And they do. Like *young* human beings with a short span of attention and high distractability. A college classmate of mine once told me about having been selected, as the most likely ten-year-old in town, to present the key to the city to some visiting dignitary. He wrote his own brief speech and rehearsed it until his parents complained that he was keeping them awake by declaiming it in his sleep. But when the moment came, when he and the stranger were alone on the platform with the entire town goggling at them, he searched his mind for the speech and found himself deserted, not only by the speech, but by his mind too. So he handed over the symbolic key, saying "Here!"

You'll be lucky if you have a child actor that good.

There is still another problem for the budding dramatist, but it deserves the fuller treatment given in the next chapter. It is the problem of *exposition*.

CHAPTER 19
EXPOSITION. ALSO OTHER MECHANICS

One of the things a fiction writer doesn't worry about much is the question of how you find out what has been happening that has caused the initial situation of the story. Oh, there is the problem of hooking the reader, all right, but as soon as he's hooked, you can pedal backwards and tell the reader directly what happened. In fiction the writer is allowed to do that. In drama there is a different problem. There is no communication between the playwright and his audience once the play has started except by what the characters say and do plus what can be inferred from the stage setting.

Some playwrights, notably Arthur Miller and George Bernard Shaw, have published their plays in a form intended to be read rather than performed. These editions contain a great deal of background material and characterization details. Shaw has stage directions obviously not intended to be played adequately on stage. Take the closing stage direction for his play *Candida: They embrace. But they do not know the secret in the poet's heart.* It's fairly obvious that only the first two words can be performed on the stage, and that the addition of expository material into a printed copy of a play cannot mean that the playwright will be able to convey it directly to an audience in a theater.

And there is another allied problem. How does the playwright expose the inner thoughts of his characters? In fiction we have a choice of several points of view, and by using them carefully we can generally manage to tell the reader the most important thoughts of the most important characters, at least. A playwright has only one point of view—third person objective. And although characters in plays tend to be among the frankest and most outspoken people we are ever likely to meet ("open" is the current word), there are still a few things they can hardly be expected to tell each other—particularly characters with ulterior motives which won't be ulterior any more if they are stated honestly.

These twin problems together are called the problem of exposition. They have the same kinds of solutions.

THE CHORUS

The ancient Greeks, who wrought the earliest plays of which we have a written record, used an expository device called the *chorus*. The chorus was a group of actors who formed a sort of background for the play in a manner somewhat like the chorus of an opera or musical comedy. They did not portray characters in the primary action of the play, and they were unable to do anything which would affect the outcome. But they could observe what was going on, they could comment on the action, they could advise and remonstrate with the characters, and, most important of all, they could speak directly to the audience, filling them in on the necessary background details. For this purpose the chorus was very effective. They even help somewhat in the other problem, that of showing the secret thoughts of a character, for the character can confide in them when there is no other actor on the stage.

There are modern variations on the chorus principle. The Stage Manager in Wilder's *Our Town* is a chorus. So is the character Tom in Tennessee Williams' *The Glass Menagerie* when he steps out onto the fire escape and speaks directly to the audience. This is probably the simplest and most effective of the techniques, or it would not still be used. The playwright has a representative who can carry his message directly to the audience. Its only problem is that of verisimilitude. It does not do much to enhance the feeling that what is going on up there is a part of real life, and that the audience is merely eavesdropping.

DUSTING SCENES

One of the major differences between fiction and drama construction is in their beginnings. I have advised you to grab the reader by the throat right on the first page of a fiction story, before he has time to put it down. The opening of a play is different. In the first place, once the audience have paid admission, found their seats, and listened to the overture (if any), they are not going to get up and storm out in the first ten minutes. Besides, the first few minutes are generally lost motion anyhow. Latecomers are still tripping over feet and mumbling apologies, early-comers are winding up whispered conversations with their neighbors, and the whole audience is getting accustomed to the acoustics. So the first five minutes is frequently devoted to sound effects (circus calliope music, wind and thunder, etc.) or visual effects (a crowd milling around a marketplace, a squad of soldiers practicing precision drill) to get the atmosphere set up. And then, since the audience is still not ready for anything very heavy in the way of action, is as good a time as any to run in the background exposition.

Shakespeare used a chorus in several of his plays, but he also developed a new technique, that of having "two gentlemen" or other minor characters, come in and talk over the news and gossip of the day, thus giving the eavesdropping audience the expository information they needed and at the same time reducing the artificial and obtrusive effect of a chorus.

Later, notably in the late nineteenth century, when the demand for verisimilitude had reached its peak, and when stage sets were made to represent, as closely as possible, the room of a house with one wall removed for the audience to see in, the "two gentlemen" technique was developed into the so-called *dusting scene*. Nowadays it doesn't seem very realistic, because domestic servants are rare in the normal household, but in those days everyone important enough to have a play written about him would have had at least a couple of servants.

Consequently, about the time the last playgoer has stepped on your corns en route to the last empty seat in Row R (or 18), a little maid appears onstage with a feather duster in her hand and starts going over the furniture. (It would have to be modified for today's use—not only are maids hard to come by, but a vacuum cleaner would be too noisy.) Just before she finishes, the butler comes in and they continue their work while commenting on the fact that Old Master and Mistress had been so happy at the prospects of Young Master's return from Italy yesterday, and how strange it was that within an hour after his arrival Old Master had suddenly become his usual unbearably grouchy self and Mistress had withdrawn to her boudoir with a sick headache. By the time they get through, you are briefed and ready to start the play. It takes artistry to get all the necessary information into a dusting scene without making it seem as contrived as it really is. Perhaps the ultimate in dusting scenes is the beginning of Ibsen's *Ghosts,* and I recommend it for study by any prospective playwright.

FLASHBACKS

A technique often used in fiction is the *flashback*. One character or another simply thinks back to what happened at her eleventh birthday party, and there you are with her. If all else fails, it may be used in plays. It is obviously desirable, since it has the same immediacy that the play itself has, and it can be a very compelling way to explain the background to the present play. It does, however, often have the disadvantage of requiring changes of scenery, and often costume or even make-up, which can slow things down considerably. Certainly it will not often be feasible to make multiple flashbacks to the same scene, as is often done in fiction.

Perhaps the most sophisticated way to handle the multiple flashback requirement is to develop a theme during the original flashback. Perhaps it can be a musical one, like "Bali Hai" in *South Pacific* or "Go Home with Bonnie Jean" in *Brigadoon,* which are so impressed on our minds in association with portions of the musicals involved that only a few bars will bring us back. Or it could be a color motif or a certain trick of speech. At any rate, a flashback is an effective device for exposition in a play, but it must be used sparingly.

SOLILOQUIES

In many plays we will suddenly find only one character left on stage, and as we are squirming in our seats trying to get a better view, he will open his mouth and start talking. Not to the audience, as a chorus would, but to nobody in particular. He is talking to himself, although in tones that reach the far corners of the theater. Perhaps it would be more accurate to say that he is thinking aloud, for what he says is really what he is thinking. It is a somewhat clumsy device to duplicate what a fiction writer can do by simply going into the mind of a point-of-view character. Obviously it cannot be a complete Joycean stream-of-consciousness exposition of the character's thoughts, but only so much as is essential to the plot of the story. The device is not truly realistic, but it is an economical means of handling the inner-thought problem of exposition. Shakespeare was probably the outstanding user of the soliloquy: you probably have been required at some time in your school career to memorize one of Hamlet's.

ASIDES

If you have ever had a chance to watch *The Drunkard, Ten Nights in a Barroom,* or one of the other turn-of-the-century melodramas that are revived from time to time as burlesqued period pieces, you will probably recall seeing the man in the black hat, waxed moustaches, oily voice, and half-crouched carriage (the villain, who else?) (Booo, hissss!) slouch up to stage front, lean sideways across the footlights, hold up his hand to shield his mouth from any would-be lip readers, and announce in a stage whisper that rattles the peanut gallery, "Little do they suspect that I have fair Rosalie trussed up in the old sawmill, where the teeth of the buzz-saw will any moment begin to tear her delicate flesh. . . ." What you have seen is an *aside* in one of its less subtle forms.

An aside is somewhat like a soliloquy, except that it is spoken thoughts of the character put into words for the audience's ears only. Several variations on it have been tried. In Eugene O'Neill's *The Great God Brown,* the characters wear masks while talking to one another. The masks depict their public characters, the view that other people get. Their faces without the masks are their real selves, which are quite different. When the actor has his mask on, what he says is assumed to be audible to the other people on stage. If he talks with the mask off, he is saying what he really thinks. Another variation is used often in movies such as *John and Mary.* If the actor's lips moved, he was speaking aloud. If his face was still, anything he might say was only in his mind. This method is obviously better adapted to the screen or tube than to the stage.

HARANGUES

Occasionally in a play a character will appear to halt all competing conversation and launch into a lengthy and frequently dull statement of his own opinions or an attack on that of others. Such a speech is called a *harangue.* It differs from an aside or a soliloquy in that there are other characters present and that they can hear him. Sometimes they can even understand him. The melancholy Jaques in Shakespeare's *As You Like It* delivered a number of famous harangues. They are often used in modern Theater of the Absurd plays like Albee's "The Zoo Story" and Beckett's *Waiting for Godot.*

Harangues seem more probable than asides, but they often reveal more about a character's thoughts than it seems likely that a character would show. Perhaps that is why the harangue is so popular in Theater of the Absurd, in which no character really understands another, and is generally so tired of trying that he quits listening anyhow.

STAGE CONVENTIONS AND TERMS

In order to get your play on paper, it will be necessary to know a little about terminology generally used by theater folk, so that we will all be talking about the same thing. The terms *right* and *left* (or *stage right* and *stage left*) mean to the right or left of an actor *facing the audience*. From your eighteenth row vantage point they will seem just exactly the opposite. (I suppose it wouldn't matter much if you got them backwards; it would only mean that the stage would be the exact reverse of what you intended. But whatever you do, be consistent, or your stage directions will be utter chaos.)

Upstage means toward the back, away from the audience. *Downstage* means toward the audience (or the footlights). When one actor "upstages" another, it means that he backs off toward the rear of the stage, so that to continue facing him the other actor will have to turn away from the audience, losing voice volume and the effect of facial expression. (Turning one's back to the audience is not the disaster it was considered before the advent of speaker systems, but it still is undesirable.)

When a play is put on "in the round" with the audience on all sides, the actions will have to be completely redesigned to fit the changed situation. But that is something for the director to worry about. Most theaters still have stages at one end, so that is how you should plan your set and action.

The five terms, upstage, downstage, stage right, stage left and center stage (often abbreviated to up, down, right [R], left [L] and center) are used in describing your sets and in stage directions. They are often used in combination: up right, center left, down center, etc.

I have mentioned the desirability of making a scale diagram of your stage set. When you have done that and labeled the four sides of the stage up, down, right, and left, you will be able to see where all your doors, chairs, tables and other furniture are, and be able to figure out how to describe its location.

Probably if you have seen many plays you will have noticed that living rooms are customarily set up in a most fantastic manner, with the sofa put right in the middle, facing the audience, instead of against a wall, as it is in my house. Generally there is lots of room behind it for people to slink in unnoticed by the couple occupying the sofa, or for George to stand and talk to Gladys, who is seated on the sofa. The setting is certainly not realistic, but it does allow the actors to point their noses toward the audience, which they could not if the sofa were pulled up in front of the fireplace located in the upstage left corner. I suggest you avoid that precise center location of the sofa—it is pretty hackneyed by now—but keep in mind that actors' faces should be visible to the audience most of the time.

ACTION

After you have diagrammed your set, the most important thing of all is to make sure there is plenty of room between the furniture and props for your actors to move around freely. For move they must. Because when we read a play most of what we read is dialogue, we are inclined to think of a play as consisting mainly of people sitting and talking to one another. This is not true: if it were, we might as well listen to it on the radio. The play must have motion in it. Even if half your cast are paraplegics, they should be doing wheelies with their wheelchairs. The characters must be doing something all the time; in fact, movement is most important on the stage to make up for the fact that the more subtle facial expressions cannot be seen from the eighteenth row, and body language is used to fill the gap.

Write in as much of the action as you can visualize. The director and actors will no doubt modify your ideas and add more action of their own, but it is unlikely ever to get as far as the director and cast unless the playwright has pretty clearly indicated that it is not a sit-still play.

FORMAT

The way in which plays are printed or typed seems to vary even more widely than fiction, and is almost as varied as poetry. Primarily the objective is to make three portions of the script distinctive enough so that they each can be recognized instantly: (1) The name of the character speaking or performing the action, (2) spoken dialogue, and (3) stage directions, or narrative.

It is essential that the name of the character stand out so that the actor playing the part can see instantly when he has the responsibility of saying or doing something. The commonest way to do this is by capitalizing the name whenever it is used. When it is used to introduce a line of dialogue, it should be made even more visible, possibly by centering it on the line above or by having it jut out into the left margin a few spaces.

The name of the character should appear at the head of each speech he makes, and in the stage directions each time he does something, except that stage directions interspersed into the spoken lines or between the name of the speaker and the beginning of the spoken line may be assumed to be actions of the speaker without your saying so. Thus

MARIAN: *(Moving toward center stage)* I cannot let you do it! *(more softly)* My poor father would twist in his grave if he saw me dependent on your charity like this. *(waves for* NORMAN, *who is coming toward her, to keep away)* Please leave me. Go.

A stage direction is usually distinguished from spoken dialogue by setting it off with parentheses and underlining it or putting it in italics. This may seem overcautious, like wearing both suspenders and a belt, but it is better to be safe than to have some idiot actor read the word *(brokenly)* aloud instead of saying the speech that way.

Since there are several different possible formats for plays, it might be well to ask a producer or publisher if he has a format sample or specifications before submitting a play to him. Whatever format he uses, you can be pretty sure it will distinguish the three components somehow.

AN OPENING

The following student example may be helpful to show how to get over the preliminaries and present the first dramatic question, so that the audience will stay and see some more.

THE STRATEGIST
A Play in One Act

Cast of Characters

LEROY HENDY: *a Burglar*
JACK BRIGHTWELL: *a Bachelor Sportsman*
EDITH NORMAND: *the Wife of a Friend*

Time: *the present*

The entire action takes place in the living room of FRANK and EDITH NORMAND's apartment.

Scene: The living room of the NORMANDS' *apartment. The wall-to-wall carpeting is white, to match the upholstery on the blond wood furniture. The walls are charcoal, and on them are half-a-dozen bright modern abstract paintings. One of the paintings is hung at exact center rear, over the right end of a large sectional divan. Two end tables flank the divan, but when the scene first becomes visible, the one at the right has been pushed aside to allow* LEROY *to stand where it was. Further right, against the rear wall, is a book case filled with books, mostly still in dust jackets. At right rear is a door to the rest of the apartment, and near the right wall are an armchair and a chaise longue, with a large round coffee table holding a formal flower arrangement downstage at extreme left. Behind it, large French doors on the left wall look out onto a small ornamental balcony.*

The set is in total darkness as the curtain rises. There is a sharp cracking sound as the French doors are forced open, then little sounds of movement, the soft collision of shins with furniture, and, finally, the scrape of a small table being moved. Then the sudden beam of a flashlight illuminates the picture in the center of the rear wall. Footlights now come on, dim, but enough to let the audience see the figure of LEROY *as he carefully lifts the picture off the wall and puts it on the end table, revealing a wall safe behind it. He is a small man, wearing canvas sneakers, tight chino trousers, an old Army field jacket, and a black baseball cap with the monogram "SFG" printed on it. He leans toward the safe, focussing the light on the combination knob, and starts to manipulate it. The door, right, swings open noiselessly, and* JACK *steps in quietly.*

JACK: Who's there?

LEROY drops the flashlight and starts to run toward the French doors. There is the sharp report of a pistol, and he screams and falls to the floor. Then the lights come on full, to show LEROY *writhing and moaning on the floor at center left.* JACK *stands by the door where he has entered, one hand on the light switch, the other still holding a smoking pistol. He is a man of about forty, balding, but heavily tanned and looking almost offensively healthy. He is dressed in a flamboyant red brocade robe, blue silk pajamas, and red moccasin type slippers.*

LEROY: Ooh! You've killed me.
JACK: 'Fraid not, worse luck. I only winged you.
EDITH: *(From offstage)* Jack! What was that?   *(She appears behind* JACK, *wearing a revealing black nightgown and carrying a pale blue pegnoir over her arm. She is an attractive woman of thirty-five, with suspiciously blonde hair.)*
         What on earth is going on?
JACK: We seem to have a burglar. I caught him trying to get into Frank's safe.

EDITH: Oh, no! *(She steps back out of the doorway to put on her pegnoir.)* Did you kill him?

JACK: *(Apologetically)* No. I was trying to pot the bugger in the belly, but only got his leg. A bad shot, but of course it was dark.

LEROY: Ooh!

EDITH: You shouldn't have taken such a chance. Suppose he had been armed?

JACK: By George, maybe he still is. Here, Edith, you hold the gun on him. I'll go frisk him. *(He hands the pistol to* EDITH, *who takes it gingerly, with her fingertips, and stands looking at it as if it were a dead mouse.* JACK *crosses to* LEROY.

LEROY: Don't touch me. I never owned a gun in my life.

JACK: We'll see. *(He pats* LEROY's *pockets expertly.)*

LEROY: Ooh. You're hurting me.

JACK: Stop your blubbering. It's only a flesh wound; I doubt if it even touched the bone. Wiggle the leg a little; see if you hear a grating sound. *(He twists the leg brutally.)*

LEROY: Oaaow! My God, I'm bleeding to death!

JACK: Ridiculous. You've got lots more blood than that. I've trailed deer for twelve hours that were bleeding worse than you are.

EDITH: He *is* ruining my brand new carpet, though. What can we do about him?

JACK: Call the police. They'll take him away.

LEROY: No, for God's sake! Not to jail. Who'd take care of my wife and kiddies?

EDITH: But we can't do that. How would we explain your being here? Oh, why couldn't you have just scared him away?

JACK: *(Brightly)* I'll just jump into my clothes and leave. Then you can call the police and tell 'em you shot him.

EDITH: *(Nearly dropping the pistol)* You wouldn't leave me alone with him?

LEROY: *(Raising up on one elbow)* If you turn me in, I'll spill my guts about him being here.

· · ·

Chapter 20
Hallmarks of Drama

It is fairly obvious whether a literary work is a story or a play; one can tell by the format, just as one can tell poetry from either one by the irregular right margin. But how can you tell whether an idea is best suited to fiction or to drama? There should be some way to tell which it is without having to write it both ways to find out. Let's look together at some of the characteristics of drama which may differentiate it from fiction.

SPECTACLE

The first thing that a play should have is the ability to be displayed to advantage on a stage, a peculiar characteristic of being spectacular. The play *Cyrano de Bergerac,* for example, would make a pretty feeble story, at least for anyone older than fifteen. The longnosed but silvertongued swash-buckler himself is completely incredible; the heroine, Roxanne, is incredibly colorless. But on the stage, Cyrano manages to carry it off like a fast-ball pitcher, throwing the ball past the audience so rapidly that there is no time to think. His heart and character are so large that they seem to take up the entire stage. His sweeping gestures certainly do.

The same is true of Oedipus Rex, with commingled blood and tears streaming down his face from his eyeless sockets; of the Emperor Jones, tricked by the beat of the native drums into running back into the arms of his motionless pursuers, and of Ionesco's anti-hero Berenger, at bay in his lonely bedroom, cut off by swarms of rhinoceros. (Ionesco originally wrote "Rhinoceros" as a short story. If you doubt my thesis that some stories are best told as plays, try reading the short story and comparing it with the play, which is powerful even when read.)

Of course there are limits to the scope of a play, as we saw in Chapter 19. Some plots require so much spectacle that they need cinema, with a battery of lenses and movable cameras. And a wide screen if possible. I question, for example, if the chariot race in *Ben Hur* would be particularly effective on a stage. Or the burning of Atlanta in *Gone With the Wind*.

CONFLICT

Conflict is important in fiction—essential, in fact. It is difficult to say that it is even more essential in drama, but I will have to say it. The word *protagonist*, meaning the hero of a play, comes from two Greek words meaning "first contestant." (The opposing character may be called the *deuteragonist*, or second contestant, but so few Americans can count up as high as two in Greek ordinals any more that the term is seldom used.) The word *agony* is derived from the same root, so you can see that this kind of contest, or struggle, can be a pretty grim one.

Although the conflict may not be joined as early in a play as in a story, as was indicated in Chapter 19, from the time it is developed, there must be a dramatic question before the audience at all times. Who will win the battle of wills, or *agon*? Sometimes, as in *Oedipus Rex*, for example, the struggle may be between the protagonist and the gods, or the forces of natural law, in which case the outcome would seem to be predictable, but the protagonist must have such power of will that we can wonder if things cannot be made to work out for him. In other cases, such as *Antigone*, the struggle shapes up as a contest of wills between two strong characters, each apparently invincible. Or in more complex drama, like Shakespeare's *Hamlet* or *Macbeth,* there are other characters who oppose the protagonists, but they are conceived as so inferior to him that the actual contest is between the divided motives of the hero himself. But in all cases we must be so intent upon finding out who will win and how that we often forget to breathe and realize the neglect only after the crisis, when we resume all vital processes.

Sometimes there are more than two forces involved. We may find three or more characters or groups, each wanting something which will keep any of the other agonists from having what they want. This permits temporary alliances between sides, like the coalition cabinets in European politics. And it further permits unraveling of the alliances and the forming of new partnerships. Let's take a look at the opening of a student-written play which will serve to illustrate multilateral conflicts.

Kitty in the Tree

A Play in Three Acts

ACT I: The living room of a large suburban home
ACT II: A few days later
    Scene 1: Elizabeth returns
    Scene 2: Dora and Agatha leave
ACT III: Agatha's triumphant return

CAST		
Agatha:	A yellow female cat that the audience never sees
Will:	Head of the house, head of a large company, a man in his middle 50's
Ella:	Will's wife
Dora:	Will's sister, several years younger
Elizabeth:	Daughter of Will and Ella
Walter Stone:	Company lawyer

TIME: Now

PLACE: The living room of a large suburban home

SYNOPSIS: *The large living room gives an impression of comfort and status. The room is smartly furnished with a sofa and chair downstage; an end table with phone next to sofa. To the left is a bar and next to the bar a small utility room or closet. Upstage through a wide archway is a hall leading to the front door and stairs leading off left. To the right and up a step is a glass partitioned solarium, full of plants. On stage right there is a window and downstage from window is a door leading to dining room. It is after dinner on a Friday evening. (*WILL *found out during the day that the Government is investigating his company for failing to pay Federal taxes, but he has not told the family about the investigation.)*
(WILL's *daughter,* ELIZABETH, *has been gone two weeks on her honeymoon.)*
The play opens with WILL *at his favorite pastime, chasing* AGATHA.

ACT I

WILL: Kitty, kitty, here kitty, you stupid cat. I know you're here somewhere.   *(he gets down on his knees and reaches under the sofa)*   Ouch!   *(he jerks his hand out fast, and puts his thumb in his mouth, then stands up)*   Bastard cat, wait till I get the broom.   *(starts toward the closet on stage left)*   Bite the hand that feeds you. I'll fix you.   *(gets broom from closet and walks hurriedly back to sofa, saying with a menacing look)*   Nice kitty, nice kitty.   *(dropping to his knees as he jams the broom under the sofa)*   Meowee   *(cry from the cat.* WILL *jumps up with broom and runs around in back of sofa and chases cat, hitting the floor with the broom, toward the front door upstage hollering)*   I'll get you, you bastard cat.   *(*ELLA *enters through dining room door)*

ELLA: *(sharply)*   Will! Stop chasing that poor cat.

WILL: That slinky beast attacked me. Look what she did to my thumb.   *(putting the broom back in the closet, he walks over to the bar)*

ELLA: *(walks over and sits down on sofa; picks up a magazine and starts looking through it)*   If you'd be nice to poor Agatha, she wouldn't bite you.

WILL: *(puttering around the bottles at the bar)*   All I want to do is hold her and show her that I love her. But that stupid cat stopped loving me a year ago. What happened to the vodka? I just bought this bottle and it's almost empty.

ELLA: *(matter of fact, but sarcastic)*   You mean like last night when you had both hands around Agatha's neck? Fix me a scotch and soda, will you, dear? You had better talk to your alcoholic sister about the vodka.

WILL: *(mixing the drinks)*   I don't think you should call Dora an alcoholic. She may drink a little, but she is not an alcoholic.

ELLA: All right then, a drunk.

WILL: *(setting Ella's drink on the end table)*   There you are, dear.   *(he walks toward the window on stage right)*

ELLA: *(speaks softly, still glancing at the magazine)*   But Will! I think you should talk to Dora. After all, she is your sister, and she is drinking quite heavily.

WILL: *(looking out the window, he mumbles something inaudible and sips his drink)*

ELLA: What did you say, dear?   *(takes a sip of her drink)*

WILL: *(loudly)*   I said, there's that damn cat in the tree, staring in the window at me, just waiting to get her claws in me. A little arsenic. . . .

ELLA: Will, forget the cat and tell me what's to be done about Dora's drinking.

WILL: All right, Ella. I'll talk to her.   *(he walks over and looks out the window again)*   It's starting to get dark. Hmmn . . . looks like Agatha has come down from the tree.

ELLA: Thank you, dear.   *(still sipping her drink)*
(DORA enters through archway, walks over and sits down in the easy chair)

DORA: Good evening, Ella. And what mischief have you been up to today? Have you measured all the bottles? Please make me a drink, Will.

ELLA: *(disgusted)* I should think you'd had enough today.

WILL: *(to placate)* We can do without that now . . . Dora . . . can drink a little.

ELLA: Well, I have things to do. *(she finishes her drink and departs through door to dining room)*

DORA: *(quietly)* Well, brother, what is it? Is Dora getting to be too much of a boozer? Maybe I'll embarrass your rich friends. . . .

WILL: No, no Dora, that isn't it. I just don't want anything to happen to you. Last year you were in the hospital. . . .

DORA: Sanatorium.

WILL: It was still a hospital.

DORA: They were wringing me out. Did you know I was in there during National Health Week? That was nice.

WILL: I just don't want you to have to go back there. Think what you are doing to yourself, and to all of us. Dora, if you wish, I'll get rid of all the bottles, the bar, the whole works, if it will make it any easier for you, Dora, dear.

DORA: *(finishing her drink)* I am not an alcoholic, Will, I drink no more than anyone else in this house, but if you want me to stop, I will. I'll take up knitting or fancy needle work and become your spinster sister. *(Dora starts crying and exits through archway upstage)*

WILL: *(at the bar now mixing a drink, then walks over to window. ELLA can now be seen watering plants in the solarium. She is now wearing a robe)* Damn cat!
    (Telephone rings, Will walks over to the end table, and picks up the phone) Hello . . . Hello, Walter. . . .

ELLA: *(calling from the solarium)* Who is it, Will?

WILL: *(putting his hand over the mouthpiece, saying loudly)* It is Walter Stone, dear.

ELLA: *(loudly)* I thought it might be Elizabeth. *(ELLA goes back to her watering)*

WILL: *(softly)* Hello, Walter, what did you find out?

(pause) They are going for an indictment in a couple of weeks. . . . Personal income too *(excited)* Five years for your slip . . . ten thousand dollar fine. . . . No, I haven't told the family yet. . . . Don't get excited? I could go to jail for five years, and you tell me not to get excited. I'm sorry, Walter, but keep at it. Call me if anything turns up. I'll be home all week-end. Goodbye, Walter. *(He puts the phone down and picks up his drink and is finishing it as ELLA enters through archway and sits by him on the sofa)*

ELLA: I thought surely Elizabeth would have called us by now.

WILL: *(taking ELLA's hand)* Dear, they are on their honeymoon. They have only been gone two weeks now. I doubt if they are thinking about us now.

ELLA: *(relaxing, lays her head on WILL's shoulder)* What did Walter want?

WILL: Just company business. It seems the Government wants to check some of the records. I'll let you know if anything comes of it.

ELLA: Well, I'm going to bed. Will, feed Agatha before you come up. *(WILL makes a disgusted face, but says nothing. ELLA kisses WILL on cheek and stands up)* Goodnight, dear. *(the telephone rings. ELLA answers it)* Elizabeth, dear, I was hoping to get a call from you. Will, it's Elizabeth.

WILL: I heard you. Where are they?

ELLA: *(loudly)* Where are you, dear? . . . New York? We thought you were going to Paris. . . . Only got as far as New York? *(pause)* No! I don't believe it. That is just awful. . . . You're leaving him? *(pause, then soothingly)* You come on home, baby.

WILL: What's happening?

ELLA: *(shushing him with her hand)* You'll be home the first of the week. Now, now, baby, don't cry. You just pack your things and come on home. We'll be waiting for you. Bye, bye, baby. Call me if you need me. We'll see you the first of the week. *(ELLA puts the phone down)*

WILL: *(loudly)* Ella, for God's sake, what is the matter?

ELLA: *(still standing, pulls her robe around herself tighter and starts pacing back and forth in front of the sofa)* I knew it! I just knew it! I never did trust that Tony, and this just proves it.

WILL: *(quietly)* Ella, what did he do?

ELLA: *(still pacing and beginning to sob)* He said my poor Elizabeth is like a cold fish in bed. Now he is chasing some chorus girl in New York. My poor darling. *(ELLA hurriedly exits through archway, sobbing)*

WILL: *(standing up now and walks toward the bar, talking as he goes)* Married two weeks and already separating. That must be some kind of a record. *(He sets his small glass aside and picks up a balloon glass)* All we need now is for Agatha to have kittens. *(pours a double shot of scotch in the balloon glass, adds ice and soda water and walks toward the sofa, still talking aloud)* A year ago all we had to worry about was Dora. *(standing now in front of sofa looking out at the audience, rocking gently on his feet)* We've come a long ways in a year. Now Dora is an alcoholic. . . . Wonder what will happen next. *(He turns and walks toward the window, still sipping his scotch and soda. He looks out the window and holds up his drink.)* Here's to you, kitty in the tree. When things get rough just go climb a tree. *(He finishes the drink, turns and walks toward the bar)* I may soon be in the tree with you, kitty. *(He sets the glass on the bar and turns toward the audience and says loudly)* Income tax evasion? God!

CURTAIN

There are a few points that might be made about the play. First, the playwright slipped in some exposition in his opening stage directions: the portion included in parentheses.

(WILL found out during the day that the Government is investigating his company for failing to pay Federal taxes, but he has not told the family about the investigation.)

(WILL's *daughter*, ELIZABETH, *has been gone for two weeks on her honeymoon.*)

This might be printed on the program in hopes the audience will read it before curtain time, but the best thing to do will be to make sure that they can tell from the play itself. Do you think that the telephone conversations with Walter Stone and with Elizabeth are adequately self-explanatory?

Next, the playwright has considered the undesirability of having a cat on the stage and made her an unseen presence, like Harvey, the six-foot rabbit in the play of the same name.

Third, the action is too swift for a play. You have just read the entire first act, which would probably play in about fifteen minutes. In a story, it might work, for if the reader misses something he can turn back a couple of pages and look at it again. There is no way to turn back on a stage. Each plot development should be presented so clearly and completely that even your brother-in-law Joe, who drank three double martinis before the play, can follow what is going on.

Finally, there is plenty going on. If we count up the conflicts, we have (a) Will against the cat, Agatha; (b) Ella, the wife, versus Dora, the bibulous sister; (c) Will against the United States Government (perhaps comparable to the gods of Greek tragedy), and (d) Elizabeth against her sex-starved husband. Whether they will intermesh or continue as interesting but unrelated sub-plots, we cannot tell. Perhaps we will never know, for the playwright has never gotten around to writing any further.

SUDDEN REVERSALS IN ACTION

The plotting of a play, like that of a story, does not proceed on a smooth course, with the dramatic tension increasing and building up at a uniform rate until the climax is reached, but humps along with a series of minor climaxes before the main one. If you are writing a play of two or more acts, arrange it so that a substantial climax coincides with the end of each act, particularly if there is an intermission between acts. (Intermissions are ideal times to sneak out unnoticed.)

In drama, the resolution of a crisis is most likely to be in the creation of another one. As you approach a crisis, it becomes more and more apparent that one of your agonists is about to prevail over the other(s). The audience is sitting, waiting for the kill. Then, just as their breath has been held almost to point of asphixiation, there is a twist of the plot, and suddenly the other is on top. If you have ever witnessed a well-staged professional wrestling match, you will have seen the technique at its simplest level.

I once attended a high school senior play, most of which was quite forgettable, but I can still recall the curtain scene of Act One. In the play a bored but wealthy vacationer (played by the son of the local bank president) picks up a jobless but presentable bum. (This is a standard plot gimmick, probably symbolizing the longing of penniless playwrights for an "angel" with money to finance production of a play that will make the penniless playwright wealthy and famous.) Wealthy Vacationer is explaining to Jobless Bum that it is not really necessary to have money or talent to get along in the world, just so people think that you have them. To prove his point, he introduces J. B. to everyone as a millionaire friend. The moment of truth arrives when J. B. reaches into his pocket and states, with a little amusement in his voice, that he seems to be temporarily out of money. Several bystanders whip out their wallets with offers to tide him over, as Wealthy Vacationer looks on, smirking. J. B.'s exclamations of "Oh, you mustn't" only make the suckers more eager, until J. B. finally says, "I certainly thank all of you for your offers, but I think I'd rather take a loan from the only person here who *really* knows me." With that, he turns to W. V., hand outstretched. CURTAIN.

Perhaps the best example of sudden reversals in action is Edward Albee's play *Who's Afraid of Virginia Woolf?* in which the two principals, George and Martha, are continually alternating in momentary victories in their eternal and destructive game of One-Upsmanship.

DRAMA CHARACTERS

You may recall that in a play or movie you have seen, you appear to notice a particular person, even in a mob scene, perhaps before you know that he is going to be the protagonist. This may be partially because of technical tricks of lighting or costuming, or even because you recognize the actor from having seen him before somewhere. But mainly it is because he is more noticeable. The leading characters of a play, at least the protagonist and deuteragonist, are made "larger than life." This doesn't mean that they are actually taller and heavier (although leading men in ancient Greek plays and modern opera have been known to wear elevator shoes or the equivalent, especially when their leading ladies are tall). It is just that all their characteristics, although normal human ones, are exaggerated. Tragic heroines suffer more than you and I would. Comic clowns fall harder than anyone else, and with more flourishes. In the example shown, *Kitty in the Tree*, Will seems to hate his cat more passionately than most felinophobes, and he certainly seems to have a fantastic array of troubles.

This is not to say that dramatic characters are superhuman. Their virtues may be exaggerated, but so are their faults. Superman makes a fine comic strip character, but he would be a poor character for a play, since he is short on weaknesses. (Kryptonite, as I recall, is his only Achilles heel.) Charley Brown, from *Peanuts*, would do much better. His catastrophies are as complete as Superman's triumphs. Still better would be Linus, whose triumphs and disasters are equally earth-shaking. (See *You're a Good Man, Charlie Brown*.)

THEATER OF THE ABSURD

The kind of plays loosely entitled *Theater of the Absurd* are to drama as free verse is to poetry, or experimental writing is to prose. In general it might be said that they share all the hallmarks of drama listed above to some extent, and are hard to judge until they have actually been put before an audience. (Even then, it's hard to tell for sure. *Waiting for Godot* was unsuccessful before its initial audiences of sophisticated upper middle class people who are the more or less typical theatergoers, but has been an outstanding success before audiences of convicts or black sharecroppers, who have been waiting for something like Godot all their lives.) Finally, such plays should be avoided by playwrights who are not already pretty well-grounded in conventional theater, as playwrights, actors, directors, or backstage workers.

Theater of the absurd makes little effort to look like real life. The characters are unconventional people who rarely are much more like the folks next door than are the clowns at a circus. Their motives may be perfectly clear and reasonable, but their actions frequently are not. Like other dramatic characters, they are larger than life, but the characteristic many of them have more than real people is their absurdity. Often they can be considered caricatures rather than characters.

Theater of the absurd has conflict at least as strong as that in conventional plays. And it has a plot, or at least all the ingredients of a plot. Sometimes the plot is hard to follow, because it may not be developed logically, or even chronologically. A strong strain of irony is usually present, frustrating or unexpectedly helping the desires of the characters. And the conflict is not always resolved: the play often ends on a note that indicates that essentially the same action is destined to be repeated forever.

There is usually a heavy use of symbols in the absurd play—often to the extent that it overshadows any non-symbolic action and leaves one to wonder whether to follow the action as one would in a standard play or to forget what is going on and concentrate on what it all is supposed to mean. As a matter of fact, probably neither is the most appropriate way to watch such a play.

The total effect of most good absurd plays is emotional rather than intellectual, and the stage, as we have seen, is particularly suited to affecting emotions. And in combination with the emotional stress—we feel angry, frustrated, confused, or amused without quite knowing why—there is the effect of a giant inkblot, which is continually changing shape like an amoeba, so that there is a series of Rorschach effects on our minds. Perhaps those are what should be watched, rather than either the overt action or the symbolism.

CHAPTER 21
THE PROOF OF THE PUDDING

The best way to tell if you have a successful play, of course, is to have it staged before an audience and see what they think, and/or what the critics say. Neither of these criteria is infallible—Chekhov's serious plays had a habit of opening to what are euphemistically called "mixed reviews" and only achieving success when revived a couple of years later. However, if the opening night audience is enthusiastic, you are off and running.

PRODUCTION—BIG TIME

Who produces plays, and where? Well, the highest prestige, and the most money, is from a successful Broadway (New York) production. Note that I say a *successful* production. Only a handful of plays open on Broadway each year, and not more than a couple of fingerfuls last the whole first season. It is a fiercely competitive market, and unless you are extra-well endowed with talent, luck, and thickness of skin, you will be better off with your sights set lower. But plays *are* produced on Broadway, though rarely the first plays by a playwright. *Writer's Market* has a listing of professional play producers operating on and off-Broadway and in various other cities. Several of the most prestigious state that they accept only plays submitted through an agent.

The listing of agents in *Writer's Market* indicates which ones specialize in plays. Getting an agent interested in handling a play for you may be almost as much of an effort as getting a producer interested in producing it, but in this field an agent could be worth at least his weight in gold, because of the chance that a successful play could bring in all sorts of subsidiary rights, such as book, TV, or movie rights, matters in which your agent should be qualified to advise you. If your play is really a hot item, by all means go through whatever steps are necessary to obtain the agent you want. For details on how to interest agents, and what to look for or avoid, look in Chapter 15.

PRODUCTION—SMALL-TIME

Let us assume that your play is of more modest caliber than required for Broadway or other high-prestige production, or that your personality is too sensitive to take the buffets and rebuffets certain to come in those fields. Are there no other possibilities? Of course there are. Some of the producers listed in *Writer's Market* handle plays for summer circuits or small theaters off-Broadway or in other parts of the country. And most sizeable cities have semi-professional or excellent amateur theater groups which are often hungry for fresh new scripts at bargain prices. Even small cities often have "little theater" amateur groups, more often than not in financial straits (I speak from bitter experience) who would be glad to consider a play by a local playwright, particularly if he will accept a couple of free tickets in lieu of a cash royalty.

Nor should you overlook the school stage. The drama coach of your local high school or college may be eager to have material for classes in acting or directing, or for staging. If your play is appropriate for younger children, even junior high or elementary schools might be interested.

The above possibilities are particularly good because they

would give you an opportunity to work with the director as he is shaping the play during rehearsals, to do any necessary rewriting yourself—and more important, to see the reason for it. And nothing can beat the experience of seeing your own work on its opening night. The experience may be a bummer, but there are almost always some good moments when you can see the audience react to your words. (We won't remember things like the play I was once associated with which opened with the two major male actors both bleary-drunk. Fortunately, one of them had lost his false teeth as well, so the audience couldn't understand any of his crossed-up lines. But that wouldn't happen to *your* play.)

Another possibility is one of the numerous contests sponsored by colleges or foundations, usually with cash prizes as well as opportunity for production. Your creative writing instructor or the drama department will probably get notices of several of these. Winning or placing in one of these contests might mean a cash prize of some kind, and it very possibly could mean having your play produced by whoever is putting on the contest. This would be nice, particularly if the place of production is close enough for you to observe at least the opening night. If you live in Portland, Maine, and the play is being put on in Portland, Oregon—well, you will at least get the honor, and possibly the director will be willing to write you a brief critique on how it staged.

SKITS AND BLACKOUTS

There is always a market for *skits,* which are brief plays generally intended to teach or propagandize. They are usually funny. (It is a strange thing, but the best plays to be performed by amateurs are comedies, preferably slapstick. Probably it is because if the leading lady in, say, *Lysistrata* or *The Taming of the Shrew* trips over her own feet and falls on her face, the audience will laugh and possibly even think that it was done on purpose. But if the leading lady in *Antigone* or *Hedda Gabler* trips and falls, the audience reaction will still be to laugh—and in those plays we cannot afford it.) Anyhow, skits may be used by factory management to impress the necessity for taking safety precautions, by political campaigns to lampoon the opposition, by schools to demonstrate the need for rules and regulations, by churches to kick off campaigns for financial pledges, or by social improvement groups to demonstrate the necessity for inter-racial understanding, environmental laws, consumer protection, or sex equality. If you are connected with an organization of some kind, see if they need a skit or two. Better still, convince them that they do—possibly using a skit for the convincing.

And don't downgrade skits as a means for getting experience in playwrighting. They are short, which means that you will get practice in striving for effect in every line. They are didactic, which means that you will have to learn to put across a theme, but by soft-sell methods, so that the audience will be impressed, but not turned off. They are exaggerated, which means that they give practice in making larger-than-life characters. And they have to be playable, which means that the skitwright will learn a lot about the capabilities of the stage (or dozen square feet of floor) as a medium.

The great Russian playwright, Anton Chekhov, started his career as a joke writer. Some of his jokes got expanded and became short stories (many of which don't look very funny to an American readership); others developed into comic one-act plays. By the time Chekhov tackled his first full-length play, he already knew quite a bit about the theater and about creating plays that would work.

A *blackout* is a punch-line joke put into dramatic form. It gets its name from the custom in burlesque, where the form was developed, of turning off all the lights abruptly at the end of the punch-line. It is a faster way to finish than drawing a curtain, and it serves as a punctuation to make sure that there is no time for an anticlimax to develop and obscure the line. It also gave the actors a chance to make their getaway in case the more prudish members of the audience took offence at the line, which in many cases was quite possible.

There is clearly less market for blackouts than for skits, since they require lighting capabilities not always available in living rooms, school gymnasiums, or church recreation halls. But if you can find an appropriate place for one, writing and staging a blackout is marvelous training for the development of a sense of timing. And not all blackouts are obscene, any more than all limericks are.

PLAY PUBLICATION

Most publishers of plays are not primarily interested in selling their books to the general public through book stores, as publishers of novels do. Their audience is almost exclusively groups who intend to produce plays—amateurs, predominantly. As has already been indicated, there are lots of different kinds of amateur groups who put on plays, so one might expect different publishers to concentrate on different segments of the market, and in many cases this is true. Consequently it is essential that you research your publisher, just as you would a market for poems or fiction. Read the squib each publisher puts in *Writer's Market,* and in many cases it will tell you whether they cater to the elementary school trade, church groups, high schools, or miscellaneous little theaters and other adult organizations. Then, when you find one which sounds as if it were going the same general direction that you are, write and ask for one or two of their more successful plays. Read them. See what format they use. Check the type of action they contain, the general kinds of characters they seem to like. See the nature of the dialogue. It is improbable that the dialogue will be replete with earthy four-letterisms and the action be bedroom farcical if the publisher is out after the church group or elementary school business. On the other hand, if it is slanted toward the little theater trade, you wouldn't expect the plots to be based on whether Sister should stay home and take care of Little Brother as she promised her parents, or take off to the drive-in with her boyfriend. These and more subtle types of slanting will become evident as you read the plays.

The one almost universal hope, if not requirement, be that your cast contain *at least* as many female parts as male. This stems from the fact that almost uniformly, starting in the days of the ancient Greeks and through the much later ones of Shakespeare, during both of which times all parts for people of either sex were played by men, and on down to the present day, with the Japanese Takarasuka Theater in which all parts for characters of either sex are played by women, the majority of *great* plays have always had more male than female parts—and this is usually true even when the protagonist is a woman!

This manifestation of male chauvinism would not be so bad if it were not for the fact that there tend to be more women interested in theater (at least amateur theater) than there are men. I do not know why this is; perhaps a graduate student of psychology or anthropology should write a doctoral dissertation on the subject. But I do state it as a statistical fact. So in order to cast the average amateur play, it is necessary to disappoint several girls and women who really wanted parts and go out and beat the bushes for bored boys and men who would rather be watching the late show than rehearsing every night. So the world is more likely to trample a path to the door of the playwright who makes a play with two women for every man in the cast than to honor one whose play follows the sexist tradition.

How do you get paid? How, in fact, does the publisher get paid? Let's start with the second question. If the play concerned is a "name" play—successful on Broadway or the equivalent—the publisher will demand payment of a royalty in return for permission to produce. The size of the royalty may depend on such factors as the popularity of the play, the size of the prospective audiences, and the number of times to be performed. The playwright will get a cut of this royalty, the size of which will depend upon the amount contracted for before the play was published.

In the case of comparatively "unknown" plays, the publisher will give any group permission to produce the play provided it buys the scripts from the publisher. This would probably amount to a copy for each actor plus copies for the director, the stage manager, prompter, light operators, etc. And a few spares to replace ones lost when someone left the cast in a huff and forgot to throw his script into the director's face. The playwright may get a royalty based on a percentage of the price of the books sold. Or he may simply sell his play outright for a lump sum. Different publishers operate in different ways.

It is interesting to note that at one time the play which had been produced more than any other play on the American stage was one of these "unknowns" entitled *Aaron Slick of Pumpkin Creek* (or possibly it was *Punkin Crick*). Not only was it a play that worked out on the stage, but it was the sort of slapstick farce that could get even funnier if an amateur cast blew a few lines. And the cast included more women than men. When you add on the fact that it was the very first play on the alphabetical listing of Samuel French's publications, how could it miss?

CHAPTER 22
EPILOGUE

Rules are good guides, but they are intended to be broken if they stand in the way of the final goal. I hope none of you would hesitate to ignore a KEEP OFF THE GRASS sign if ignoring it would enable you to save a life. I also hope you would bravely ignore anything this book says if that will enable you to write a better poem, story, or play.

The one rule I think you should save for last, however, is to *persevere*. Don't break this one until you have to. If you know you have an idea that is basically sound, don't give it up until you have rewritten it every conceivable way. If you have written something that you think is spectacular, don't give up trying to get it published or produced until you have exhausted yourself and all the possibilities. Great American Novels were written by people who kept on trying.

If you miss fame by breaking this rule, I hope you also have children who will pour sand into your stereo record jackets.

Appendix A

Robert Frost: The Way to the Poem[*]
by
John Ciardi

Stopping by Woods on a Snowy Evening[**]
By Robert Frost

Whose woods these are I think I know.
His house is in the village though;
He will not see me stopping here
To watch his woods fill up with snow.

My little horse must think it queer
To stop without a farmhouse near
Between the woods and frozen lake
The darkest evening of the year.

He gives his harness bells a shake
To ask if there is some mistake
The only other sound's the sweep
Of easy wind and downy flake.

> The woods are lovely, dark and deep.
> But I have promises to keep,
> And miles to go before I sleep,
> And miles to go before I sleep.

The School System has much to say these days of the virtue of reading widely, and not enough about the virtues of reading less but in depth. There are any number of reading lists for poetry, but there is not enough talk about individual poems. Poetry, finally, is one poem at a time. To read any one poem carefully is the ideal preparation for reading another. Only a poem can illustrate how poetry works.

Above, therefore, is a poem—one of the master lyrics of the English language, and almost certainly the best-known poem by an American poet. What happens in it?—which is to say, not *what* does it mean, but *how* does it mean? How does it go about being a human reenactment of a human experience? The author—perhaps the thousandth reader would need to be told —is Robert Frost.

Even the TV audience can see that this poem begins as a seemingly-simple narration of a seemingly-simple incident but ends by suggesting meanings far beyond anything specifically referred to in the narrative. And even readers with only the most casual interest in poetry might be made to note the additional fact that, though the poem suggests those larger meanings, it is very careful never to abandon its pretense to being simple narration. There is duplicity at work. The poet pretends to be talking about one thing, and all the while he is talking about many others.

Many readers are forever unable to accept the poet's essential duplicity. It is almost safe to say that a poem is never about what it seems to be about. As much could be said of the proverb. The bird in the hand, the rolling stone, the stitch in time never (except by an artful double-deception) intend any sort of statement about birds, stones, or sewing. The incident of this poem, one must conclude, is at root a metaphor.

Duplicity aside, this poem's movement from the specific to the general illustrates one of the basic formulas of all poetry. Such a grand poem as Arnold's "Dover Beach" and such lesser, though unfortunately better known, poems as Longfellow's "The Village Blacksmith" and Holmes's "The Chambered Nautilus" are built on the same progression. In these three poems, however, the generalization is markedly set apart from the specific narration, and even seems additional to the telling rather than intrinsic to it. It is this sense of division one has in mind in speaking of "a tacked-on moral."

There is nothing wrong-in-itself with a tacked-on moral. Frost, in fact, makes excellent use of the device at times. In this poem, however, Frost is careful to let the whatever-the-moral-is grow out of the poem itself. When the action ends the poem ends. There is no epilogue and no explanation. Everything pretends to be about the narrated incident. And that pretense sets the basic tone of the poem's performance of itself.

The dramatic force of that performance is best observable, I believe, as a progression in three scenes.

In scene one, which coincides with stanza one, a man—a New England man—is driving his sleigh somewhere at night. It is snowing, and as the man passes a dark patch of woods he stops to watch the snow descend into the darkness. We know, moreover, that the man is familiar with these parts (he knows who owns the woods and where the owner lives), and we know that no one has seen him stop. As scene one forms itself in the theater of the mind's-eye, therefore, it serves to establish some as yet unspecified relation between the man and the woods.

It is necessary, however, to stop here for a long parenthesis: Even so simple an opening statement raises any number of questions. It is impossible to address all the questions that rise from the poem stanza by stanza, but two that arise from stanza one illustrate the sort of thing one might well ask of the poem detail by detail.

Why, for example, does the man not say what errand he is on? What is the force of leaving the errand generalized? He might just as well have told us that he was going to the general store, or returning from it with a jug of molasses he had promised to bring Aunt Harriet and two suits of long underwear he had promised to bring the hired man. Frost, moreover, can handle homely detail to great effect. He preferred to leave his motive generalized. Why?

And why, on the other hand, does he say so much about knowing the absent owner of the woods and where he lives? Is it simply that one set of details happened-in whereas another did not? To speak of things "happening-in" is to assault the integrity of a poem. Poetry cannot be discussed meaningfully unless one can assume that everything in the poem—every last comma and variant spelling—is in it by the poet's specific act of choice. Only bad poets allow into their poems what is haphazard or cheaply chosen.

The errand, I will venture a bit brashly for lack of space, is left generalized in order the more aptly to suggest *any* errand in life and, therefore, life itself. The owner is there because he is one of the forces of the poem. Let it do to say that the force he represents is the village of mankind (that village at the edge of winter) from which the poet finds himself separated (has separated himself?) in his moment by the woods (and to which, he recalls finally, he has promises to keep). The owner is he-who-lives-in-his-village-house, thereby locked away from the poet's awareness of the-time-the-snow-tells as it engulfs and obliterates the world the village man allows himself to believe he "owns."

Thus, the owner is a representative of an order of reality from which the poet has divided himself for the moment, though to a certain extent he ends by reuniting with it. Scene one, therefore, establishes not only a relation between the man and the woods, but the fact that the man's relation begins with his separation (though momentarily) from mankind.

End parenthesis one, begin parenthesis two.

Still considering the first scene as a kind of dramatic performance of forces, one must note the poet has meticulously matched the simplicity of his language to the pretended simplicity of the narrative. Clearly, the man stopped because the beauty of the scene moved him, but he neither tells us that the scene is beautiful nor that he is moved. A bad writer, always ready to overdo, might have written: "The vastness gripped me, filling my spirit with the slow steady sinking of the snow's crystalline perfection into the glimmerless profundities of the hushed primeval wood." Frost's avoidance of such a spate illustrates two principles of good writing. The first, he has stated in "The Mowing": "Anything *more* than the truth would have seemed too weak" (italics mine). Understatement is one of the basic sources of power in English poetry. The second principle is to let the action speak for itself. A good novelist does not tell us that a given character is good or bad (at least not since the passing of the Dickens tradition): he shows us the character in action and then, watching him, we know. Poetry, too, has fictional obligations: even when the characters are ideas and metaphors rather than people, they must be *characterized in action*. A poem does not *talk about* ideas; it *enacts* them. The force of the poem's performance, in fact, is precisely to act out (and thereby to make us act out empathetically, that is, to *feel out*, that is, *to identify with*) the speaker and why he stopped. The man is the principle actor in this little "drama of why" and in scene one he is the only character, though as noted, he is somehow related to the absent owner.

End second parenthesis.

In scene two (stanzas two and three) a *foil* is introduced. In fiction and drama, a foil is a character who "plays against" a more important character. By presenting a different point of view or an opposed set of motives, the foil moves the more important character to react in ways that might not have found expression without such opposition. The more important character is thus more fully revealed—to the reader and to himself. The foil here is the horse.

The horse forces the question. Why did the man stop? Until it occurs to him that his "little horse must think it queer" he had not asked himself for reasons. He had simply stopped. But the man finds himself faced with the question he imagines the horse to be asking: what *is* there to stop for out there in the cold, away from bin and stall (house and village and mankind?) and all that any self-respecting beast could value on such a night? In sensing that other view, the man is forced to examine his own more deeply.

In stanza two the question arises only as a feeling within the man. In stanza three, however (still scene two), the horse acts. He gives his harness bells a shake. "What's wrong?" he seems to say. "What are we waiting for?"

By now, obviously, the horse—without losing its identity as horse—has also become a symbol. A symbol is something that stands for something else. Whatever that something else may be, it certainly begins as that order of life that does not understand why a man stops in the wintry middle of nowhere to watch the snow come down. (Can one fail to sense by now that the *dark and the snowfall symbolize a death-wish,* however momentary, *i.e.,* that hunger for final rest and surrender that a man may feel, but not a beast?)

So by the end of scene two the performance has given dramatic force to three elements that work upon the man. There is his relation to the world of the owner. There is his relation to the brute world of the horse. And there is that third presence of the unownable world, the movement of the all-engulfing snow across all the orders of life, the man's, the owner's, and the horse's—with the difference that *the man knows of that second dark-within-the-dark of which the horse cannot, and the owner will not, know.*

The man ends scene two with all these forces working upon him simultaneously. He feels himself moved to a decision. And he feels a last call from the darkness: "the sweep / Of easy wind and downy flake." It would be so easy and so downy to go into the woods and let himself be covered over.

But *scene three* (stanza four) *produces a fourth force.* This fourth force can be given many names. It is certainly better, in fact, to give it many names than to attempt to limit it to one. It is *social obligation,* or *personal commitment,* or *duty,* or just the *realization that a man cannot indulge a mood forever.* All of these and more. But, finally, he has a simple decision to make. He may go into the woods and let the darkness and the snow swallow him from the world of beast and man. Or he must move on. And unless he is going to stop here forever, it is time to remember that he has a long way to go and that he had best be getting there. (So *there is something to be said for the horse, too.*)

Then and only then, his question driven more and more deeply into himself by these cross-forces, does the man venture a comment on what attracted him "The woods are lovely, dark and deep." His mood lingers over the thought of that lovely dark-and-deep (as do the very syllables in which he phrases the thought), but the final decision is to put off the mood and move on. He has miles to go before his sleep. He repeats that thought and the performance ends.

But why the repetition? The first time Frost says "And miles to go before I sleep," there can be little doubt that the primary meaning is: "I have a long way to go before I get to bed tonight." The second time he says it, however, "miles to go" and "sleep" are suddenly transformed into symbols. What are those "something-elses" the symbols stand for? Hundreds of people have tried to ask Mr. Frost that question and he has always turned it away. He has turned it away because *he cannot answer it.* He could answer some part of it. But some part is not enough.

For a symbol is like a rock dropped into a pool: it sends out ripples in all directions, and the ripples are in motion. Who can say where the last ripple disappears? One may have a sense that he knows the approximate center point of the ripples, the point at which the stone struck the water. Yet even then he has trouble marking it surely. How does one make a mark on water? Oh very well—the center point of that second "miles to go" is probably approximately in the neighborhood of being close to the meaning "before I take my final rest," the rest in darkness that seemed so temptingly dark-and-deep for the moment of the mood. But the ripples continue to move and the light to change on the water, and the longer one watches the more changes he sees. Such shifting-and-being-at-the-same-instant is of the very sparkle and life of poetry. One experiences it as one experiences life, for everytime he looks at an experience he sees something new, and he sees it change as he watches it. And that sense of continuity in fluidity is one of the primary kinds of knowledge, one of man's basic ways of knowing, and one that only the arts can teach, poetry foremost among them.

Frost himself certainly *did not ask what that repeated last line meant*. It came to him and he received it. He "felt right" about it. And what he "felt right" about was in no sense a "meaning" that, say, an essay could apprehend, but an act of experience that could be fully presented only by the dramatic enactment of forces which is the performance of the poem.

Now look at the poem in another way. *Did Frost know what he was going to do when he began?* Considering the poem simply as an act of skill, as a piece of juggling, one cannot fail to respond to the magnificent turn at the end where, with one flip, seven of the simplest words in the language suddenly dazzle full of never-ending waves of thought and feeling. Or, more precisely, of felt-thought. Certainly an equivalent stunt by a juggler—could there be an equivalent—would bring the house down. Was it to cap his performance with that grand stunt that Frost wrote the poem?

Far from it. The *obvious fact* is that *Frost could not have known he was going to write those lines until he wrote them.* Then a second fact must be registered: *he wrote them because, for the fun of it, he had got himself into trouble.*

Frost, like every good poet, began by playing a game with himself. The most usual way of writing a four line stanza with four feet to the line is to rhyme the third line with the first, and the fourth line with the second. Even that much rhyme is so difficult in English that many poets and almost all of the anonymous ballad makers do not bother to rhyme the first and

third lines at all, settling for two rhymes in four lines as good
enough. For English is a rhyme-poor language. In Italian and in
French, for example, so many words end with the same sounds
that rhyming is relatively easy—so easy that many modern
French and Italian poets do not bother to rhyme at all. English,
being a more agglomerate language, has far more final sounds,
hence fewer of them rhyme. When an Italian poet writes a line
ending with "vita" (life) he has literally hundreds of rhyme
choices available. When an English poet writes "life" at the
end of a line he can summon "strife, wife, knife, fife, rife," and
then he is in trouble. Now "life-strife" and "life-rife" and
"life-wife" seem to offer a combination of possible ideas that
can be related by more than just the rhyme. Inevitably,
therefore, the poets have had to work and rework these combinations until the sparkle has gone out of them. The reader is
normally tired of such rhyme-led associations. When he en-
counters "life-strife" he is certainly entitled to suspect that the
poet did not really want to say "strife"—that had there been in
English such a word as, say, "hife," meaning infinite peace and
harmony," the poet would as gladly have used that word instead of "strife." Thus, the reader feels that the writing is
haphazard, that the *rhyme is making the poet say things he does
not really feel*, and which, therefore, the reader does not feel
except as boredom. One likes to see the rhymes fall into place,
but he must end with the belief that it is the poet who is
deciding what is said and not the rhyme scheme that is forcing
the saying.

So *rhyme is a kind of game*, and an especially difficult one
in English. As in every game, the fun of the rhyme is to set one's
difficulties high and then to meet them skillfully. As Frost
himself once defined freedom, it consists of "moving easy in
harness."

In "Stopping by Woods on a Snowy Evening" Frost took a
long chance. He decided to rhyme not two lines in each stanza,
but three. Not even Frost could have sustained that much
rhyme in a long poem (as Dante, for example, with the advan-

tage of writing in Italian, sustained triple rhyme for thousands of lines in "The Divine Comedy"). Frost would have known instantly, therefore when he took the original chance, that he was going to write a short poem. He would have had that much foretaste of it.

So the first stanza emerged rhymed a-a-b-a. And with the sure sense that this was to be a *short poem,* Frost decided to take an additional chance and to redouble: in English three rhymes in four lines is more than enough; there is no need to rhyme the fourth line. For the fun of it, however, Frost set himself to pick up that loose rhyme and to weave it into the pattern, thereby accepting the all but impossible burden of quadruple rhyme.

The miracle is that it worked. Despite the enormous freight of rhyme, the poem not only came out as a neat pattern, but managed to do so with no sense of strain. Every word and every rhyme falls into place as naturally and as inevitably as if there were no rhyme restricting the poet's choices.

That ease-in-difficulty is certainly inseparable from the success of the poem's performance. One watches the skillman juggle three balls, then four, then five, and every addition makes the trick more wonderful. But unless he makes the hard trick seem as easy as an easy trick, then all is lost.

The real point, however, is not only that Frost took on a hard rhyme-trick and made it seem easy. It is rather as if the juggler, carried away, had tossed up one more ball than he could really handle, and then amazed himself by actually handling it. So with the real triumph of this poem. *Frost could not have known what a stunning effect his repetition of the last line was going to produce.* He could not even know he was going to repeat the line. He simply found himself up against a difficulty he almost certainly had not foreseen and he had to improvise to meet it. For in picking up the rhyme from the third line of stanza one and carrying it over into stanza two, he had created an endless chain-link form within which each stanza left a hook sticking out for the next stanza to hang on. So by stanza four, feeling the poem rounding to its end, Frost had to do something about that extra rhyme.

He might have tucked it back into a third line rhyming with the *know-though-snow* of stanza one. He could thus have rounded the poem out to the mathematical symmetry of using each rhyme four times. But though such a device might be defensible in theory, a rhyme repeated after eleven lines is so far from its original rhyme sound that its feeling as rhyme must certainly be lost. And what good is theory if the reader is not moved by the writing?

It must have been in some such quandary that the final repetition suggested itself—a suggestion born of the very difficulties the poet had let himself in for. So there is that point beyond mere ease in handling a hard thing, the point at which the very difficulty offers the poet the opportunity to do better than he knew he could. What, aside from having that happen to oneself, could be more self-delighting than to participate in its happening by one's reader-identification with the poem?

And by now a further point will have suggested itself: that the human-insight of the poem and the technicalities of its poetic artifice are inseparable. Each feeds the other. That interplay is that poem's meaning, a matter not of *what does it mean,* for no one can ever say entirely what a good poem means, but of *how does it mean,* a process one can come much closer to discussing.

There is a necessary epilogue. Mr. Frost has often discussed this poem on the platform, or more usually in the course of a long-evening-after a talk. Time and again I have heard him say that he just wrote it off, that it just came to him, and that he set it down as it came.

Once at Bread Loaf, however, I heard him add one very essential piece to the discussion of how it "just came." One night, he said, he had sat down after supper to work at a long piece of blank verse. The piece never worked out, but Mr. Frost found himself so absorbed in it that, when next he looked up, dawn was at his window. He rose, crossed to the window, stood looking out for a few minutes, and *then* it was that "Stopping by Woods" suddenly "just came," so that all he had to do was cross the room and write it down.

Robert Frost is the sort of artist who hides his traces. I know of no Frost worksheets anywhere. If someone has raided his wastebasket in secret, it is possible that such worksheets exist somewhere, but Frost would not willingly allow anything but the finished product to leave him. Almost certainly, therefore, no one will ever know what was in that piece of unsuccessful blank verse he had been working at with such concentration, but I for one would stake my life that could that worksheet be uncovered, it would be found to contain the germinal stuff of "Stopping by Woods"; that what was a-simmer in him all night without finding its proper form, suddenly, when he let his still-occupied mind look away, came at him from a different direction, offered itself in a different form, and that finding that form exactly right the impulse proceeded to marry itself to the new shape in one of the most miraculous performances of English lyricism.

And that, too—whether or not one can accept so hypothetical a discussion—is part of *how* the poem means. It means that marriage to the perfect form, the poem's shapen declaration of itself, its moment's monument fixed beyond all possibility of change. And thus, finally, in every truly good poem, "How does it mean?" must always be answered "Triumphantly." Whatever the poem "is about," *how* it means is always how Genesis means: the word become a form, and the form become a thing, and—when the becoming is true—the thing become a part of the knowledge and experience of the race forever.

Appendix B

Exercises

The following exercises may be used to strengthen various muscles in your cerebrum (or wherever creativity comes from) or as pump-primers when your idea-well seems to have run dry.

After each exercise title there is a notation of which chapter(s) the exercise might be associated with; however, these notations are not meant to suggest that the exercise must only be done while you are studying any particular chapter.

EXERCISE A—SIMPLIFICATION (CHAPTER 2)

Select a passage from a textbook on some other subject —Anthropology, Biology, or Criminology will do—and try to rewrite it making it as simple as any other ABC, so that a young child could understand it. Insofar as possible, use only words found in Appendix C, and avoid or define any horrendous technical jargon. Simplify and resimplify.

EXERCISE B—PROSE PARODY (CHAPTER 2)

A parody is to a writing as a caricature is to a face. Select some well-known writer with a markedly characteristic style (like Faulkner, Hemingway, Henry James, or the translators of the King James Bible) and write a brief piece in a burlesque of the style. This is a good way to write satire on politics or other current events.

EXERCISE C—GUT REACTIONS (CHAPTER 3)

Close your eyes and sit outdoors for about a half-hour (preferably in a light breeze). Open your eyes only as necessary to make notes. Identify as many *smells* as you can, and try to identify your emotional reaction to each odor. What were your internal visceral reactions to each (mouth watering, belly rumbling, stomach tightening, tears starting, going into the fetal position, etc.)?

Repeat the same process, using sounds instead of smells.

EXERCISE D—HEAD AND GUT REACTIONS (CHAPTER 3)

Sit down to write an assignment for this or any other class. Have a spare sheet of paper divided into two columns and a pen or pencil available. Make a note in the first column of each distracting or extraneous thought you have while trying to work. Opposite it note your emotional reaction to the thought.

EXERCISE E—A NOSTALGIC STORY-STARTER (CHAPTER 3)

Go through a storage place in your home (a catch-all drawer, a closet, medicine cabinet, etc.). Itemize what you find and try to recall why each thing is there. Write out the story behind any single item. Put your story into dialogue to get an extra exercise in.

EXERCISE F—CHILDREN'S POETRY (CHAPTER 5)

Go through Appendix C, which contains 769 of the words most likely to be known by children beginning to read, and find five sets of words, each containing five words which rhyme with each other. One set might be *buy, by, cry, eye, lie.*

EXERCISE G—CHILDREN'S POETRY (CHAPTERS 5, 8)

Using only words found in Appendix C, write a simple rhyming poem of at least four lines. Keep in mind that it does not have to have a deep meaning, but that it must be catchy, and that any imagery must refer to things within most children's experience.

EXERCISE H—POETIC PARODY (CHAPTER 5)

A parody is an imitation of the style of another writer, generally written in a light vein to make fun of the style or subject matter. Lewis Carroll wrote several famous ones, such as

> Twinkle, twinkle, little bat
> How I wonder what you're at
> Up above the world so high
> Like a teatray in the sky.

And *Mad* Magazine is full of them.

Write a parody of the words to a song. If you have any trouble selecting a song, I suggest using one from a Gilbert and Sullivan light opera (the Judge's song from *Trial by Jury,* any of Koko's songs from *The Mikado,* etc.). They are pretty light-weight themselves and they lend themselves well to use in satire. The poems of Longfellow and Poe also lend themselves to parody, and both poets (three, including Gilbert) are too dead to object.

EXERCISE I—POETRY FORM (CHAPTER 5)

A ballad stanza has four lines, with a rhyme scheme of a b a b or a b c b. Like this

> Mary had a little lamb
> Its fleece was white as snow
> And everywhere that Mary went
> The lamb was sure to go.

Rewrite Lincoln's Gettysburg Address (Chapter 6) in ballad stanzas. Keep the meaning and spirit as close to the original as you can, but feel free to pick your own words.

EXERCISE J—POETRY FORM   (CHAPTER 5)

A sonnet is a 14-line poem with a rhyme scheme. The first eight lines generally rhyme a b b a a b b a. The last six have several varying rhyme schemes, notably c d e c d e or c d c d e e. Elizabethan sonnets, written by Shakespeare and his contemporaries, have a variant rhyme scheme: a b a b c d c d e f e f g g (three quatrains and a couplet). Here is John Milton's famous sonnet on his blindness:

> When I consider how my life is spent,
> Ere half my days in this dark world and wide,
> And that one talent which is death to hide
> Lodged with me useless, though my soul more bent
> To serve therewith my Maker, and present
> My true account, lest He returning chide,
> "Doth God exact day-labor, light denied?"
> I fondly ask. But Patience, to prevent
> That murmur, soon replies, "God doth not need
> Either man's work or his own gifts; who best
> Bear his mild yoke, they serve him best. His state
> Is kingly: thousands at his bidding speed
> And post o'er land and ocean without rest;
> They also serve who only stand and wait."

Rewrite the Lord's Prayer (Our Father) in the form of a sonnet. If that seems sacrilegious to you, try it with the Twenty-third Psalm, which was originally written as a poem.

EXERCISE K—POETIC IMAGERY   (CHAPTERS 2, 6)

Make up a list of similes or metaphors that are so unusual (or even absurd) that you are sure that you have never seen them used before, e.g.

(1) The moon rose full and orange, like a Union 76 sign.
(2) The translucent afternoon moon looked like a communion wafer pasted on the sky.

EXERCISE L—RORSCHACHS (CHAPTERS 6, 7, 8)

Take a sheet of paper and drop on it a blob of India ink,
finger paint, or other colored substance (ketchup will work, in a
pinch). If you have two colors together, all the better. Fold the
paper over the blob, and press the halves together. Unfold, and
as it dries, look at the blot you have made. Squinting your eyes
if necessary, figure out what it looks like. Write a brief free-
verse poem describing the scene and whatever emotional effect
it may give you.

EXERCISE M—WRITING NARRATION (CHAPTER 10)

Re-read "A Quickie." Rewrite the sketch, using all *narration* instead of dialogue. *Or,* write as dialogue a conversation
between two persons of different sexes. They do not have to be
husband and wife or a couple on a date. Grandmother and
grandson, housewife and supermarket checker, diner and wait-
ress, pop-singer and fan—all would be satisfactory.

EXERCISE N—CHARACTERIZATION AND NARRATION (CHAPTERS 10, 11)

Go to some place where there are usually a number of
people to be found (a bus station, a public beach in season, a
crowded restaurant). Select one person (an older person
generally works out best) and think up a name and personality
that will fit his appearance. Imagine why he is there and where
and why he is going when he leaves. Do not follow him (that's
cheating). *Do* take notes covertly, so you will not get punched
in the nose or suspected of being a plainclothes dick. When you
get home, write out in narrative and description the episode
you have built up around the character.

EXERCISE O—PLACE DESCRIPTION IN DETAIL (CHAPTER 10)

Select a small area of ground (floor or parking lot will do if
there is no ground available) not more than a yard square and
examine it closely. Ask yourself questions like: What color is it?

How does it smell? Is there any vegetation on it? What does it look like? Taste like? Is there any animal life? What size and shape? Does it make a noise? What kind? Does the plot have any features that would distinguish it from any other area of the same size? Jot down a list of your detailed observations. From the list, write a sketch description of the area.

EXERCISE P—SLANTED DESCRIPTIONS (CHAPTER 10)

Write a description of a place, making it appear as pleasant and inviting as possible, like a real estate prospectus. Now write another description of the same place, changing none of the basic facts, but substituting adjectives and adverbs with a bad connotation for those which are favorable. See how *un*inviting you can make it sound.

EXERCISE Q—MORE SLANTED DESCRIPTIONS (CHAPTER 10)

Write a description of a person, creating as favorable an impression of him as possible (like a job résumé). Now write another description of the same person, with the same characteristics, but giving them names with bad vibes (*stingy* instead of *thrifty*).

EXERCISE R—DESCRIPTION OF A PERSON (TO BE DONE IN CLASS) (CHAPTER 10)

Divide the class into pairs. Study your partner closely, using all of the senses he will permit. Write a list of details about his appearance (looks, sound, taste, smell, and feel). Concentrate on those features which will serve to distinguish him from any other member of the class—moles, freckles, dimples, hairline, distinctive coloration of eyes (it's surprising how many people have one segment of an iris that is different from the rest). How are his ears shaped? Do they both stick out from his head at the same angle? Are both his shoulders the same height? Are his fingernails chewed short? Is he right- or left-handed? Are the palms of his hands moist or dry? Soft or callused?

After you have made the list, arrange it into some logical order and write a brief description. It will probably not be necessary to use all the details you have noted, so select the most distinctive ones carefully.

EXERCISE S—POINT OF VIEW (CHAPTER 10)

Think of a fictional situation involving conflict. Tell it in 500 to 1,000 words from the point of view of one of the characters involved, using first person, third person as a camera, or third person limited omniscient point of view technique. Then go through the same chain of events from the point of view of another, conflicting character. You may, if you desire, use a different point-of-view technique in the second part. It would give you extra experience.

Or, take another situation involving conflict. Write it in *alternating points of view* as seen by two different characters as above, but with the p.v. characters alternating several times as they do in "Craftsman." This time you should use the same p.v. *technique* (first person, third person as a camera, etc.) throughout, to avoid confusion insofar as possible.

EXERCISE T—SITUATION TO PLOT (CHAPTERS 11, 14)

Take the following initial situation and write a story based on the subsequent action. Develop your own characters, setting, and plot, to include climax and resolution.

> *Two young men, A and B, are going steady with two young women, X and Y (remember the acronyms AX and BY). A and B are happy with the arrangement, but both girls would prefer to change partners, though neither has confided her desire to the other nor, of course, to the boys.*

Take it from there.

EXERCISE U—SITUATION TO PLOT (SCIENCE FICTION) (CHAPTERS 11, 14, 16)

Assume a world quite like our own except that all male babies are either "altered" or destroyed at birth except for a few with superior genetic characteristics who are saved for stud purposes. All enterprises are operated by women, with the neutered men in comparatively menial jobs. The stud men are permitted to associate with women only long enough to perform their function. The heroine, a successful executive, finds herself in love with the man who has fathered her two children (and those of hundreds of other women).

Take it from there.

EXERCISE V—WRITING FROM A SKELETON PLOT   (CHAPTER 14)

Take the following simple plot and write a story with characterization, motivation, necessary description, and dialogue:

> *An eleven-year-old boy runs away from home. He has several adventures and meets several people, including some hippies, all of whom urge him to go back, until he meets understanding and sympathy in the person of a middle-aged panhandler who laughs delightedly and assures him, "That's how I got my start." The boy, able to visualize his own possible future, declines to act as a shill for the panhandler and heads for home.*

EXERCISE W—CHILDREN'S FICTION   (CHAPTER 16)

Write a story no more than 400 words long, composed as nearly as possible of words found in Appendix C. Forget about verisimilitude, but strive for sensory (particularly visual) effects suitable to go with illustrations, and for lots of action interesting to small children. Keep a record of words used outside the list.

EXERCISE X—MOTIVATION   (CHAPTER 18)

Write a synopsis for a play, emphasizing the motivation. For every important action performed by any character, write an explanation beginning with the word "because."

EXERCISE Y—STORY BOARD FOR A PLAY   (CHAPTER 20)

A *story board* is a device to help you keep track of the action in a play (or story) so that you will know everything that is going on at any one time. It keeps you from giving stage directions that will put actors on a collision course, or writing a scene that just "won't play." Divide each scene of your play into the shortest possible fractions, called "frames." A frame may be a single speech (or even part of a speech), an entrance, or the movement of a character across stage. Write the primary action of the frame on the left side of a divided sheet of paper. Then, in the right half, write down every *other* action that is going on onstage at the same time. What are the other actors doing? Is the cigarette still smouldering in the ashtray? What is the maid doing with the newcomer's coat? Do all the other actors turn and look at the newcomer, or do some of them pantomime continuing their own conversation?

EXERCISE Z

Write an *ending* to an act, such that the action will close at a critical point. Summarize the previous action briefly so that the reader will be able to understand what you have written.

Appendix C

A List of Easy Words

a	angry	bad
about	animal	bag
above	another	bake
accident	answer	ball
across	ant	balloon
afraid	any	band
after	apple	bandage
afternoon	are	bang
again	arm	bank
air	around	bark
airplane	arrow	barn
all	as	basket
almost	ask	bath
alone	asleep	be
along	at	bear
already	ate	beat
also	awake	beautiful
always	away	became
am		because
an	baby	bed
and	back	bee

been
before
began
begin
begun
behind
being
believe
bell
belong
beside
best
better
between
big
bigger
bill
bird
birthday
bit
bite
black
blew
blood
blow
blue
board
boat
book
both
bottom
bow
bowl
box
boy
branch

bread
break
breakfast
bright
bring
brother
brought
brown
bug
bump
bunny
bus
busy
but
butter
button
buy
by

cage
cake
calf
call
came
camp
can
candy
cap
car
care
careful
carry
cat
catch
caught

cause
cent
chair
chance
chick
child
children
circus
Christmas
city
clap
clean
climb
close
clothes
clown
coal
coat
cocoa
cold
color
come
coming
cook
copy
corn
corner
could
count
country
cover
cow
cried
cross
crowd
cry

cup	else	flag
cut	end	flew
	engine	floor
dance	enough	fly
danger	even	follow
dark	ever	food
day	every	foot
dear	eye	for
deep		fork
did	face	found
dig	fair	four
dinner	fall	fresh
dish	family	friend
do	far	frog
does	farm	from
dog	fast	front
done	fat	fruit
don't	father	full
door	feather	fun
double	feed	fur
down	feel	
dress	feet	game
drink	fell	garden
drive	felt	gate
drop	few	gave
dry	field	get
duck	fight	girl
	fill	give
each	find	glad
ear	fine	glass
early	finish	go
earth	fire	goat
east	first	going
easy	fish	gold
eat	fit	gone
egg	five	good

good-by	hid	jet
got	hide	joke
grade	high	juice
grandfather	hill	jump
grandmother	him	just
grass	his	
gray	hit	keep
great	hold	kept
green	hole	kill
ground	home	kind
grow	honey	kiss
guess	hop	kitchen
	hope	knew
had	horn	knock
hair	horse	know
half	hot	
hall	house	lady
hand	how	land
happen	hungry	lake
happy	hunt	large
hard	hurry	last
has	hurt	late
hat		laugh
have		lay
he	I	learn
head	ice	left
hear	if	leg
heard	I'll	let
heart	in	letter
heavy	indoors	lie
held	inside	life
hello	instead	light
help	into	like
hen	is	line
her	it	lion
here	its	listen

little

live

log

long

look

lost

lot

loud

love

lunch

made

mail

make

man

many

march

matter

may

me

meat

meet

men

met

mice

middle

might

mile

milk

mill

mind

minute

mirror

miss

money

monkey

month

moon

more

morning

most

mother

mouse

mouth

move

movies

much

music

must

my

nail

name

near

neck

need

neighbor

nest

never

new

next

nice

night

no

noise

north

nose

not

note

nothing

now

number

nut

of

off

often

old

on

once

one

only

open

or

orange

other

our

out

over

own

page

paint

pan

pants

paper

park

part

pass

pay

peach

peanut

peep

penny

people

pet

pick

picnic	rain	school
picture	ran	seat
pie	read	see
piece	ready	seem
pig	real	seen
pillow	red	sell
place	rest	send
plain	ride	serve
plant	right	set
play	river	seven
please	rode	shadow
pocket	roar	shake
point	robin	shall
policeman	rock	shape
pond	rocket	she
pony	road	sheep
poor	roll	shell
post	roof	shine
pot	room	shirt
present	root	shoe
press	rope	shop
pretty	round	short
pull	row	should
puppy	rub	show
push	rug	shut
put	run	sick
puzzle		side
	said	sign
question	salt	silver
quick	same	sing
quiet	sandwich	sister
quite	sang	sit
	sat	six
rabbit	save	size
race	saw	skate
radio	say	skin

skirt	store	thank
sky	storm	that
sled	story	the
sleep	straight	their
slide	street	them
slow	strike	then
small	string	there
smell	strong	these
smile	such	they
smoke	sugar	thick
sniff	suit	thin
snow	summer	thing
so	sun	think
soap	sunshine	thirsty
soft	sure	this
sold	surprise	those
some	swam	though
song	sweater	thought
soon	sweet	three
sore	supper	threw
sound	swim	throat
soup		through
space	table	throw
squirrel	tail	thumb
stand	take	ticket
star	talk	tie
start	tall	time
station	taste	tired
stay	teach	to
step	tear	today
stick	teeth	toe
still	television	together
stocking	tell	told
stone	ten	tomorrow
stood	tent	tongue
stop	than	too

took   walk   wind
tooth   want   window
top   war   wing
touch   warm   winter
town   was   wise
toys   wash   wish
train   watch   without
tree   water   woman
trick   wave   wonder
trip   way   wood
tried   we   wool
trunk   weak   woke
try   wear   wolf
turn   weed   word
turtle   week   wore
twelve   went   work
two   were   world
              west   worm
ugly   wet   would
umbrella   what   wrap
uncle   wheat   write
under   wheel   wrong
until   when
up   where
upon   which   yard
us   while   year
use   white   yellow
              who   yes
              whole   yesterday
valley   whose   yet
vegetable   why   you
very   wide   young
visit   wife   your
voice   wild
              will
wait   win   zipper
wake   zoo